A NORTH LIGHT

A North Light

*Twenty-five years in a
Municipal Art Gallery*

John Hewitt

Edited by

FRANK FERGUSON AND KATHRYN WHITE

FOUR COURTS PRESS

Set in 10.5 pt on 14 pt Janson Text for
FOUR COURTS PRESS LTD
7 Malpas Street, Dublin 8, Ireland
www.fourcourtspress.ie
and in North America for
FOUR COURTS PRESS
c/o ISBS, 920 N.E. 58th Avenue, Suite 300, Portland, OR 97213.

A catalogue record for this title
is available from the British Library.

ISBN 978-1-84682-364-0

SPECIAL ACKNOWLEDGMENT

This publication received financial support from
the Office of Innovation, University of Ulster.

Printed in England
by Antony Rowe Ltd, Chippenham, Wilts.

Contents

Illustrations

Acknowledgments

The editors would like to thank, first and foremost, the John Hewitt Estate, and Dr Keith Millar in particular, for their support and encouragement with this publication. We also wish to acknowledge our appreciation to Tony Kennedy, Patricia McCooe and the John Hewitt Society for their help and advice in the editing of the book. Special thanks go to the University of Ulster Library and to Frank Reynolds and Jayne Dunlop, whose pivotal assistance with the original manuscript was invaluable. We would also like to acknowledge Jennifer Cook, Frank Lyons, Anne Jamison and the Office of Innovation, at the University of Ulster, for initial project funding, along with Mike Wilson from the Research Office for his assistance with the project.

Acknowledgments are due to the Public Record Office Northern Ireland for permission to view and use material from the John Hewitt Archive. We would also extend our appreciation to the Heritage Lottery Fund, the Ministerial Advisory Group on the Ulster-Scots Academy (MAGUS) and the Ulster-Scots Agency for their generous encouragement and enthusiasm for this project.

Special thanks go to our colleagues at the University of Ulster. In particular, we are grateful for the constant support of our Dean Pól Ó Dochartaigh and Head of School of English and History, Jan Jedrzejewski. We would also wish to acknowledge the help and support of members of the Ulster Poetry Project, Carol Baraniuk, Adrian Henderson and Averill Burchanan for their assistance with this book. We would also wish to extend our gratitude to Sarah Chestnutt, Joanne Taggart and Janetta Chambers for the vital administrative duties they performed for the project. Thanks go also to Damian Smyth at the Arts Council Northern Ireland, and to Chris Spurr and Laura Spence at the BBC.

We would like to thank the following representatives of author's estates and their publishers for permission to reprint extracts of their work in this book. All efforts were made to contact the copyright holders in this collection. Extracts from John Hewitt's 'The Modelled Head', 'O Country People', 'The Municipal Gallery Revisited, October 1954', 'From the Chinese of Li Wang Shi', 'The Little Death', 'The Return', 'Freehold', 'Pro Tanto Quid Retribuamus', 'The Return', 'Torcello' from *The Collected Poems of John Hewitt*, ed. Frank Ormsby (Blackstaff Press, 1991) reproduced by permission of Blackstaff Press on behalf of the Estate of John Hewitt. 'Calendar' by Roy McFadden, reproduced with permission from the McFadden Estate. Permission to reproduce materials held in the Public Record Office Northern Ireland granted by the Deputy Keeper of the Records.

Finally, we extend our warmest gratitude to the staff at Four Courts Press for their patience and diligence throughout this project, and thank Martin Fanning especially for the guidance that he has provided in the completion of Hewitt's autobiography.

Introduction

JOHN HEWITT'S STATURE IN IRISH WRITING
AND CRITICISM

... and I am left with these alternatives,
to find a new mask for what I wish to be,
or try to be a man without a mask,
resolved not to grow neutral, growing old.

'The Modelled Head'[1]

John Hewitt's centrality to the arts in Northern Ireland during his adult lifetime has long been accepted. As a poet, critic, curator and observer from within and from afar during his period of 'exile' in the 1950s and 1960s, few public figures of the twentieth century have left as significant a body of work, or influenced those around him to the extent that Hewitt did. The image that pervades is of his late incarnation as a father figure and guide for the golden generation of northern writers who emerged in the 1960s, an avuncular, if some-what stubborn commentator on the politics, culture and aesthetics of Ulster; and one who could trace involvement with attempting to develop the arts within Northern Ireland from the 1930s onwards – and someone who had confronted, and occasionally lost spectacu-larly against, the intransigence of the establishment. Indeed the drafting of *A North Light* appears to have been precipitated by Hewitt's most public of losses against Ulster conservatism. In 1953 he had attempted to gain the Directorship of the Ulster Museum and Art Gallery, and was apparently passed over because of his

---

1 Frank Ormsby (ed.), *The Collected Poems of John Hewitt* (Belfast, 1991), p. 103.

alleged political sympathies with Northern Irish Catholics and socialists. *A North Light* concludes with Hewitt gaining the post of Arts Curator in Coventry – an apt metaphorical destination for one who refused all attempts at living as a neutral. This move away from Ireland, a spatial, rather than a political, emotional or cultural migration, permitted an opportunity for reflection and self-examination. It afforded him a means to explore where he had come from and examine his preoccupations as a 'museum man' but also as a poet, critic and inhabitant of Ulster.

This text, functioning in many ways like a diary in its technique of writing to the moment and its terse, arch brevity, illuminates one of Northern Ireland's lesser-explored periods of cultural and political history, and yet ironically one of the most discussed passages in Hewitt's professional life. Shrewdly, Hewitt submerges his feelings of personal injustice that he felt at the time of writing, to examine wider political, cultural and personal preoccupations. Here he explores the importance of place and the relation of man to his environment, particularly those feelings experienced by the modern city dweller who yearns for connection with the natural world. Rooted as he was in his native, industrial, Protestant Belfast, there are further Northern Irish crises of ownership and belonging to the land that required examination in his memoir. Hewitt's individual and communal trauma is also the basis of his political philosophy and his poetics. His paradoxical sense of fulfilment within and simultaneous exclusion from the Northern Irish city and countryside prepare the ground for his autobiographical narrative. In his poem 'O Country People' he details his affinity with these country folk but also acknowledges the disparity between himself and them: 'there is a wide bog between us, a high wall'.[2] This duality of self, which may be the inevitable condition of his self-ascribed Planter imagination, verges on a form of navigating his way through an identity crisis. As an essayist he often expressed a certain sense of cultural inferiority as a northern Protestant, albeit one of agnostic socialist sensibilities: 'We have no such literary heritage, no ancient language. Scotsmen, Englishmen and Welshmen have here in Ulster become clotted in

---

2 'O Country People' in *John Hewitt Selected Poems*, ed. Michael Longley & Frank Ormsby (Belfast, 2007), p. 30.

an uneven and lumpy mixture'.[3] However, for those expecting *A North Light* to operate as a wringing of hands, or of endless sanctimonious self-justification, there will be disappointment. The text highlights Hewitt's growing appreciation of his multiple cultural allegiances and conveys his sense of identity not as fractured, but as increasingly focused and unified, and able to speak articulately for itself. This is accomplished through his projection of himself as curator and collector sifting through artefacts of memory to fashion a coherent whole. And yet, while *A North Light* expresses the affirmation of locating one's voice and vision in the mid-twentieth century in Ulster, it exposes the difficult terrain that existed for writers within that cultural space. This was a stony ground that could only be negotiated by exile in many instances, even if in Hewitt's case it was a provisional exile, and one with frequent homecomings, and eventual return.

For readers expecting a poet's journal, there will be some dissatisfaction. As the title *A North Light. Twenty-five years in a municipal art gallery* suggests, the book is concerned with Hewitt as gallery man, rather than poet. Yet the title is peculiarly apt, the yoking of the poetic to the mundane is much in keeping with Hewitt's customary irony, which goes a long way to remove a sense of self-glorification in the work that follows. It provides a means for Hewitt to voice an appreciation of who he was, what motivated him to write for public audiences, and a means to chart his way out of Belfast, alluding to his time as a twenty-five year stretch employed by the council. While the book never reaches the heights of eloquent Irishry employed on *The Green Fool* or *Borstal Boy* it shares similar motivations, and deserves to stand within this company. In the case of the relationship to Kavanagh's self-styled 'green fool', there are echoes of seeing a strange, beautiful light on the hills. (Hewitt's North Light shines as an echo of the United Irishmen's Belfast newspaper, *The Northern Star.*) But Hewitt, dissenter agnostic that he was, was more suspicious of manifestations of grace than Kavanagh, particularly when that mysticism may hint of Catholic, or indeed Protestant Romanticism. His comprehension of the light

3 Tom Clyde (ed.), *Ancestral Voices: the selected prose of John Hewitt* (Belfast, 1987), p. 108.

shining on his homeland is mediated through a professional life-time's awareness of viewing Irish, British and European traditions in painting and literature, in the careful perambulation through field and glen, and in the realization that for all the preparation that aesthetic ideology may provide, in order to *see* the country one must look with diligence, patience and affection.

Hewitt might almost be criticized for being a throwback to a form of fustian antiquarianism, were it not for the pervading energy of engagement with his subject. While Kavanagh is strangely absent from the many writers that Hewitt encountered, Brendan Behan does feature within the memoir, and while Hewitt's brush with the British state is not as fraught, and by no means as violent as Behan's, there did flourish a brief but sanguine friendship between them. Both in a sense experienced a sense of emotional incarceration and intellectual stifling within their respective Irelands, which found some sort of alleviation in writing.

In Hewitt's case this resulted in work that was never executed with the same level of volatility or luminosity – for all Hewitt's affections for the vernacular of the weaver poets, one could never see him able to embrace Behan's colloquial verve. But where Hewitt shades Behan is in his measured, considered reflection on his life and writing, born out of the trinity of concerns of poet, curator and critic. It would be too simplistic to suggest that Hewitt lived longer than Behan, and therefore his later oeuvre merely reflects the concerns of a writer in more secure maturity. If anything, *A North Light* marks Hewitt's shift into a more confident, perhaps even more radical realization of the possibilities for intellectual creativity in Northern Ireland; and collateral to this, a greater desire to excoriate and satirize the political failings of the North.

Hewitt did of course experience a long career as a writer. During the 1930s he made a concerted effort to write poetry and his work during this period addresses the tortured history of the province. By 1943, he had established himself as a writer and art critic and his collection *No Rebel Word*, published in 1948, clearly conveys his views on the concept of Regionalism that preoccupied his thoughts at this time.[4]

4   John Hewitt, *No Rebel Word* (Belfast, 1948).

During the next four decades Hewitt wrote prolifically in his various roles as reviewer, art critic, poet and prose writer. Hewitt's writing brought him considerable recognition and acclaim; in 1960 his services to art and literature were formally acknowledged when he was elected a member of the Irish Academy of Letters. In 1974 he was awarded the honorary degree of Doctor of Letters from the University of Ulster, and Queen's University Belfast bestowed a similar honour in 1983, following a period of three years from 1976 to 1979 when Hewitt had been the University's first Writer in Residence. Hewitt was also offered an OBE in 1979 from the Conservative Government, but refused it; this decision was not surprising considering that a few weeks beforehand Hewitt had been elected as the first President of the Northern Ireland Fabian Society. In 1983 he was made Freeman of the City of Belfast and the following year was awarded the Gregory Medal by the Irish Academy of Letters.

Influenced by his Belfast boyhood and non-conformist background, Hewitt, in *A North Light*, provides a fascinating and authoritative insight into the world of the arts, charting the development of Northern Ireland's artistic, political and cultural temperament during the early twentieth century.

HIS RATIONALE FOR WRITING THE MEMOIR

Having been rejected for the position of Director of the Museum and Art Gallery in 1953, Hewitt initially had little imperative to write, and for the following four years there was little in the way of creative published output. This lack of agency resulted only in the penning of various newspaper reviews of theatre productions and art exhibitions. Following his move to Coventry, to take up the post of Director in the Herbert Art Gallery in 1957, Hewitt also took on the role of Poetry Editor of the Belfast-based magazine *Threshold*.[5] Not until 1967 would Hewitt begin a decade of prolific writing and publishing once more.

5 See 'Introduction Hewitt Papers (D3838)', Public Record Office Northern Ireland, 2007, p. 9; http://www.proni.gov.uk/introduction_hewitt_d3838-2.pdf accessed 15 July 2012.

However, perhaps we should not view this relative hiatus as a 'creative slump', as it was in 1961 that Hewitt began writing *A North Light* – an account of his life from his birth in Belfast in 1907 up until he left his native province in 1957. This explains why Hewitt was not publishing a great deal during this period, as evidently he was preoccupied with writing his 'autobiography'. Written four years after his arrival in Coventry, it is obvious that Hewitt's memoir constitutes a backwards glance at Northern Ireland and is an attempt to confront and examine his position as museum man, Ulsterman, poet and art critic, as well as affording him the opportunity to unreservedly provide comment on those whom he knew. Despite declaring 'Now poetry is what I'm about', in an interview with the *Coventry Evening Telegraph* in 1968, this memoir details the richness of Hewitt's experience and knowledge of art, his views on aesthetics, literature, regionalism, identity and politics – both in Northern Ireland and Europe. [6] It shines a light on Northern Irish culture, discusses prominent writers and artists, as well as providing comment on lesser-known but equally talented artists, and is undoubtedly a celebration of the wealth of history and culture of the province.

As well as enabling Hewitt to demonstrate the wealth of knowledge he had accumulated over the years and to chart the changes in his thinking with regards to art and aesthetics – the memoir functioning in many ways as the growth of his consciousness – *A North Light* allowed Hewitt to openly voice his views on the establishment and to offer his analysis of his failure to secure the Directorship of the Museum and Art Gallery in Belfast. It may have been this uncensored approach that resulted in Hewitt's autobiography remaining unpublished for so long, although many strategic chapters were printed during his lifetime and soon after his death on 27 June 1987.[7] Perhaps it functioned as a means of purging, enabling Hewitt to deal with the various aspects of his life up until that point and

6 Ibid., p. 4; *Coventry Evening Telegraph*, 28 August 1968.
7 For example, 'Secular Burial' appeared in *Honest Ulsterman* 2 (June 1968), 6–9, 'Alec of the Chimney Corner' was published in *Honest Ulsterman*, 4 (August 1968), 5–12 and 'From Chairmen and Committee Men, Good Lord Deliver us' was published in *Honest Ulsterman*, 6 (September, 1968), 16–22.

clearing space for the creative impetus that would burst forth in 1967 and produce some of Hewitt's best work. Whatever his motivations for writing this memoir, Hewitt, in detailing his life, has provided a picture of Northern Ireland's cultural history which is invaluable and unsurpassed.

OUTLINE OF MEMOIR

'I see pencils and brushes and things. This boy's future will be bound up in Art.'

A North Light can be read as following four main episodes of Hewitt's life. The first section (chapters 1–8) details Hewitt's education and his early interest in art which led to the almost fortuitous appointment as Art Assistant in Belfast's Museum and Art Gallery, after reading a job advert in a barber's shop while waiting for a haircut. He describes how art played a significant role in his youth, his family's artistic tendencies evidently casting their shadow over him, and yet confirms that as a child, 'art occupied no place in the perpetually fluctuating hierarchy of [his] ambitions'. However, the trips abroad with his father, to places such as Bruges and Brussels, undoubtedly fuelled his passion for art and he describes in the initial chapters how the works of artists such as Landseer and Michelangelo became 'the furniture of [his] mind'. If his appointment may appear to be delineated with the easy fatalism of a young man in his early twenties, he makes apparent quite quickly the seriousness with which he approaches his personal vision of what constitutes great European art. He combines the idealism of a writer coming to maturity in 1930s Ireland, imbued with all the attendant international concerns of someone of leftist temperament with a particular northern Irish dissenter's individualism. Hewitt's dissent, while not religious, still shares the political and cultural facets of his compatriots. This manifests itself in his passion for art being circumscribed by his 'disappointment' with masterpieces such as the *Mona Lisa* and Rouault's *Head of Christ*. And yet Hewitt acknowledges throughout the memoir how his appreciation of aesthetics was fluid, detailing how his opinion of art changed over time as he matured. It is a testimony to Hewitt's knowledge of the arts and contribution to Northern Ireland's art scene that the Convenor of the Royal Ulster Academy of Art in Belfast, upon hearing the news that Hewitt was to leave his native city for the post of Art Director in Coventry, wrote that 'No one has done more for the Arts in Ulster'.[8]

Following his appointment as Art Assistant, Hewitt describes the 'Declaration of Allegiance to His Majesty King George 5th', which he was required to make, and conveys signs of his political position which would eventually draw him to the concept of regional identity within the island of Ireland. Hewitt acknowledges how the 'Declaration of Allegiance', the only oath he would ever take, was cited 'plainly to affront or, if possible, to exclude Roman Catholics', providing comment on Northern Ireland's political structure at the time. The Northern Irish poet Francis Davis is discussed (Hewitt considering him to be one of the most important poets), along with the Museum and its exhibitions – including the acquisition of Belfast's famous 'Mummy', Kabooti. Hewitt details his first exhibition which consisted of Post Impressionist paintings and also discusses the Sir John Lavery Collection (1856–1941). Lavery, who was the official artist of the First World War and whose collection comprised of portraits of eminent politicians and churchmen, including Lord Carson, Lord Craigavon (Northern Ireland's first Prime Minister) and Cardinal Logue, was commissioned to paint the state visit of Queen Victoria; Lavery was tangentially involved in the Irish War of Independence and the Irish Civil War and painted the portrait of Michael Collins on his deathbed, entitled *Love of Ireland*. Hewitt speaks of lost history, a theme that would become prominent in his poetry, and describes how the young people of Belfast were growing up with no knowledge of the famous faces painted by Lavery, and no awareness of what their significance had been:

> my heart, dejected, wondered which of these
> may hold a meaning that will long endure [9]

8 Letters relating to John Hewitt leaving Belfast for Coventry (D3838/7/34/1-20). Public Record Office Northern Ireland.
9 'The Municipal Gallery Revisited, October 1954' in *John Hewitt Selected Poems*, p. 48.

The second section of the narrative (chapters 9–16) details the period of transition in Hewitt's poetry, when he began to actively address the tormented history of the province and examine his own identity. It discusses Hewitt's holiday on Rathlin Island in 1935, with his wife Roberta, a place he describes as 'a microcosm of the Irish past', where he consolidates his identity.[10] Indeed, Hewitt's deepening awareness of his sense of place corresponds to his meeting and subsequent marriage to Roberta Black in May 1934. Until her death in October 1975, she was to remain a constant and vital companion – an equal who shared his humanitarian vision and belief in accompanying this social action. Her wisdom and, at times, refreshingly blunt common sense punctuates the memoir, and provides a touching, if tangential, record of a marriage.

Hewitt as demonstrated in his marriage and his friendships was a man of conversations. Conversations with various artists are discussed, including those with Belfast-born artist John Luke who, along with Colin Middleton, became a close friend of Hewitt's and contributed to the shaping of his aesthetic values and 'response to [his] age.'[11] Hewitt discusses his time at Queen's University Belfast, where his interest in poetry intensified and he began imitating the style of James Joyce and Liam O'Flaherty.

This section also details Hewitt's political life, his interest in 'left-wing' politics, including his brief time as literary editor for the political journal the *Irish Democrat*, when he wrote under the pseudonym Richard Telford, and his involvement in Belfast's Peace League. He describes the time spent with 'lively likeable comrades' at the Summer School of the Independent Labour Party in Welwyn Garden City, 1933, which was attended by James Maxton, the Scottish Socialist politician and Leader of the Independent Labour Party. It was here that Hewitt first met the poet Shelley Wang who would become a close friend, and following his death, behind Japanese lines in 1939, Hewitt wrote an elegy for the man he describes as ranking first in essential humanity.

This section discusses Hewitt's friendship with Paul Henry who he describes as 'the best Irish landscapist of the half-century' and

10 P. 65.
11 P. 55.

mentions the talents of his wife Grace, an artist who was accredited, by some, as being more talented than her husband. Grace Henry's friendship with James Joyce's daughter Lucia is mentioned, and Hewitt records Grace's opinion of Joyce's handling of his daughter. He details 'Unit One', 'a momentary banding-together of a handful of English painters, sculptors and architects' whose exhibition had a significant impact on local artists and inspired 'The Ulster Unit', a group consisting of artists such as Lady Mabel Annesley, W.R. Gordon, John Luke, Colin Middleton and George MacCann. This multi-disciplinary group staged an exhibition in Belfast's Locksley Hall in December 1934, which was a testimony to the vibrancy and progressiveness of artists in Ireland during this period. Part II concludes with 'The Fair at Kilrea', an intriguing little section which details Hewitt's journey to the small town of Kilrea, County Londonderry, to meet with the sister of Hugh Thomson (1860–1920), a well-known illustrator who provided the illustrations for Mrs Gaskell's *Cranford* and Jane Austen's *Pride and Prejudice, Emma, Sense and Sensibility, Mansfield Park, Northanger Abbey* and *Persuasion*.

The third section (chapters 17–26) encompasses Hewitt's responses to the rise of fascism in Europe and his role in the war as a lecturer to troops, interspersed with his sense of his own growing maturity as a writer and critic. In these chapters he describes a feeling of frustration with some of his leftist and radical cliques, his description of the pacifist farm set up by John Middleton Murry as a 'steaming fish tank of supercharged egos' underscores his annoyance at the pettiness and short-sightedness among these groups prior to and during the war.

Alongside his irritation at the perceived failings of some, is a recognition of his own rising reputation as a well-regarded critic. This brought with it certain unwelcome attentions – particularly the satirical squibs visited upon him by the novelist F.L. Green, who depicted Hewitt as a know-it-all Northern Art Curator, Griffin, in his novel *Odd Man Out*. It appears here in an episode in 'The Sour Laugh' (chapter 21) and evidently chagrined him.

As someone listed in a reserved occupation, Hewitt took no part in the hostilities, but was drafted in by the government to explain the finer points of Marxist dialectic to the troops stationed in Northern

Ireland. Despite this somewhat bizarre undertaking, he appears to have enjoyed the opportunity for public speaking and spent a productive time in travelling around the army bases. The bureaucracy of wartime particularly irritated Hewitt, and when various parties dragged their heels on paying damages to a friend who was injured by falling debris after a bomb raid, Hewitt characteristically claimed himself to be 'an uncharitable and savage antagonist of those enemies of life, the grey men with asterisks for eyes and footnotes for feet'.[12]

The war provided him the opportunity of meeting and corresponding with a number of writers who were stationed in Northern Ireland and whose letters from the front provided him with vital news about the Allied mission. In typical Hewitt fashion, much of his second War Year's chapter is given over to a discussion of the Buddhist and vegetarian painter John Luke, a good friend and 'a belated Florentine', whose perceptive and poignant strictures on observing life and the craft of the artist act as profound statements to individual humanity, set against a backdrop of world conflict. Such discussion on the interplay between the individual and the state stimulated Hewitt's adaptation of a regionalist mentality in his outlook as means to steer beyond the difficulties of the national question in Northern Ireland politics, culture and identity after the war.

The fourth section (chapters 27–37), charts Hewitt's awareness of his maturity in his professional and critical life in the immediate post war years. His growing confidence in his capabilities is evidenced in the public recognition of his poetry and criticism, often cited in a modest or self-deprecating manner. His self-assurance is further demonstrated in a number of chapters where he feels able to comment upon key moments in mid-century Irish history. 'The Funeral of Mr W.B. Yeates' provides a vivid tableau of Yeats' funeral, where a moment of marking time for the state and Ireland's poet is humorously undercut by a local shop's inability to spell the name of the deceased. These chapters also develop his personal views on popular art and indicate a softening towards Modernism and the other movements of the twentieth century which had generated so much of his early critical resistance ('Annus Mirabilis' 31).

12 P. 134.

Also evident, perhaps paradoxically, alongside his theorizing of regionalism, is a deepening consciousness of sharing a European sensibility, enhanced by undertaking international P.E.N. conferences and research trips to The Netherlands and Austria. It is on these journeys where Hewitt develops his observational gaze on paintings, artists, writers and the often barbed or fragile ego of the public literary figure. The establishment of his reputation leads to a number of humorous and painful incidents. In a jocular vein, he recounts Brendan Behan phoning him up one evening requesting a bed for the night. But Hewitt's notoriety as a man of the left and an upholder of non-sectarian, cross community ideals, Hewitt suggests, was the main reason for his being passed over for the Directorship of the Ulster Art Gallery ('From Chairmen and Committee Men'). This traumatic experience that ultimately, in his mind, precipitated his move to England, is told frankly and without self-pity, demonstrating his stubborn refusal to run away from a fight or yield any room to his opponents.

This, of course, is Hewitt's narrative of events, yet for all of his sense of personal injury, the text concludes with a strong impression of rediscovered energy in moving physically and symbolically to Coventry. It could be argued that this 'exile' provides the major impetus in Hewitt's development as a curator and writer, providing him a new environment for reflection and a stimulus to complete this important stocktaking of his personal history and myth. The convenient detection by Hewitt of other Hewitts buried in the local cemetery on the very day of his interview provides a symbol of discovery of new ancestral and emotional roots in a foreign place that he embellishes into a very powerful conclusion of invigorated purpose and mission. This finale suggests a working through of painful issues and an emergence into a state of creative vitality: John Hewitt had found again his northern light.

THE APPENDIX AND A NOTE ON THE TEXT

Hewitt composed a number of chapters that were rejected from the final copy of his intended version of 'A North Light'. The copy-text for the memoir is taken from two ring-bound folders that Hewitt had privately typed up in two sessions between September 1963 and March 1964.[12] This appears, provisionally in the very least, as the near finalized outcome of a considerable process of revision of the autobiography materials. The manuscript box of 'North Light' files in the Special Collections at the University of Ulster contains several unbound folders of a variety of early permutations of the book. Hewitt spent much time in crafting the memoir, initially recording on tape, then writing the chapters in long hand, and then typing them up, occasionally changing a word here and there, before choosing a final working list of chapters to be professionally typed and bound.[13] Many of these chapters may have been discarded as they exposed friends, acquaintances and enemies, either too forcibly to public acclamation or censure. Others read as perhaps too affably parochial in their approbation of friends and colleagues. Other chapters such as 'What is My Nation', a sustained drafting of Hewitt's conception of his Irishness, appear more developed in other publications.

Hewitt's memoir constitutes one of his most extensive works in prose, and suggests that his years in Coventry, rather than a retreat or exile, were ones of a substantial creative middle period in his working life that now requires extensive revision in literary criticism.

The editors have reprinted the original final version of the memoir with minimal changes to the copy-text. In particular, they have retained Hewitt's use of compound words. This almost-Joycean turn in Hewitt's style portrays a much more experimental, Modernist ambition than perhaps Hewitt had been allowed in his poetry. The preponderance of these words throughout the writing meant that any revision would have made for a plainer, less authentic text. They emphasize that this is no muted autobiographical musing of an exile, but a serious endeavour to push for clarity of expression and to creatively envision his past as much as record it journalistically. This

12 Receipts, Box 5, John Hewitt Collection, University of Ulster.
13 Several chapters did not make the final selections; these include the following: 'Edinburgh 1950', 'The Sun Dances', 'Zoltan Frankl', 'Multum in Parvo', 'Alec of the Chimney Corner', 'Dublin 1953', 'Poets Party 1952', 'Paul Nietzsche', 'The Clothes Horse', 'E.N. Carrothers', 'Geoffrey Taylor 1900–1956', 'Donegore', 'Politics', 'What is My Nation' [incomplete], 'Odd Man in', 'The Night of the Bath or The Shallow End', 'E.M. Forster', 'Misfit' and 'Secular Burial'.

edition aims to provide the reader with as close a replication of the final version of Hewitt's 'A North Light' as is possible. Only obvious grammatical omissions have been silently changed, as have occasional lapses in spelling and Hewitt's occasional preference for certain archaisms. The editors have assembled the version that Hewitt had professionally typed and bound; and now, after the reasons for his exile have passed into history and myth, Hewitt's own narrative is finally revealed.

A NORTH LIGHT

How It All Started

One forenoon in late July 1930 I was sitting in the barber's shop waiting my turn for a haircut. I was in my twenty-third year, about twelve stones in weight, five feet nine inches standing up, of a clear complexion, the hair to be cut was fair; son, with an elder sister, of Robert Telford Hewitt and his wife Elinor born Robinson; they had been married in 1900, and I had followed seven years after. Creature of habit, I had always had my hair cut here, since that far first day when the barber lifted me on to the narrow board across the chair-arms and my mother watched the blond curls fall and saved one of them. Even when we left the neighbourhood, at some inconvenience, I came back at the necessary intervals.

This morning the barber himself was not in; it was his son who was at work, a tall young man whom I could remember as a little chap with a shaggy head, lathering chins for his father's razor. Though of a friendly disposition, he had not yet achieved his father's easy and fluent affability, and so, save for the snip of his scissors round an old man's head, the sunlit shop was quiet.

I picked up one of the local morning papers – Belfast had then three, none of which we took at home – read through the cricket scores, and the news; and since I have always been a thrall to print of any kind, I glanced over the advertisements too. Suddenly my attention was gripped by a surprise. The Belfast Museum and Art Gallery required an Art Assistant, and offered a salary of two hundred and fifty pounds a year, rising by five annual increments of ten pounds to three hundred.

Although I had graduated at the University a few weeks before, I was not really looking for a job. It had been assumed and I had accepted the assumption that I should readily find something in the teaching line to suit me. I had finished my teacher's training course a year ago, and, by now, was qualified to take on work in primary or secondary schools as I pleased. My father was Principal of a public elementary school. My mother until her marriage had been a teacher too. Her elder sister had also taught until she too had married a Principal. A third in my mother's family, her adored eldest brother, although dead now for a dozen years, was still remembered as a highly successful school teacher.

His bachelor's degree had been the only one in the connection to precede mine. So a lifetime in education seemed my destiny.

That evening at home it needed little discussion before we decided that I should apply for the Gallery job; it could do no harm, either way.

I have been, so far, carefully circumstantial in my account of this, because it appears to me an interesting example of the effect of chance on a man's direction in life. That July morning, in a normal situation, I was, it seemed, firmly meshed in an inevitable net of tradition; and yet, with a rectangle of newsprint I was cut loose and set out on a path far beyond my imagination or ambition.

I find it interesting to search back for the clues, the determinants, which turned me to this unexpected gate when everything pointed the other way. Art as a means of earning a living did not rate high in our estimate of careers. A younger brother of my father, Sandy, had, late in the last century, been an art student, but the hazards of his craft drove him over to the commercial side, and even there his struggle had been hard. Once, falling out of work, like so many others, he had gone to the United States where an elder brother had prospered in the thread business. In New York Sandy got word of employment in Virginia as a lithographer. But when he arrived there he discovered that a long-standing strike was in progress, and that he would be taken on as a blackleg. This he could not do. So, penniless, he made his way back to New York, tumbling in at Tom's door in very poor shape. This is one of those family anecdotes which is now woven into my personal myth, my imaginative pattern of truth. It has played no inconsiderable part in making and keeping me a man of the Left.

Later Sandy fared much better, married a capable Scotswoman and settled in London. From time to time, he would send us posters which he had designed and drawn 'on the stone'. One was a marvellous representation of a retriever with a shiny coat and a bird in its jaws. Another was of a pretty young woman in a long skirt and wearing a tam-o'-shanter, playing golf. It was, my father averred, this lithography, with the long hours of leaning against and drawing on the wet stone which gave Sandy his stomach trouble. But that trouble was insufficient to keep him out of the London Artists' Rifles, when he joined-up under the Derby Scheme, to be killed in France in 1917. We always had on our walls a couple of lush green watercolours and a pair of sepia costume figure-compositions, to keep his skill in memory; and in my grandfather's drawing room was his masterpiece *The Snake Charmer.*

My father was always playing with watercolour, more consistently, though still without any distinction, in his later years when he had more time. For, in the days when his salary was small he spent two or three evenings a week teaching Commercial English and Book-keeping in the Technical Institute. He also wrote articles and reviews for the educational journals and ran little correspondence courses, using the gelatine-duplicator to multiply the specimen lessons. Out of one of his series of articles grew a little book, *Drawing for Schools*, his sole essay in authorship. It was kept in print for a good many years, through two editions, and the tiny trickle of royalties from the publisher every six months amused and pleased him, although in time the amounts became very small. It was not a very good book, for it fell in the period between the old rigid system of object drawing and the new upsurge of Child Art; but, from his correspondence, I know that it helped many a lonely teacher in Donegal or Kerry to face the inspector with a little more assurance. I was touched, some years ago, when looking for something else, to find its title in the Catalogue of the National Library in Dublin. I could not resist applying for, and handling the copy, for I do not possess one of my own.

My mother had, at some time, before my sister and I kept her hands full, taken painting lessons, but never got further than copies of Highland Lochs and wicker baskets bulging with melons and grapes, which hung in heavy fluted gilt frames in the front parlour. Later, I can remember when, to earn herself some pin money, for one winter, at home, she ran a ladies' class in the ephemeral craft of pen-painting. You bought a pattern-transfer of, say, a floral basket surrounded by sprays of blossom, or a crinolined lady with a parasol, and by ironing it on to a piece of fabric, silk or satin, secured the design to be followed with the pigments. These were ordinary oil paints mixed to the tint required and applied by pen, the nib of which was very broad and flexible. This was well adapted for producing petal-forms or ribbon-like scrolls; and when the paint was dry, the decorated fabric was used as a table centre or runner or mat, according to size and shape; more elaborately sometimes as a cushion-cover; though this last had evident disadvantages. I remember picking at one of these – I was an inveterate picker – and removing the rose-petals one by one. A short-lived undertaking, it left me with the smell of oil paint and turpentine in my nostrils forever, forever exciting.

On my father's bookshelves was a large bound volume of *The Art Teacher's Monthly*, for what year I never noticed; and in this, issue by issue, someone called W.E. Sparkes contributed an article on a famous painting, always accompanying it with a diagrammatic analysis of the composition. So even before I could read comfortably I could grasp the structure of such works as *The Last Supper* with its radiating lines of perspective which could be extended to converge in the central figure, as *The Fighting Temeraire* with its sagging tent-rope rhythms of hull-rigging, and tug-funnel. So, too Landseer's *The Bay Mare* and Michelangelo's *Prophets* and *Sibyls* were, in monochrome, part of the furniture of my mind. When I saw *The Bay Mare* at Burlington House in Derek Hill's Landseer Exhibition early in 1961, and in the May of that year, the Sistine Chapel, I could not help thinking on each occasion that it had all been a long way round. Indeed, the principles underlying these analyses are still the spine and bone of my aesthetics, as natural and as easily acquired and firmly maintained as my Belfast accent and my lurching gait.

I left the National School in my twelfth year, but in the boys' school where folk of my surname but no kin were famous foot-ballers, and a year later in the co-educational Methodist College, apart from the drawing lessons I profited little in general knowledge or appreciation of art; for, in those days, there was no thought of allowing painting or modelling or any other creative self-expression in school, or any place on the time-table for art history.

What I learned I picked up from books at home; from artists' biographies discovering the much jeered at Samuel Smiles' *Self Help* to be a treasure island of which Cellini and Palissy were as heroic denizens as Arkwright or Stephenson. *The Children's Encyclopaedia*, the eight volumes of which I borrowed, for extended periods and in proper sequence, from my more prosperous cousins, the Martins, with its multitude of reproductions, though conventional to a fault in its emphasis of the academic and the anecdotal, was an abundant source of information.

So I grew up to accept that Painting and Sculpture had their places in the world of general knowledge, that the exceptional persons who achieved masterpieces were among the most praiseworthy of mankind; but since I had only a small talent for drawing and a little more for modelling, I realized that I should never be an artist of any consequence myself: and, consequently, Art occupied no place in the perpetually fluctuating hierarchy of my ambitions.

Yet further back there had been an odd happening in my experience, a brief incident, which, in the light of my subsequent career, has a peculiarly numinous quality. Sometime in the spring or summer of 1916 when I was not yet nine years old, and when we were living with my maternal grandmother in Bangor, County Down, for some obscure reason or on a sudden impulse – she was a woman of impulse – my mother took me to a clairvoyant or, to be more precise, what we should now call a psychometrist, a Mrs. Smeltzer, for 'a reading'. When I had been introduced, the lady, tall, English, grey, serious, asked me for something from my person. I unlatched and gave her my belt, one of those striped canvas-elastic belts with the catch shaped like a snake. She held this in her hands on her lap and closed her eyes. After an enormous silence, she began, slowly and then with greater vigour, to describe forms which hovered about me. My mother recognized from the description that her father, dead nearly twenty years before, was one of them. They all communicated goodwill toward me and offers of help 'from their side'. Then Mrs Smeltzer said 'I see pencils and brushes and things. This boy's future will be bound up in Art. Yes. They are nodding approval.'

When we returned home, we told my father. He laughed and said, 'Not likely. Think of what art has done for Sandy. Jack will be given as good an education as we can afford. After that he'll be able to turn to teaching or medicine, even'. My own dream at that time was to become a medical missionary, or failing that, an explorer.

Because of this strange encounter which I can remember so vividly and for which I can suggest no rational explanation, although generally of a sceptical turn of mind, I keep room in my philosophy for George Fox and William Blake and Thomas Traherne, and listen respectfully when, once in a while, a man may tell me of his visions or his visitors.

2

The Free Library

The Museum and Art Gallery for which the Art Assistant was required had only been open a twelve-month. But Belfast's Museum history was longer than that. There had been a museum founded in 1851 by the local Natural History and Philosophical Society, one of those worthy cultural groupings of the commercial and professional classes typical of the time, which had, among its members, a hardware merchant who was a first rate zoologist, clergymen who were antiquarians, a College professor who was a renowned Egyptologist, medical doctors who were experimental scientists. The Museum, the first to be erected by public subscription in Ireland, still stands, its decent regency facade rather outfaced by the high College of Technology across the street. Here, every Easter Monday, swarms of the town's inhabitants elbowed in and paid their pennies to see the mummy, the five-legged sheep, the Hawaiian feather-cloak, the fragment of the Great Eastern's Atlantic cable, the stuffed penguin which Captain Crozier brought back from the Antarctic, the twisted glass walking stick, and the hoof of a mule killed in the Jameson Raid when an expanding Empire provided the trophy.

Much later in the century, due to the prodding and nagging of an irrepressible agitator, William Gray, the City Council, reluctantly, after a protracted campaign of delays, finally accepting the permissive legislation of the Libraries and Gymnasiums Act, built the Free Public Library, in 1888, in which the Library proper occupied the ground and middle floors. The ground floor annex was used to exhibit antiquities and natural history, the top floor was the Art Gallery. The building, a solid sandstone block, the architect of which had some Italianate notion in his head, was set in a main thoroughfare about a quarter of a mile from the city centre.

During my school days, when I had regularly to cross town, this was a notable haven of refuge for those days when I felt like mitching, usually at the beginning and the end of term when the roll call has not yet any, or has given up authority. In the entrance hall, the tall plaster cast of William Pitt, after Flaxman, faced, beside the staircase, the large plaster *Lorenzo de Medici* after Michelangelo, all detail choked with successive coats of white paint. Along the corridor ahead was the Grainger Room, called after the Canon whose bequest it housed. Here cinerary urns, stone axes, bronze swords, lay exposed in their impenetrable silence and mystery, and here too one had to be alert to the amorous approaches of elderly tramps, for there were several doss-houses just around the back of the building. Upstairs, the landings displaying *The Veiled Lady*, *The Christian Martyr* and *Pensiero*, in alabaster, you came to the galleries, several dingy rooms with worn and splintering floorboards and dusty plaster Metopes round the friezes. Here we saw, my father and I, for he early established the habit of taking me, the annual exhibitions of the leading local art society. In one of these I had my first excitement of seeing a work publicly shown which I had previously seen in the making; the little bust of my father's brother Sam, by his wife, Hannah. For not long before he had broken what was beginning to appear like a vow of celibacy, to marry, in middle age, his spinster-neighbour, an amateur artist and a prominent member of the society.

It was here, although I cannot date it more accurately than some-time shortly after the War, that Professor Cizek's Exhibition of Austrian Children's Art broke, for me, like a marvellous dawn, the uncoiling of a dynamic spring. In an age like ours now, deluged with Child Art in all degrees of sophistication, from the world's ends and the next street, browbeaten and intimidated by the authority of ten-dentious tomes like Sir Herbert Read's, it is almost impossible to recreate the effect which this exhibition had upon those ready to be kindled to a new world of experience; so much joy, so much spon-taneity, so much vitality. Yet, trying hard to visualize any single pic-ture or group of pictures after what must be forty years, I can only conjure up vague Christmas-card-like, flat pattern images, snug and cosy as bowdlerized folktale, embellished now and then, though here I may well be wildly wrong, with a timid flourish of *L'Art Nouveau*.

There were coloured postcards and illustrated booklets on sale, for the benefit of child refugees and war-orphans, which we brought home in bundles to brighten many a winter afternoon.

Later, in, I think, 1925 or '26, there was another important exhibition, this time of the paintings and sketches of Nathaniel Hone, that grossly neglected landscape master. Because he spent his life in France, in Egypt, and back at home in Ireland, he never impinged upon the London opinion makers, and his painterly qualities, worthy to set beside those of his comrades of the Barbizon School and higher than those of any English landscapist of the same period, are unknown outside the small number of his visually educated fellow countrymen. In this exhibition I was confronted for the first time with the full range and variety of a mature artist's life work. It was this, I now realize, which gave me a glimpse of the nature and essence of style, of the assured personal gesture of the loaded brush and the selective vision of the disciplined observer. The tiny sketches in watercolour demonstrated too how a moment of visual pleasure, curiosity, or suggestion of these may be caught and held without hazard or hesitation.

Then in 1927 Belfast took its place in the much-trumpeted series of exhibitions of British Art organized by Sir Joseph Duveen. This was the first display on any scale that I had ever seen of contemporary work. Tame enough now in retrospect; few of the participants still have names outside the journals of the time; the unaccustomed brightness of the colours and the variety of the styles, the surprising impact of which one would hardly notice now in the current distortions, hit me with considerable force. Art at once had become not merely something valuable in the heritage of our Western civilization, but a lively activity of today.

There was much public interest, newspaper denunciation and argument, but before the show shut about sixty works had been sold; I have sometimes wondered where they went, for, apart from the Gallery's own timid half dozen, I only saw one of them again, a pencil drawing by Colin Gill which the proud possessor believed to be by the better-known Eric. I made my own contribution to the debate with a very adolescent and bright eyed letter to *The Belfast Evening Telegraph*, never dreaming that I should for a period in the future be the art critic for that very journal and be paid for it. I defended the intentions of the exhibitors – the chief *pièce de résistance* was a painting of an excessively pneumatic coalminer at work in a narrow seam, by George Bissill – and, in particular, aimed my heaviest blows at a local doctor who had expressed his sense of outrage and indignation at the repeated insults to True Beauty and The Human Form Divine.

The Exhibition was reinforced by a series of lectures by Frank Rutter, Hubert Worthington and Dr Thomas Bodkin. The best, that by Rutter, had an immensely important effect on the shaping of my ideas. I can still see that tall spare figure with the large jaw and the enormous horn-rimmed spectacles; but as my visual memory is so much better than my auditory, I cannot recollect the sound of his voice. What he said I do remember, for it was for me the first telling of the story of Modern Art, from the Impressionists to Picasso and Matisse, which, not long after, I was to read in his own book and hear so often from others and to reproduce so frequently myself.

Later I was to discover that Frank Rutter's visit had another more material consequence. A local collector, Sir Robert Lloyd Patterson had recently bequeathed his pictures to the city, together with six thousand pounds to ensure that they be adequately housed. The collection was a thoroughly discreditable jumble of Victorian trash. *The Favourite of the Harem*, a close but incompetent imitation of *When Did You Last See Your Father?*, a knee-breeched gentleman and a lady in fancy costume on a *chaise longue* with a fan lying on the polished floor before them, these were the most memorable. It has always been a deep satisfaction to me to discover how very stupid rich and clever businessmen can be when they fall into the dealer's nets. Nowadays, usually across the Atlantic, very wealthy men to avoid the more obvious risks of untutored impulse, employ expensive art experts to form their collections for them; but when the resultant hoards are placed on public view – 'he lends them unto nations/ Until he is sure that nations know them his', as old Gordon Bottomley, that fine poet, once wrote – the lack of personal taste or conviction cannot be blanketed by the ostentatious parade of famous names; and I sometimes find myself longing, in such a context for a tablet with an unfamiliar name, the name of a living artist not yet accoladed by the suave viziers of the Bond Street Bazaar, or even for a real 'howler', to give a touch of individuality to the display.

On Sir Robert's bequest, by whose inspiration I never discovered, Rutter was engaged to report, specifically with regard to its suitability for inclusion in the collections of the New Art Gallery, then in the process of being built. He assessed them fairly if much less ruthlessly than might have been expected, and suggested that for the sake of the benefactor's good name and for the future reputation of the Gallery, the whole bag of tricks should be disposed of, and any sums accruing from the sale added to the six thousand pounds, the total to be used to buy worthwhile contemporary pictures which should be labelled to commemorate the benefactor's name.

The executors agreed, with what seemed a sensible proviso, and the High Court modified the terms of the bequest, writing-in the stipulation that the purchase of the works should be placed in responsible hands, nominating the Contemporary Art Society for this. The pictures were sold, few reaching double figures, a Val Prinsep doing much the best to reach nearly one hundred pounds; the lot coming to nine times that figure. Later, one item was returned by its purchaser, who, on removing the glass had found it to be merely a chromolithograph: a circumstance not to anyone's credit, not to the man who sold it to Sir Robert; not to Sir Robert, although his battered reputation as an art connoisseur could take the blow without any possible worsening of its condition; not to the Curator who failed to spot the fraud; not to the auctioneer who sold it again, hardly even to the man who finally found out.

The nine hundred pounds added to the cash in hand was laid out, not as it would have been had the choice been left to the Libraries, Art Gallery and Museums Committee of the Belfast Corporation, on Arnesby Brown, Munnings, Tuke, but on about thirty English Post Impressionist paintings; two first-rate Sickerts, Stanley Spencer's *Betrayal*, two Johns, an Innes, one each of the Nashes, a Matthew Smith, a fine Steer, two William Roberts, the best of these; the others being, many of them, then popular with the C.A.S., and not now of much account, Roger Fry, Vanessa Bell, Duncan Grant, Keith Baynes, Elliott Seabrooke, Edward Wadsworth, Neville Lewis. This collection has indeed remained the principal attraction of the Belfast Art Gallery ever since, although most of the Committee out of whose hands the purchasing had been taken were openly contemptuous of the brash modernity of the paintings.

About the Steer painting there is an interesting story. This was of a naked woman sprawled on a bed with a small child sketched-in at her side: it could be called, if you so cared, *Woman in Childbirth*, but the whole thing was carried out with a quiet tenderness and in no way offensive to any who would not be offended by nakedness. When the new Gallery was opened and the Sir Robert Lloyd Patterson Collection given a room to itself, several aged females, among them Lady Meyer, the wife of the Town Clerk, were scandalized by the inclusion of the Steer, and raised a gaggle of protests. Losing his nerve completely, the Curator, instead of taking the painting off exhibition and hiding it until the old creatures had died, got the willing authority of his committee to have it exchanged for something less provocative. Credit is due to the Contemporary Art Society who stood by their choice and refused to be involved in any exchange-retreat. So the Curator found someone more accommodating who swopped him an indifferent Steer landscape and a couple of pencil drawings for it. The nude was forthwith acquired by Sir Michael Sadler. When his collection was dispersed years after, the same painting came into the hands of my friend Zoltan Lewinter Frankl and hung in his drawing room less than half a mile from the Gallery. In fact, the aged ladies did not long survive their successful agitation.

The building of the new Museum and Art Gallery was the culmination of a long sequence of events. The Society which owned the Old Museum and its collections made them over to the city at the beginning of the century, and a curator was appointed to organize the bringing together of these and the city's own, housed in the Free Library. Arthur Deane, the first custodian of the joint collections, had had some experience in Warrington where the museum and art material was and still may be housed in the floor above the public library. Of his predecessors in the Old Museum and in the Free Library premises little record has been left. One, the most notable, was a good field botanist kept in mind by *The Flora of North East Ireland* of which he was large part author. Another was a Quaker vegetarian who kept a bag of nuts in his desk. A third is reputed to have faked his own suicide, leaving his jacket and boots on the river bank, but it is declared, being briefly glimpsed years later in a crowded street. There is still a very interesting group of Fuseli drawings in the Gallery, of which he is recorded as having been the donor, a rather odd circumstance.

By 1910 Arthur Deane was given a twenty-three years old assistant, J.A.S. Stendall, a naturalist from Chester interested in owls and spiders. The next year developments speeded up. A competition was held for the design of a new building to be erected in the Botanic Gardens, one of the city's very few parks, adjacent to the University. The competition was assessed, and the winning design selected. But the City Council, like so many other councils tardy in spending money on non revenue-producing departments, was slow to move. The Great War came before a stone was laid. After the War nothing happened. Then in the late Twenties the mounting economic depression, endemic in Northern Ireland, where the unemployment figure has never fallen below six per cent of the employable population, made public works a necessity, and so work was started on the pre-war design. Even then only one wing of the full project was set a-building. Actually two-fifths was contracted for.

The new building was opened in 1929, eighteen years after the design had been accepted; so it has a sturdy Edwardian, 'Board of Works money-box' look, served by a narrow and unimposing entrance at one corner, with tall narrow windows set in rusticated stone walls. On the side facing the park proper at the first storey level are a couple of carved pseudo-classical ship's figureheads of no decorative value, but hospitable to pigeons. The rump of the edifice where the incompleteness shows, remains toothy with jutting and receding brick courses.

It seems impossible now with rising costs that the plan will ever be fulfilled. Nor would the appearance, perhaps towards the end of this century or the beginning of next, of an Edwardian pastiche have much to commend it. So, structurally the Museum and Art Gallery remains, though very recently taken over by the Government of Northern Ireland and renamed The Ulster Museum, perhaps as a prelude to the unification of the country when it will be able to serve the three other counties of Ulster, now part of the Republic, a teasing problem for architects and a monument to civic indecision and lethargy; its original cost ninety thousand pounds, just the cost of a wartime bomber. During the war, every time I heard on the radio of a bomber being lost, I thought 'There goes the other bit of the Museum and Art Gallery'.

3

My Application Goes In

So I got the application form and filled it in. The questions on education were straightforward enough, and my testimonials from the Professor of History at Queens and the Vice-Principal of the Training College were consistent with my claims. But for actual practical art work there wasn't much I could say.

In my last year at school with matriculation behind me, and nothing to occupy the summer term but cricket – I was wicket-keeper and opening bat for the First XI – I received permission to attend the Art School. As I was, from the Principal's point of view, simply filling-in time, he fobbed me off with a class in drawing and another in modelling.

It may be hard to believe now that the first included drawing from the cast, that is, laborious and carefully shaded renderings of a plaster hand or foot, and that the modelling was the tedious copying in clay of a plaster relief of bulbous flowers. And, drudging drearily at this task work in the stuffy classrooms of that early summer, when the world was bright outside, I often felt that art schools had nothing to do with art, that, at least, there must be some other path of initiation into the Mystery.

By some odd coincidence the staff at that time consisted almost entirely of little, seemingly-elderly men. The Principal, a small Yorkshire man, with the long dark jaw of a knockabout comedian, had a mad passion for Roman lettering and for the genius of Frank Brangwyn and Gerald Moira. It was not until I was in Scotland in 1936 that, apart from lettering, I encountered any original work from his hand, rather dull pencil drawings of boats in a harbour, in the Annual Exhibition of the Royal Scottish Academy. There was also a painting master with rimless glasses, a large moustache and a high wing collar. I already knew his big watercolours of the Cornish coast in local society exhibitions, and I learned later that he had, because his wife was a suffragette, figured with her on the list of suspected persons whose visits to the Art Gallery had to be carefully supervised as a precaution against any local imitation of the slashing of *The Rokeby Venus*. This man lived in the tense expectation of having a show in London. He had. It was a flop, and all the spirit went out of him. Another little man with hair tufts sprouting from his ears, also padded the corridors purposefully, reputed a past master, even more, a philosopher of perspective, painter and metal worker, he was then and for many years after in the leisurely process of designing and building a house with his own hands at a rocky cliff foot in North Antrim. My modelling master was of average height so that he looked tall in this company; he had a fine shock of greying hair, and had been sculptor of an excellent bust of William Gray, the pioneer of museums in the city. As a young man, the modelling master had been one of the small band of enthusiasts which represented the North's contribution to the Gaelic movement of the turn of the century, changing his Christian name, as they all did, to its Irish form; thereafter being known, as Seumas. In the first decade of the century he had gone to France and come back a convert to Impressionism. This fairly demonstrates the existence of the time-lag between Continental usage and its being taken up in our westernmost island. That forty years evident at the century's start became progressively shortened, decade by decade, with the increase in travel and in the availability of the mass media of communication, so that now the delay in adopting the latest mode of executing or assembling a work of art, has, for the quickest of talents, narrowed to a bare twelve months. Another member of the staff, who had been abroad with him and who had surprised local exhibition visitors even more with the yellow and mauve colour schemes of his new found faith, I only saw at a distance. Over him hung a great shadow. Years before, in a life class, stepping back to examine a student's drawing, he had brushed against a curtain and accidentally dislodged a large plaster figure behind it, which lurched forward and killed the student by his side, instantly. Certainly, I felt a brooding atmosphere of depression there, and my memory of the top floor of the Technical Institute, where the Art School was housed, is of long empty corridors across or along which sad little men perpetually appeared or disappeared soundlessly and unpredictably like gnomes in some Kafka fantasy. But the brief sentence and date in my application form could carry no hint of this, being at once an understatement and an overstatement. I had taken courses in drawing and modelling during the summer term.

But what had given me incomparably richer experience of and enthusiasm for art had been my brief trips abroad with my father. In 1927 he took me to the Continent for the first time, to Belgium, where I found the Ghent *Adoration of the Lamb* and Memling's *St Ursula* casket in Bruges highly exciting, and, in Brussels, oddly enough enjoying the paintings of people by De Braekeleer, Laermans, and van Rysselberghe so much that I still respect those unfashionable names; particularly the second, for the class conscious proletarianism of his themes. Meunier too in sculpture, with his sinewy bronzes of miner, harvester and fisherman, took my taste.

It was, however, the surprise of foreignness which had the chiefest impact, with its new world of belfries and bridges and canals and quays and long beaches with sand hills – on the ship to Ostend I had been talking to a young Belgian returning for a holiday, and as we leaned on the rail, suddenly he looked up and pointed and cried, 'Look, look there is my country', and all I could see was a darker line along the grey horizon, my first experience of another man's nationalism. The Bruges students with the great peaked caps, and the collie-dogs harnessed to the axles of the handcarts, and the beautiful old faces in the Béguinage, these, and, most of all, that festival in Ghent, when men in fancy costume danced in the streets with great prancing ostrich feather headdresses, their shoulders humped with straw, and, afterwards, plucked out the straw and threw it on the big bonfire, gave me my first sharp wounding awareness that the folk culture of my own people was visually a poverty-stricken thing, that architecturally we were barbarians without either taste or breeding.

On our way back passing through London we spent an afternoon at Lords, and were lucky to see Holmes and Sutcliffe, the greatest of all county opening pairs, put on 110 for the Players' first wicket.

Holmes with the strong jaw and the peak of his cap against his nose, playing forward to be caught and bowled by J.C. White;

Sutcliffe, with sleek black head, facing Vallance Jupp at the other end, with Percy Chapman hunkered at cover; and when Holmes was out, he was followed by the sombre Charles Hallows, the Lancashire lefthander, who played out time.

In 1929 we went abroad again, to Paris. My sharpest reactions were the usual disappointment at the *Mona Lisa* in the Louvre, and consternation at Rouault's *Head of Christ* in the Luxembourg, which I found clumsy and coarse in handling, not nearly so commendable as a painting of a young woman in a pink dress by an artist whose name I have completely forgotten. The Matisse *Odalisque* I could accept. The Impressionists, particularly Monet, seemed far brighter and more immediate than the reproductions and the coloured slides had foretold. Here and there too were items which struck a familiar and friendly note: Mercié's *David* sheathing his sword, because there was another cast of it in the Gallery in Belfast; Barye's snarling carnivores, for Belfast had a dozen of these too; Le Sidaner's pale Pointilliste *Table*, for there was another table of his with people round it in Belfast, and a street scene in Dublin too. Because of this set of circumstances, I have always been inclined to put him higher on my list than he deserves. My personal discoveries were Rodin's watercolours of Siamese dancers, Puvis de Chavannes' *St Genevieve Looking Over Paris* in the Pantheon, Carrière's portrait of *Verlaine* swimming in its dull golden light, and, uncomfortable twins for enthusiasm, Courbet and Ingres. I liked, but felt a little guilty in liking, *La Source* by the latter. *The Stormy Sea* by the former seemed one of the most powerful images I had ever experienced. For sculpture, Pompon's *Polar Bear.* Bourdelle's *Herakles* drawing the long bow, and his mask of *Beethoven*, the essence of popular romanticism, dominated the rest. Epstein's flying Assyrian *Memorial to Oscar Wilde*, I sought for in Père Lachaise, but more for the sake of the man whose *De Profundis* was my prose model just then. Even yet it is with some difficulty that I remember to include this sculpture in the Epstein canon.

It was during this visit that I had a strange experience which began my desultory meditations on reality and appearance. I came on a Japanese artist or student copying a romantic nude by Henner, one of those painters in whom the influence of the camera produced the urge to present his figures out of focus. It was a very good copy, but the eyes were distorted and given an Oriental obliquity, which in the original they did not possess. The problem was then, did the artist see them so, as they were or as he thought they ought to be; or, more simply was he making the copy for the home-market and styling it to suit? At the time the economic determination appeared the readier answer, but now I am much less positive, becoming more and more of a mind that we see in the style of our age, modified by race and education certainly, but within the conventions of the period. This did not matter much, when society jogged along at the pace of the packhorse or the ox-drawn wagon; but now, at jet speed and with the endless oscillations produced by the pressures of mass communications, it becomes more and more difficult to isolate and analyse the constituents of the accepted vision of our midcentury. In art particularly, the steeplechase of styles leaves many of us floundering at the cubist fence, the suprematist fence and the tachiste water-jump.

Staying in the same hotel in Rue de Vaugirard were a journalist from Chicago, Karl Pretscholt by name, and his wife. Years after I came upon a reference to him in a book by Malcolm Cowley. He was a small bright wise-cracking man with large horn rims and a wide brimmed hat. Much of his lively talk I could follow fairly easily, since I had been for some years a weekly reader of the *New Masses*, and had from this some acquaintance with the current names, reputations and events. In retrospect, however, it is not the prose of Michael Gold or the verse of Horace Gregory which remains with me; it is rather the lively outlines of William Gropper's drawings, the stylized industrial lithographs of Louis Lozowick and the merry notation of Otto Soglow's cartoons. These, particularly the first, must have had great influence in establishing my personal canon, saving me from the easy overestimation of much English graphic work.

But to return to Pretscholt: frequently he and his wife hooked me off with them when my father wanted to pad a slower pace. From Karl I learnt a great deal, for he had a quick mind and a verbal freshness unlike any I had yet encountered. He was indeed, the first alien adult to enter my experience; and of the shreds and snippets of his talk where everything given his American accent had, in that, a head-start in humour, one sentence has remained with me, a sentence which has proved to be what I have heard Middleton Murry describe as 'one of those great imaginative utterances by which I live'. This sentence 'Life can be very amusing once you get over your indignation', has, in some measure, saved me from the dryly doctrinaire or the rigidly sectarian.

In went my application by the date required, and I set about the other side of the business. All press advertisements for municipal employment carry as an integral part, the warning 'Canvassing will disqualify'. Belfast is, I fancy, unique in this admonition. It is, of course, a standing joke, a signal that one should go ahead and start canvassing right away. We did; I say we, for the kinship network is important in Ireland. An influential member of the appointing committee belonged to the same church as we did. My father had a word with him, a very useful word, for he proved, in this, my chief support. One of the co-opted members of the committee was on the staff of the same school as my brother-in-law's father. The mother of a young woman of my acquaintance knew an Alderman well. So those lines were secured.

I myself called on another co-opted member, a trades union official and for some time a Labour MP in the local Parliament. I called on another trades union official too, and although he was far to the Right I admitted my leftist views which he told me to keep to myself till the appointment was made. I called with the Chairman of the committee, an ancient, stooped, shuffling, bearded man. There was current then the story of another Committee Chairman who spoke out against a particular candidate because the latter had not had the good manners to call and show himself and solicit the Chairman's support. Certainly my Chairman did not take my visit amiss. By these and other courses contacts were made or chain-reactions shunted-off, so that in a fairly short space of time many members of the Council were acquainted with my interests and hopes.

But in these affairs the things not to do are frequently more important than those which must be done. Several persons I was warned not to approach, one in particular who might later remind me of any obligation I was under; it was well-known that this individual had more relatives in Corporation employment than any other member of the City Council.

As interviews would not be called or the appointment made before the early autumn, and as I had set in motion those forces which I thought could best serve my purpose, I went off, this time alone, to Paris for the third time. On my previous visit as my father got enough exercise in the daytime sightseeing I had been free most evenings and had covered long distances in the city and come to have a fair grasp of general directions and features. So, although I was now alone, it was not in a completely strange place. I was able to move around with some confidence, running into a skirmish between a cyclist and a Negro taxi driver. The Negro drew a knife in the scuffle, but a waiter from a nearby cafe ran across and kicked him neatly in the wrist and the bright blade tinkled and shot into the gutter; a piece of timing I shall never forget. During this visit too, I met an eccentric little Scot, – he had a red beard, wore a straw boater, a purple woollen cardigan and carpet slippers. He was a Jacobite, a French Royalist, and a Moslem. What he carried in his briefcase I never found out. He took me to interesting places, the Mosque for instance, and knew cafes where the food was palatable and cheap. With him at the Gobelins factory I saw how the tapestry weavers worked with a mirror on the other side of the web. One weaver, I noted with interest, could work and read, his book, *The Poems of Rupert Brooke.*

Without my Scot I discovered Sylvia Beach's *Shakespeare Head* bookshop. The many photographs of Joyce and his circle and the various relevant volumes gave the little place something of the quality of a shrine to one who like myself had already experimented with the interior-monologue and the stream of consciousness. It was the oil-painting by the ill-fated Patrick Tuohy which made the strongest impression. This was the occasion I bought *Pomes Penyeach* for the equivalent of two shillings; and there too I met and talked with the young American poet Selden Rodman known nowadays as a leading anthologist and an authority on the painters of the Caribbean. Although the Depression was setting in and the great days of *Le Dome* and *La Rotonde* drawing to a close, when I read of the Exile Generation, I feel that I caught the last thinning evaporating whiff of it.

On the gallery side this visit was rather a deepening and an extension of my earlier experiences than a new chapter. Monet perhaps gained importance, and Ingres widened his appeal and Courbet too.

Félix Ziem was discovered, a contemporary of Nathaniel Hone, but more vivid, more overtly romantic than he. Manet occupied more time and attention. One show or group of shows was entirely new: The French Colonial Exposition; but apart from the general pleasure of wandering around the native pavilions and the sunlit alleys brushing against gigantic negroes billowed in white cotton, it was above all the unimaginable varieties of timber, hardwoods of marvellous grain and subtle colour, which held my glance. These and Maurice Denis' enormous mural reputed to be the largest in the world, although I cannot remember it well enough to measure it against Tintoretto's *Paradiso* in the Ducal Palace in Venice. I did not, of course, know then that it was the end of another empire which was being celebrated.

4

Sworn In

I had been back from Paris some weeks and there was still no word of an interview. A councillor, well canvassed, on my side, raised the question of the delay, at the September monthly meeting, and he was told by the Chairman that it seemed highly probable that a local candidate would be appointed. I had heard of a local rival, a commercial artist, but this was no worry. Yet the business was dragging on, and if I failed to secure the job, I would have been hanging around for nothing, missing a term's teaching at least. I was naturally becoming impatient and fretful. Although my parents were as openhanded as possible, my feeling of obligations was settling down within me, a permanent weight.

The delay was in fact due entirely to the Curator attempting to organize support and pushing hard for his own candidate, an ex-army officer who was living in Paris, and whose mother had, for a short time, been in charge of an art gallery in another Irish town. I could not then guess what the interlocking mechanism was in this intrigue. However, many years later, reading Douglas Goldring's *Nineteen Twenties* (1945) I spotted the names of several persons who could well have participated. It seemed, anyhow, that a man living in Paris should *ipso facto* be an art expert, and if his mother had had some experience, then by some strange device of heredity, that man, the son should also be a first rate gallery operator. Later I learned that our soldier did indeed turn up for interview just a day or two before I did. But whether he was not as sober as the occasion warranted, according to one report, or whether the thought of the translation from the Seine to the Lagan looked less attractive when investigated, as might more charitably be assumed, the gentleman withdrew his application and I have never heard a word of him since.

Perhaps it was simply that meeting the Curator face to face and considering a career of subordination to him, was sufficient to provoke instant retreat.

At last, towards the end of October, I was called and presented myself before Arthur Deane, a clean shaven middle aged man of medium height, with receding hair and chin and a hangdog expression. He interviewed me alone, prefacing his remarks with the blunt warning that just because I was a local lad, I must not feel too sure that I should be appointed, an admonition which took on a wry significance a quarter of a century later, but which, at the time, I took without blinking, believing that my canvass had been as thorough as I could have engineered, and feeling that my interviewer was making encouraging noises to himself. There were a few questions in which the names of Lavery, John and Brangwyn were bandied about. Then I was taken up to the Art Gallery, shown a couple of stacks of paintings, face to the wall, and asked to arrange them for hanging. Two young men stood by, to assist with the lifting and carrying. Both of these, Alfred George and Harold Bryans, have remained my friends ever since. The paintings were a strangely assorted lot. A couple I put aside altogether. Orpen's *Resting*, that good early painting of a laundress, I centred, and built and balanced around. Nevinson's *Welsh Landscape*, I remember, bothered me greatly, its dimensions and shape making it difficult to place. In his report to the Committee Arthur Deane stated that my hanging lacked experience, a not very perspicacious judgement.

I was duly appointed by the Committee and their decision was ratified by the Council at the November meeting; but before I could take up my employment I had, another Belfast ritual, to equip myself with a duly attested declaration of allegiance to His Majesty King George the Fifth, his heirs and successors by law.

I had seen His Majesty only once, when he drove in an open carriage from the docks to the City Hall in July 1921, there to open the first session of the Parliament of Northern Ireland. I have always respected his courage on this occasion, as at that time the country was astir with civil disturbance, and there was a chance that some terrorist outraged by the partition of the land, might have attempted his assassination. Snipers' bullets had been aimed at and hit less exalted personages. But, most of all I have admired his speech from the Throne, the statesmanlike text of which was largely from the pen of General Jan Smuts, so wise about every nation's problems but his own. If the King's words had been heeded by the politicians of both parts of Ireland, a better future would have been ours. Certainly, the bland manner in which the Monarch's advice and aspirations were ignored by the Government of the North was not the least effective lesson I have learned in how the term loyalty may be interpreted.

To make my own declaration I called upon a Justice of the Peace, an acquaintance of my father, a grey capable man with a grey moustache, in a well cut grey suit. He had known the families of both my parents for many years and had been a neighbour of ours for a long time. Remarking on the day it was, the Fifth of November, he enquired with a smile if I meant to respect my undertaking. This proved the only oath I have ever taken. In the rare instances since, in which any testamentary predication has been necessary, I have held to my right to affirm, much to the confusion of the Commissioner for Oaths involved, who has always had some trouble finding the right book with the proper form of words.

This insistence on a declaration of allegiance on entering local government service was, plainly to affront or, if possible, to exclude Roman Catholics whose religion was deemed to postulate loyalty to their native land rather than to a potentate overseas. But, even with this, you cannot be too careful. There was once a tricky situation when it was discovered that an Englishman just appointed to a senior City Hall job, while not himself a Catholic, had contracted a mixed marriage. He was quickly made to realize the embarrassment which he might unwittingly have caused the city.

Many years later, I had once to deputise for the Director at a meeting of the Libraries, Museum and Art Gallery Committee. The then City Librarian – not an Irishman, Belfast has never had an Irish librarian in this century – reported that he had just engaged a new janitor. The Chairman, a former commercial traveller in ladies' underwear who had married a woman who owned a shop, enquired if, by any chance, the new employee was 'a Mussalman'. This odd term shocked me. But presently I understood. The librarian, a very shrewd and efficient functionary whom I had thought to have liberal views, replied that it was a principle of his never to ask any man his religion, 'but', and here he smiled knowingly, 'it was on Saturday morning that I interviewed him; and he said he was in a bit of a hurry as he was going with the boys to Bangor'. At this the Chairman expressed his satisfaction, for, as everybody who read the local newspapers realized, the librarian had let us know that the man in question was some sort of officer in the Junior Orange Order, an organization which supported the Unionist Party and whose loyalty was unimpeachable.

When I entered the Museum and Art Gallery, one of our controlling committee members was a Nationalist councillor, a publican, a giggling, red-faced, white-haired silly fellow. Practically all publicans in Northern Ireland are Roman Catholics; the wholesale side of the traffic has no such limitation. The first Prime Minister had some interest in it, for at this remove the contagion has abated. In the Museum and Art Gallery we employed two charwomen, and, by custom, one of these posts was in the gift of the councillor, and he invariably nominated a Catholic widow for the job. When the Protestant charwoman came to retire, she was, of course, succeeded by one of her own faith. But when during the war the councillor died, his right died with him; and we had no more Catholic charwomen. The number of uniformed attendants and cleaners increased over the years as working hours were shortened, but throughout my sojourn only one Catholic, out of a dozen or more, was employed. He had come originally from the Parks Department when redundancy there and the staffing of the new building had offered an easy transfer. This man remained the single representative of a section of the community which forms about one quarter of the city's population, and, for historical reasons, a much larger fraction of the unskilled labour-force.

The professional staff was small. There was the Curator, already mentioned, with, I discovered, the disconcerting habit of flinging open the door of his spacious office and clapping his hands to demand attention of an underling. Sometime in his career subsequent to coming to Belfast, a period about which nobody knew very much, he had learned about timbers and picked up a smattering of botany, as an earnest of which he was forever digging a pocket-lens out of his vest with a flourish. This lens-play seems to have been some sort of symbol of the craft among the older Museum men. I noticed the trick when visiting other museums and meeting senior members of staff. Deane's deputy, the Assistant Curator, also already referred to, had the same habit, and early in my career I made a firm resolution that, while I might, from time to time, use a lens or a magnifying glass if absolutely necessary, these articles would remain in a drawer until required.

In the leading art shop of the town where the usual objects of merchandise were academic nineteenth-century oil paintings by Faed or Leader, elaborate late Dutch flower pieces and groups of florid cardinals or hilarious monks, an enormous magnifying glass, more than a span in diameter, used to lie on a low table, to be taken up by the proprietor to demonstrate the minuteness of detail, the reflection in the dewdrop, the authentic wild flowers and mosses of the foreground, the intricacy of the lace cuff, the eyelash, the fin-gernail, to the prospective customer, and for a simple or ignorant mind such obvious magic was difficult to resist.

The Assistant Curator, besides being a younger man than his chief, had a livelier extrovert intelligence, and had made himself a competent naturalist, an ornithologist of the older type, and an ama-teur of archaeology. His most useful achievement, while strictly extramural, had its relevance to his calling, the editing for many years of the local naturalists' journal. The two juniors were those who had helped me with my picture hanging. Alfred the elder, already by some trick of pigmentation growing white-headed in a handsome fashion, although only the same age as the century, was a quiet, gentle person, a vast compendium of local history, the true custodian of the Museum's tradition, a man without guile and full of charity, careful of his words, lacking in all temper or rage. Harold, almost my own age, less equable in temperament, but embarrass-ingly eager to do anyone a service, was the general technician, pho-tographer, mounter of specimens, as enthusiastic about his male choir as Alfred was about his church work.

After being introduced all round, meeting the typist, and the girl in the library where the pamphlets, reference works and exchange runs of specialist journals were shelved, I was set down in a store room, for, with the complexities and excitement of making a staff appointment, it had not occurred to anyone to find me a proper place to work. Here, on a trestle table, were placed several metal drawers from a filing cabinet, containing the card-catalogue of the art collections, so that I might familiarize myself with their contents.

Very soon, stopping in the entrance hall on my way to the gallery, with the Hall Porter, top-hatted William Paul, I was given my first piece of advice. Billy told me never to leave my nest in the back store, or walk about where I might be seen, without a bit of paper in my fist. 'They all do it. It looks as if you are on business'. I have found that this is true.

William Paul and Mrs Wilson the Protestant charwoman were, by far, the oldest employees in the place; they had worked in the Royal Avenue premises since early in the century. When I first met him, Paul was a robust looking man with a large moustache and red cheeks, but, in fact, a year or two earlier, when engaged in the transfer of material from the Public Library to the new building, he had had a serious accident, when the antiquated rope-manipulated hoist in which he was coming down with a load of plaster casts, fell. From this set in a slow progressive physical deterioration, first the lame foot, then the slurred speech, till he finally retired, a mumbling shuffling husk. But before this decline had become overpowering, while he yet could be communicated with, I learned much of the older artists in the community with whom he had been popular in the old Public Library days.

Mrs Wilson seemed immortal. A stout pleasant faced widow, her thinning hair twisted in a top knot, she accomplished her daily tasks with robust good humour, standing no nonsense from any, revered by all; even Arthur Deane was in some awe of her. Her widowed son had gone to America, so she brought up the orphaned grandchildren with cheerfulness and skill. Apart from her work with us which left her free in the afternoons, she charred outside. During the Thirties when there was talk among my literary friends of the Proletarian Novel, she was, for me, the archetype of that monolithic figure, the Working Class Mother, the deep bosomed, the understanding, her strength, her good nature, her permanence giving her a symbolical quality. Her son died in the States, and friends sent home a photograph of him in his open, up-ended coffin. And for a few weeks after she had received it, if you met her in a passage-way with mop and bucket, she was liable to draw it out from the complicated recesses beneath her coarse hessian apron, or 'rubber', and disclose it for your admiration. Unfortunately, the man had been dressed up with dinner jacket and bow-tie and laid in a casket with satin frills round the inside, for all the world like a grotesque doll in a giant's toyshop, or, since the ensemble was surrounded by enormous floral wreaths, a surrealist sweetmeat. This was before our general knowledge had been enriched by Evelyn Waugh's evocation of Whispering Glades, before I had read that description in Faulkner of a gangster's obsequies, so I had difficulty in concealing my horror from that brave old woman.

5

Men My Brothers, Men the Workers

The night watchman I met on Wednesday and Saturday evenings when we were compelled to be around until the building closed at nine o'clock, for he came on duty at that hour. A tall, robust fellow, rather like an ex-policeman, his name was Bob Molyneaux, which to me always seemed at variance with his appearance and job, for Molyneaux is a name known to Irish historians as that of an early eighteenth-century economic reformer, a friend or, maybe, just an acquaintance of my hero John Toland, the deist and biographer of Milton. Bob worked a seven-day week which included a twelve-hour stretch from Saturday night till Sunday morning. Arduous as this seems, it accorded well with his other avocation, that of a green grocer, for his wife and he kept a wee shop in a backstreet, hardly a stone's throw from where I first went to school. When he went off duty he could go straight to the early morning vegetable market and haggle for supplies.

The seams and creases of the old industrial area where the little red brick houses of the workers cowered in the long shadows of the tall bleak factories, an area which lay in a drab arc, on a mile radius from the city centre, to the north and west, was hiving with little shops such as his. Every street had its backyard population of horses and asses for the two wheeled carts.

In the years when I walked to school by my father's side, on the last lap going down Agnes Street there were three establishments which always kept my attention: the leather shop with that characteristic smell, its windows decked with shining saddles and long whips and brass studded head harness; the blacksmith's with the smell of burning horn and the banging of hammers on anvils and the dull glow at its cavernous entrance; the hay store, a mere doorway in the wall, out of which tufted a spiky barricade of straw, while across the fronting pavement there was dusted a splay of oat grains usually worked over by jerking pigeons. The little man who owned the hay store had a large red swelling on his neck, and his short legs were given frequent exercise by the boys out of school at lunch time or from the neighbourhood, filching and snatching handfuls of grain for their birds at home. He was found drowned one morning in a stream up in the dark hills where the town straggled to its end, and the hay store never opened its narrow door again. But while it prospered with the saddlers and the farriers, it was tied-up with the warren of small shops and carters; harness, shoes and fodder for the beasts, rims for the cart wheels, and reins and whips for the drivers; a whole traditional, paleotechnic pattern, in a few years to be superseded by the internal combustion engine, the filling station and the smudge-faced apprentice in overalls.

What Bob did during the daylight hours I could readily imagine: I even knew a tea-traveller who was also an exponent of Major Douglas' Social Credit, one of whose regular customers Bob was. But how he filled the long hours between his clock rounds of the building I never knew. There were no portable radios then, and it is unlikely that he read anything, for he could only spell with difficulty, as some of the bizarre reports circumstance forced him to make evidenced.

The superintendant, or foreman, who had been employed when the building opened, had left before I became a Local Government Officer. He had been found to be deeply engaged with the suppliers of furnishings and working materials, as, for example, when, with an official order for turpentine for the Museum, he had secured a tea-service for himself.

He had at first obtained his appointment because of his military bearing, his waxed moustaches, and a grovelling obsequiousness to those in authority. He was succeeded by a small stout man with a round red face who wore his uniform cap at a jaunty angle and whistled party-tunes. By trade, a pattern-moulder, by hobby a player of the large Orange drums, known as Lambegs and hammered with light short canes not padded drumsticks, he was the son of the mace-bearer in the City Hall. Nevertheless, he saw to it that the building was well maintained. Particularly proud of the excellent condition in which the cork-tiled floors were kept, he was once asked to write out his recipe for the superintendent of another public institution with similar flooring. The first requisite, he wrote, was 'Wax deluded with turpentine'.

He set the pattern. Most of his subordinates were also members of the Orange Order, and many, in addition, related by marriage or kinship to members of the City Council. One man indeed, son-in-law of a councillor, coupled his Orange membership with being a Freemason; but the majority of his colleagues considered that in this he was being above himself, straying out of his class. As I was informed, 'Masonry is for gentlemen'. Like most of the others, he too was an Ex-Service man.

The Ex-Servicemen were divided into two camps; those who talked at length about their war experiences and those who ostentatiously maintained a deliberate silence. One of the first group, a bandy fellow with a flat nose, was a notorious fire-eater and self-reported hero, seemingly utterly unaware that when first engaged as night-watchman before Molyneaux came, his persona had received perceptible damage when he had been detected carrying a loaded stick on his rounds. His chief enemy was a tall gaunt man who had served in the Marines. The men had their meals in the kitchen, a small tiled room with a hot plate which always reeked of burnt toast. Here, these two, if their times off-duty coincided, used to sit back to back, ignoring each other. Now and then, when the flow of heroics became intolerable, the tall man would stride out of the kitchen in disgust. Once, when I met him in the corridor after such a withdrawal, he remarked, 'Mr Hewitt, did ye not see the blood pouring under the door?' The same man, although war epics were abhorrent to him, polished his medals till every detail was rubbed down to a blurred smoothness. He was the principal Art Gallery patrolman and I got to know and like him.

When his tuberculosis became serious and his sick leave periods lengthened, the cost of the proprietary brands of medicine which his doctor prescribed became more and more of a burden. On this point I became involved in a lengthy correspondence with the Ministry of Health. I ran the gamut from simple statement and appeal, through irony and restrained indignation to prophetic rage, but achieved nothing. Of course, the faceless bureaucrat who dealt me back the numb stereotyped replies, was bound by rule; but this did not excuse the style of those answers. If he had only written 'Look here, I know the law's full of silly anomalies, but I can't get round 'em. I would if I could'. I should have felt better about it. It simply confirmed me in my deep inherited hate for bureaucracy in any guise. The end of my friend was pitiful but characteristic. He was taken to a sanatorium, but when he knew that he must die, he insisted against all persuasion and authority that he must die at home with his wife and adopted child, and did.

His relief man in the Art Gallery patrol, a small lurching fellow with large hands, was our Catholic, alone among the male employees, and had to endure a good deal of not very amusing or kindly badinage on that score. He was noted for his strength and grudgingly admitted to be the hardest worker in the place. His exploits with the polisher, a heavy metal head with a cloth face attached to a long shaft, were much talked of, as he kept those cork-tiled surfaces to a beautiful even amber hue. Among the work people he was my truest friend.

For the rest, the men worked well enough, for these were the days of the Depression, and hundreds outside waited for their jobs to fall vacant. It was a warm indoor job, and the pay, about fifty shillings a week, reasonable at that time, and, as if they appreciated this, they seldom got involved in rows or disturbances of any depth or duration. Over my memory of them hangs only one question: where did all those foot-rules, screwdrivers, pliers, bradawls, disappear to? Perhaps they were considered expendable; and, anyhow, there was, with us, always the saving phrase 'It all comes off a broad board'. And compared to the rumoured dishonesty of the shipyards, where a piano vanished over the side into a waiting launch, from a passenger ship in dock for repairs, and where, once, a workman running for his homeward tram, fell and could not rise because of the shelving in his overcoat lining, our little losses or discrepancies were of small account.

Until the outbreak of War in 1939 there was little change in the names and faces, a few more men were taken on as increased activity justified. That man died. The hallporter retired. But till the war came and several left for the forces and others for the foundries, all remained much the same. Yet looking back on that momentary stability, I can gauge the force and direction of social change from little things. As for example, I remember that when men were screwing the pictures to the wall, one or two, when my back was turned, would whip out spectacles – the steel rimmed variety – the better to co-ordinate screwdriver and screw, and when I turned or returned, whip them off and pocket them, lest it should be thought that they were in any way physically unfit for the work. As one who had worn spectacles since leaving school, as the son of a spectacled man, this, at first, I had little patience with; but in time, I understood the old bitter body of experience which lay behind the fear, when 'the industrial scrap-heap' was no rhetorician's flourish but a poignantly exact evocation of a horrible fact, and a risk that will always remain until we have a Socialist economy.

As another consequence of the Depression, we had weekly visits to the gallery of boys and girls from the Juvenile Training Centre; these were youngsters who had just left school and for whom there was no room in the Labour market. These visits to the Art Gallery and Museum were intended to diversify the more routine instruction of the Centre. Sometimes they were given illustrated lectures, sometimes conducted tours of special loan exhibitions. When I had finished my guide lectures I observed that little groups surged off to the small gallery where the casts of classical sculpture were then displayed, to frolic and giggle and snigger at the naked Greeks and Romans and leave fingermarks and pencil scribbles behind.

So, having considered the problem, when next the trainees came, instead of marching them round an array of paintings, I herded them resolutely into the classical sculpture room, and gave them a talking to on the marvel of the human body, on the place of nudity in art, on Frankness and Shame, on Decency and Indecency. After a restless phase of embarrassment and resistance, they settled down, attentive all, boy and girl. No doubt I was rather naive, maybe rash. I was certainly unprepared for the sequel. The next day I was called in to the Curator's office. He had received an outraged letter from the Principal of the Centre, complaining that I was demoralizing his innocent charges. If the Curator could not give a firm undertaking that my offence would not be repeated, the regular visits would have to be terminated. He did. I was forbidden ever again to attempt such a shocking procedure. So that old man, who himself could never pass through a doorway or leave the elevator without fingering his fly-buttons, struck his blow for clean mindedness and purity of heart.

6

Kabooti

As I have already remarked, my first working-corner was at a trestle table in the back store. I was not long enough in the museum and art gallery profession for the word store to have assumed its peculiarly portentous associations. Storage-space is what no museum or gallery can have enough of, even, as I discovered in the years ahead, in a new building. Architects instinctively feel that their skill and reputation depend on what is seen. Committees and private benefactors want urgently to see value for their money, and consequently are only interested in what can be offered openly, accessible to the public whom they wish to impress. So that the conscientious museum or gallery man is faced with a difficult task. He may, in theory enunciate the optimistic principle that his institution should resemble the iceberg, one fifth visible: but he will, in practice, have to remain discontented and frustrated with the absurd reversal of the berg's proportions. I could not therefore appreciate that to begin my working days crammed in a store was, in a way, symbolical. I was starting among the grass roots of my craft.

Although, you might think, it was not the most appropriate setting for a new art assistant, it had a number of advantages. I was generally left alone: anyone wishing to speak to me had to make a journey of it. I could, without much interference, become adjusted to the atmosphere of the place; not the glassy front face of the exhibition galleries with the carefully composed showcases, but the old suppressed mind of it, where the memories and the mistakes, the ephemeral victories, the lasting defeats, the temporary enthusiasms, the discarded, the broken bits of experience lie silently waiting for the re-assessment, the re-discovery of purpose, or simply the continuing indifference. For everything here had, at some time, been

37

considered worth rescuing from the trunk in the attic, the packing-case in the warehouse, or the shelf in the hall.

My table was in a narrow alley between tall glass cases, stuffed with mouldering mounted birds and dusty armadillo-carapaces, or piles of odd cups and saucers and chipped bowls. These wood-membered cases with their flawed panes of glass had come from the Old Museum where they once had been on public view, the most effective display units of their day; and for all that I know may still be in use, the cracked glass stuck with adhesive tape, the shattered glass replaced by slabs of hardboard, well into their second century. I could not help imagining the faces and hands reflected in their prime, over the years, had been those of the best and most idiosyncratic men of my town; the scholarly merchants, the polymath clergy, the natural philosophers who lived on trade, the far travellers with private means or resourceful wits. It seemed now and then that I caught sight of the ghostly, distanced images of the bewhiskered Gordon Thomson, first settler at Sydney, of the spade bearded Canon Grainger, hoarder and bestower of querns and stone axes, of the bland Emerson Tennent, dedicatee of *Our Mutual Friend,* who brought back from Ceylon the painted dancing masks upstairs, and the huge limestone hand from Abu Simbel that lies on the grass verge outside, and two or three of the brave painters who formed our first Association of Artists in 1856, and, surely, the long bearded visage of the indomitable William Gray.

On the top of one case was perched a large glass fronted box containing a stuffed bulldog, his campaign medals with the faded ribbons affixed to the backboard, for he had been a regimental mascot in the heyday of the expanding Empire. On the top of the case opposite was a slender Eskimo kayak. Propped up vertically on another stood the lid of an Egyptian sarcophagus; and, on a high shelf, that surrealist delight, a large solid challenge cup buffed out of anthracite, and the small cast iron statuette of a seated man, his legs crossed. Here and there in corners too were those curiosities which had drawn the holiday concourse, the twisted glass walking sticks, and the length of the Atlantic cable.

But chief survivor of the museum's past, principal Easter Monday attraction, the mummy still possessed a glamourie that would not permit her to be hidden. She had her long glass box upstairs not far from the great headhunters' War canoe. I have written she, for the mummy was of Kabooti, daughter of a High Priest. The face had at some time fallen-in, but with coloured plaster-of-paris the concavities had been filled. The curious might, however, discover the grooved head of a screw obtruding ever so slightly from the end of the sarcophagus, and go away marvelling at the technological achievement of the Nile folk. At the centre of the Museum's tradition, it was still to wonder at that small face with the cracked lips and the mirthless smile, at the shrunken body, that visitors made Easter Monday, even in my day, the peak of the year's attendance. And in spite of conscientious attempts to systematize the displays of enthology, of archaeology, this single object which one could relate to nothing else, serenely maintained her awesome dominion. In this resides, I am convinced, an important truth for all museum men. You may seek to educate, to elucidate, by diagram, by label, by all the devices of display and presentation. You may feel that you are an instructor, a persuader with every resource of Gestalt and other psychologies. You may consciously or unconsciously shape your arrangements of specimens to the stylistic fashions of the moment – just as my first case of primitive sculpture was set out on interlocking blocks in a cubist manner, and my second, twenty years later, had backgrounds derived from Miro – but what the public need from a museum is the Mummy-Woman and all that she implies of curiosity, mystery, terror, shock.

One Saturday afternoon – for many years we were on duty on Saturdays – the bell at the office window rang and I went to attend to the enquirer. An elderly woman plainly dressed, very quietly proffered a little cardboard box, the kind of box you used to receive fragments of wedding cake in, which, when opened contained a piece of notepaper folded round a short string of half a dozen blue faience beads, a tatter of dusty stained linen, and a shard of gesso with traces of crumbling pigment. The note's pale ink still had strength enough to declare that these items had been given to Mr Francis Davis on the occasion of the unwrapping of the mummy. I accepted the donation and thanked the woman who, if I recall correctly, said that she was a daughter of the recipient; and, in my ignorance, let her go away without questioning her. This I still regret, for when I began my study of the local poets I found out a good deal about Francis Davis who was certainly one of the most important of them. He lived from 1810 until 1886, contributed in his earlier years to the famous Irish journal *The Nation*, his signature in its columns being 'Francis Davis the Belfastman', to distinguish him from that other, greater Davis, Thomas, the father of the Young Ireland movement. When I came to collect the Belfast man's volumes, I found his long poem 'Kabooti', or 'Musings over a Mummy' in his *Tablet of Shadows: A Phantasy and other poems* (1861). I also discovered among the old records that, in 1847, William Thompson, greatest of Irish Naturalists, offered him his friendship, and sponsored his visits in the spring of the following year to the Museum where he made his first acquaintance with the Egyptian princess. Further researches brought out another coincidence, that for some years around 1869, the poet lived in the Cottage which stood somewhere near the present junction of the Malone and Stranmillis Roads, say, fifty yards from the present Museum, made available to him by Alexander Crawford, Seneschal of Belfast.

So the place where my old poet mourned the untimely death of a deeply loved little child, a spot now covered by later bricks and mortar, stands not far from the centre of a triangle of lasting significance to me, the corners of that triangle being the Methodist College which I entered in 1920, the Queen's University where I graduated in 1950, and the Museum and Art Gallery which I left in 1957.

There have been those who have praised the rooted man. But of roots Roberta once said: 'They're alright if you keep them underfoot, and don't let them get round your neck.'

After maybe a month it occurred to the Curator that perhaps the back store was scarcely the proper place for me. So I was edged into a smaller but more suitable room. But every time business took me as it did infrequently to my first habitat, I always had the sense of entering the past, as one does in a country graveyard, or an English village church. My new apartment I had to share with Harold and with William Hill the label-writer and his Roneo duplicator and tins of printer's ink. William Hill was a strange man, middle-aged, clean shaven with whitening sandy hair, solid, steady, utterly reliable, with that emotional constraint which I have remarked in many Armagh men. He nevertheless spoke almost continuously in puns of the most excruciating kind. 'Ticket or leave it', he would always say, when he handed you the trial pull of an exhibition invitation which he had just set up.

In that narrow room which had been, in the architect's plans, meant for the Staff Retiring Room, I spent the best part of twenty working years. Alfred was more fortunate, for he occupied what was really a large landing at the back stairs of the Museum floor. On the high wall above his desk hung Fantin Latour's copy of Veronese's *Marriage Feast of Cana*. Smaller, of course, than the original, this painting at one time circulated among the North Country merchants who were Rossetti's and Whistler's patrons. Staff accommodation was clearly not considered a high priority in those days. When the new building had been taken over, the Assistant Curator found that no provision had been made for an office for him; so, he managed to have a slice partitioned off the general office, about six feet wide and maybe fifteen feet long. This general office housed the metal filing cabinets, the telephone switchboard, a typist's desk adjacent, and a long oak table of unknown antecedents upon which lay the timebook wherein we entered the details of our comings and goings. Only the Curator had a spacious room, with his two desks, one flat, one roll-top, and an enormous ceiling-high built-in bookcase along one wall, on the upper shelves of which were banked runs of never consulted periodicals, the Proceedings of the British Association and of the Smithsonian Institute. It was early, therefore, in my professional career that I realized the principle later to be popularized in the catch phrase 'I'm all right, Jack'.

7

My First Exhibition

The first exhibition with which I was physically engaged was of Yugo-Slav Painting and Sculpture. The paintings were roughly what we called, in those days, Post Impressionist, a blanket term for all work which betrayed any acquaintance with Cezanne, Picasso, Matisse or any of their derivatives. There were no abstractions, but a couple of still life canvasses showed, in their cavalier approach to normal shape and to gravity, the influence of the earlier distortions of Cubism. Several of the painters – I remember the names, Tabaković and Hegedušić – handled folk-subjects in a sturdy simpli-fied manner. Incidentally, when, in the summer of 1961, in Coventry, I had another exhibition from the same source, the only artist common to both was this same Hegedušić, whose burly prole-tarian figures looked cheerfully at odds with the surrounding areas of action painting and abstract expressionism, which, except perhaps a little in colour, appeared indistinguishable from current essays in the International style from anywhere in the decadent West.

Amusingly, I find, among the notes I made for my own interest, of this 1950 show, the following, 'Hegedušić who paints like a Dutch communist of the sixteenth century, in other words, like Brueghel, is represented by a fine *Fair at Koprivnoca*, *The Revolt of the Peasants*, and a striking pacifist study *Requisition*'. This was not bad for a beginner, for, nowadays, this artist, God bless him, is, in fact, high up in the Party hierarchy and is saluted as a bold and beneficent influence on the younger generations. He has survived intact.

The strength of the exhibition lay in the sculptures, principally those of Meštrović and Rosandić. The bronze bust of Sir John Lavery by the former remained in the Gallery as a gift from our famous townsman, the sitter. Rather larger than life, it presents his features, but the effect of his character has been lost in the rhetoric seldom absent from Meštrović's work. His big wood reliefs *The Annunciation* and *The Woman of Samaria* were, by the standards of those days, expensive, and had, I remember, a polished professional appearance; but the Art Sub Committee purchased, surprisingly for Protestant Belfast, a wide relief *The Deposition* by Rosandić, later entitled 'Neuralgia' by my friend George MacCann, because of Mary's gesture of grief, and a small version of the bronze *Ecce Homo* – the Tate has a life-size version – and a, less surprisingly, secular bronze bust by Fran Cota. A stone carver, Palavicini, caught my attention with his rather Gill-like figure *Summer*, a slender column incised rather than deeply cut in the form of a girl; the material respected in the contemporary dogma. When I was in Belgrade in the winter of 1959, I was pleased to see him represented in the National Museum. It was on this occasion that I saw a roomful of Meštrović's work, and appreciated, at last, the enormous reputation which he enjoyed during and just after the First World War. When I read his obituary in *The Times* in January 1962 I suddenly realized that I had taken him for dead a long time ago.

Some years after, the *Ecce Homo* was appropriately set up in an alcove on the landing between the Museum and Gallery floors. As there was a lift, the staircase was seldom used or patrolled, and, on a couple of occasions, we found little posies of wild flowers laid at its base. Someone must have been there before, and remembered and come again, to let that tense tortured figure know that he was not utterly forgotten in that unsanctified place.

Hanging these paintings was my first task, and, though I had been warned, I was surprised when the actual arrangement of the framed works was decided by the Curator's wife. Apparently, this had been the established practice. As she was a tiny woman, the pictures were hung at a height convenient for her, but much too low for the comfort of adult visitors. It was the recognized device to use a wooden board, a foot high, which when placed upon the moulded skirting, gave a firm base for the frame to be rested on while being affixed to the wall, ensuring that the pictures were shown with the bottom edges of the frames in a straight line. This was the rule for many years, and although by degrees I inched that bottom line higher and higher to a more comfortable level, it was only when Major A.A. Longden of the British Council, in the last years of the war, came and arranged an International Exhibition and set the precedent, did I take to hanging by 'the top line' in preference.

The inherent weakness of the board-method was that, as I soon found out, very few frames are made with true right-angled corners and with exactly parallel members, so that, even with the level board, frequent juggling to make the frames look right, was always necessary. For the same reason, spirit-levels are of little use. The trained eye is the safest arbiter.

After this exhibition Mrs Deane came no more to do the arranging, but slipped in now and then to inspect whatever order I had imposed. At the beginning Harold and I did most of the physical work; so that we were both very handy with bradawl and screwdriver, and it has long been my boast that it was a rare screw that could not be turned; if I could get the screwdriver to it. Then, by degrees, we had the attendants brought in; and, in my last years, I had merely to superintend.

In many other ways we were constantly kept in mind of our subordinate roles. Every title to be painted on a frame, or lettered on a mount, every label drafted for a specimen had first to be submitted to the Curator. Very soon, it became evident that he was happiest when making changes in these; and, having silently raged through the milder band of frustrations, and watching my direct prose mauled, I hit upon the easy device of deliberately placing an obvious mistake, preferably in that section of my composition in which I took least pride. So, in a few months, both the Curator and I were happy, for his heavy handed corrections produced the result I had intended from the first.

The hours were long then. We were expected to be around from 9.30 a.m. to 6 p.m. on most days; and as the building was open to the public until 9 p.m. on Wednesdays and Saturdays, we had to be on duty too. This had one consequence in bringing to an end my Saturday afternoon cricket. Those long evenings were usually spent in the drudgery of writing-up the duplicate accession book, for no one had thought of loose-leaf or carbon copy. There were, of course, no morning and afternoon cups of tea; and if we wanted to smoke, this obtained for the Assistant Curator too, we had to commit the offence in the staff lavatory. The Curator himself was a heavy pipe-smoker, and if by any chance you had to go into his office to see him or to consult one of the reference books on the lower shelves of his bookcase, after the knock on the door, there was the sound of a fumble and a slamming of drawers, and, on entering, he was to be observed sitting sullen and guilty looking, his natural features in this setting him at a great disadvantage from the start, in the midst of ascending coils and scarves of light grey smoke. His chief talent was for going with and, consequently, managing the Committee, particularly in regard to fairly regular increments of salary, but as these applied only to himself and not to his staff, this skill was viewed with little enthusiasm, particularly by his deputy, who, to be honest, carried out most of the administration, in addition to a great deal of practical work in conservation and display. The general lack of cordiality of atmosphere may be gauged from the fact that neither the Curator nor his deputy once, in the score of years I served under them, called me by my Christian name; but wider experience has made me think that this may be a trait of Englishmen who are uncertain of their own class-status. Alfred and Harold, having entered the Museum as boys were, however known by their first names consistently.

The two men, chief and deputy, were ill-matched, and it was a tragedy that circumstance had spancelled them together the better parts of their lives. When the Curator, whose health was not of the best, failed to appear of a morning, the climate mellowed, and the deputy fairly exuded relief and pleasure and walked with a springier step.

Although we were a small and largely self contained community, not even, since the building was quite a distance from the City Hall, very much in contact with our fellow local government officers, we were, of course, affected by some outside events, as when, in the first twelve months of my service, in September 1931, our salaries, like those of all public employees in the United Kingdom, were cut by the ten per cent edict of the National Government which swept into office after the Bankers' Ramp, and I found myself being paid twenty-five pounds a year less than when I had started. My sympathies were certainly with the Invergordon mutineers. But, though memories are short, I have never failed to be surprised when I am abruptly confronted with blunt evidence that events or persons once generally taken as important raise no flicker of response.

One of the Gallery's principal collections was that of Sir John Lavery, who gave the city a representative selection of his paintings, including a group of portraits of eminent politicians and churchmen specially executed; and these, then, had a room given over to their permanent display. All through my childhood, youth and early manhood, many of the subjects of the portraits were simply built-in to the fabric of our society; Lord Carson, Lord Craigavon, the Marquess of Londonderry, Cardinal Logue, Archbishop D'Arcy ...

But already some years before I left Belfast, I found that schoolchildren and young people were growing up with little or no knowledge of these framed faces and what their significance had been.

The painting of Craigavon was a very honest piece of work; the North's first prime minister, sitting squarely with a hard red face above a high white collar. 'About as spiritual looking as a ham', my friend Dr Alexander Irvine, once remarked before it. This becoming aware of the vanishing of reputation was one of my keenest experiences of growing older; for these men who had plotted, and wrought and brought into being the Six Counties State bestrode our little world with stature and authority; and my resentment at the decline has had the peculiar effect of making me eager to do justice to the memory and reputation even of those with whom I held nothing in common. Carson, the leader of the Anti-Home Rule agitation in the days before the Kaiser's War, I had seen and heard when, as a tiny boy, I went with my aunt and uncle to a great tented convocation at Six Roads End. On the partition of the country he was pushed aside by the manipulators and organizers of victory for the cause which he had articulated. But, years later, the day of his burial in St Anne's Cathedral was made a public holiday in the city. So, Roberta and I set off out of town, to Mallusk, to find and salute the grave of James Hope, that fine working-class leader of the United Irishmen, who had outlived his executed or exiled comrades, to become a main source for Madden's history of the movement. And we felt the day better spent than if we had remained on the perimeter of hypocritical mourning for the cheated leader of a wrong cause. Craigavon, who took over when Carson's use had been exploited and exhausted, to become premier for a record-breaking period, I have thought, had some right to a place in a great generation, smaller naturally than the others, Masaryk, Kemal Atatürk, Mackenzie King, but sharing something of their monolithic strength, even if his part was played out on a very much smaller stage. I detested his opinions and deplored many of his actions, but, undoubtedly, although he had little intellect and no culture, he had abundant personality, not of the mountebank or clown, but of a man who had purpose and direction and courage; and, with these qualities allied to political shrewdness, ever cunning, in a strange way, he carried through all his manoeuvres and crises his own integrity, though, as my friend W.R. Rodgers once said in a pub *apropos* of someone else, 'Integrity is a lid that covers many bins'.

8

Chance Encounter

In late September, I think, or early October 1952, we took in an interesting Rodin Exhibition, the first important display of a great sculptor's work ever to have come our way. It consisted of a few large or medium-sized and a good range of the smaller bronzes; *The Thinker, The Kiss, John the Baptist, The Man with the Broken Nose,* the praying hands of *The Cathedral* chief among them, with about a score of the lightly tinted sketches of dancers. As I had visited the Rodin Museum in Paris, and had, at that time, a lively enthusiasm for his work, the Curator acquiesced in my suggestion that I should give explanatory talks on the exhibition at stated times during its showing, and be available if any visitor asked for my guidance. To this end a boldly lettered card announcing our intention was pinned up.

So it happened that one afternoon I was sent for, as a couple of Americans, I was told, had asked for me. These proved to be a young man and a young woman. The man, a pleasant looking fellow, by the cut of his clothes was clearly from the States. The young woman, to my surprise I recognized. The youngest of the three daughters of a genial little widow who had been very friendly with my parents for many years, she had gone to Canada and then into the Republic some years previously; and now was enjoying her first holiday back home. Her companion she had met on board ship. A slight dark pretty girl with bright eyes and strongly marked brows, the only hint of her transatlantic sojourn an unselfconscious use of that comely passive particle gotten, I thought her far more interesting than on our previous encounters so long before.

The other day I asked Roberta what she remembered of that exhibition. She replied that, having seen, over the years since then, sculptures by Rodin on a number of occasions and in a variety of places, she could not honestly be sure. What she did recollect was that during my interpretive remarks I used my hands a great deal, particularly gesturing with a pressing thumb, to demonstrate the shaping of the forms. This, I am sure, is accurate, for I have never really thought of Rodin's figures as metal, but rather as clay arrested, and fixed forever when he drew back his hand for the last time.

9

Billy and Jack

How I met Billy McClughin I do not remember. It must have been very shortly after I took up gallery work when I was beginning to know local artists in any number. The same age as the century, he was a well built young man of medium height with a good head of hair, a slightly crooked jaw, and a diffident manner. An enthusiastic cyclist, he had been run down by a drunken motorist with no insurance and an address in the Irish Free State; and so he ended with a broken jaw and no compensation. His ill-luck persisted, and when I met him he was unemployed, although he had served his apprenticeship with a local firm of printers and had been until his accident employed by them as a commercial draughtsman.

Early in 1932 he told me of a young artist he knew, a former student at the Slade, just returned from London. His name was John Luke. Without more ado, I asked Billy to bring him along some evening. They came and talked for hours, for Billy and I were eager to learn something of the ways of the students in the metropolis. And that evening too, while I was reading some of my recent verse to them, Jack drew a quick pen and ink sketch of me, which, for all its slightness, remains the best likeness of the, maybe, half dozen portraits that I have sat for in pencil, chalk, watercolour, and oil. Out of that first memorable meeting developed one of the most fructifying of the earlier phases in my thought, for we three, during the next ten years, maintained a rich and complicated conversation on art, its theory, its practice, its origins, its future.

John Luke was twenty-six, six feet tall, dark, handsome, of an erect, spare build. Coming from a working-class family in which his many brothers and one sister had a high level of general ability, his eldest brother being a District Inspector in the Royal Ulster

Constabulary, he had started work as 'catch-boy' in the shipyard, one of the young helpers whose task it was to tong up and deliver the hot metal rivets to the craftsman who banged them into the holes drilled in the metal plates with his narrow hammer. There was a strike of the boys, and as a result, he never got back to the yard; but found, instead, a job in a factory warehouse. While there, some of his sketches or drawings caught the interest of an older workmate, who suggested that there actually was a place in town, in the Technical Institute, where he could get lessons in drawing. Approaching the headmaster with his little sheaf, he found his way opened by a scholarship to the College of Art. Supported by further scholarships and prizes he finished his course, and went on to the Slade, at that time under Professor Henry Tonks, where among his fellow students were William Coldstream, Rodrigo Moynihan, Claude Rogers and Geoffrey Tibble. Securing his diploma, he attended some further classes at the Westminster School of Art, and picked up a few commissions, one being for murals in a motor showroom; but with the depression hardening, and the chances of earning a living diminishing, he had been forced, at last, to return to the shelter and security of home.

This was a generation which with the leisure of unemployment learned to use the resources of the public library service to the utmost. Not only Billy and Jack, but other friends whose interests were in literature became expert at knowing in which of the branch libraries in the city certain lines were best provided for: Templemore Avenue for Irish books, Yeats, A.E., Stephens, George Moore, Lady Gregory, due to Graeme Roberts having been an assistant there, with influence over the librarian; Shankill Road where the librarian prided himself on his coverage of contemporary drama and the novel, with an extensive representation of the Americans, Sinclair Lewis, Dreiser, Cabell, Van Vechten, O'Neill, Mencken, George Jean Nathan. The Central Reference Library stood out pre-eminently for books on art subjects, and it was easy to order the most recent volumes as they came out. Even so, a number of older, more obscure books could be tracked down in the branches, so that Billy and Jack became animated Union catalogues, and could unerringly lay hands on out of the way publications. From their reading and my own – I was lucky; I could afford to buy those books that attracted me most – and out of their arguments, I became well nourished in the current works in aesthetics. After Roger Fry and Clive Bell, it was R.H. Wilenski's *Modern Movement in Art* (1927) which most strongly directed our thinking, and to this and to his subsequent books I owe a great deal. His *Meaning of Modern Sculpture* (1932) and *The Study of Art* (1934) I have laid under constant tribute; the first for its bold exposure of the academic vested interest in the myth of Greek supremacy, the second for its clarification of the categories in the examination and criticism of works of art.

Frank Rutter had been invited back for a second time to lecture and, meeting the man, though he proved consolingly human when he misread the label and mistook a painting by the Irish artist Charles Lamb for one by the better known Henry Lamb, I devoted myself to his published works, chief among them *Evolution in Modern Art* (1926). At that time the handiest compendium on popular art-history was *The Outline of Art*, edited, it was claimed by Sir William Orpen, one chapter of it, on twentieth-century British painting by Rutter. It has been superceded in our day by Gombrich's *Story of Art*, certainly an indication of progress. Quite by chance, I discovered, while I was reading Rutter's little book on *The Wallace Collection* (1913) that not merely phrases but paragraphs seemed familiar, as, for example, those on the minor Dutch painters; it was not long before I found them in *The Outline*, and I realized that, although the bulk, if not all, the writing had been done by Rutter, because Orpen's had been a much better-known name, to him was ascribed the responsibility and the credit for the total venture.

Billy introduced me to the work of W.R. Lethaby, whose *Form in Civilisation* (1922) became one of my indispensable source-books, reiterating and carrying forward William Morris' ideas in a compact and memorable prose to link up with Eric Gill's insistence on the artist as craftsman necessary to society, in *Art Nonsense*. D.S. MacColl's *Confessions of a Keeper* in several of its constituent essays provided a useful corrective to Fry's exuberant sponsorship of Matisse, and in his discussion of gallery policies for acquisitions, established, in my mind, the easy absurdity of the practice of 'gap-filling'. From him we were led briefly to Vernon Lee and Miss

Anstruther Thomson with their theory of the necessary physical response to works of art. Lisle March Phillipps' *The Works of Man*, in its new edition, I was brought to by Jack, and its suggestion that vertical and lateral extensions have been the alternating architectural modes, more particularly its success in bringing into the general pattern the Egyptian and the Moorish contributions, and its insistence on the coherence of style from the chair arm to the cupola, provided me with a set of images and frames for holding firm the visual past. Never a volume I possessed, when, in 1950, there was a re-issue with a foreword by Herbert Read, I found to my disappointment that it had become so much the mulch and subsoil of my thought I could waken no tremor of response.

Read himself was just coming forward as a popular explicator with *The Meaning of Art* which started its long and successful life in 1951. I already knew his books on *Stained Glass* and *Staffordshire Pottery Figures* but considered him incomparably more important as a literary critic. For the next twenty years I kept pace with his publications on the visual arts, irked for a while by his pedantic superrealism; surprised by his assertion in 1955 that abstract art had an interim responsibility providing an effective means of 'keeping in pickle' and well-preserved, an appreciation of the importance and nature of formal relationships until such times as the artist could turn to serve a communal function once again; somewhat astonished that he should just then conclude his essay with the heavy type slogans that Revolutionary Art is Constructive, Revolutionary Art is International, Revolutionary Art is Revolutionary; but most of all, although this was extra-aesthetic, I was astounded by his retreat from Communism because, in less than twenty years the state had not 'withered away', in the Soviet Union, this from the man who was to chide William Morris for his ignorance of the Marxist dialectic. This shook my faith in his capacity for clear and rigorous thought, and made the later acceptance of a knighthood by a professed anarchist quite in character. When I met him in Dublin at the Art Critics' Congress, I asked him why. He explained with quiet earnestness that it was not really a personal affair; it demonstrated the first gesture of Royal approval for the modern movement in art, and, as such, it could not be declined. I thought of Yeats, and Joyce and Henry

Moore, and changed the subject by inquiring about the origins of his big book, *Education*. But the crystalline innocence of the man is nowhere more evident that in his statement, in one place, (*Poetry and Anarchism* (1947) p. 8) 'In spite of my intellectual pretensions, I am by birth and tradition a peasant. I remain essentially a peasant', and in another (*Annals of Innocence and Experience* (1940) p. 19), of Wordsworth, 'We both spring from the same yeoman stock' – for not to be able to distinguish a yeoman from a peasant argues a serious lack of historical awareness and psychological discrimination.

When the English translation of Wölfflin's *Principles of Art History* came out in 1932 I took eager hold of his contrasting descriptions of the painterly as opposed to the linear, of closed to open form. This, a short time before, I had found presented in a more simplified manner in Sir Charles Holmes' *Grammar of the Arts*; and both meshed into the dialectual rhythm which my thinking was beginning to develop. I could see from Wölfflin that the English critics had a certain narrowness of approach; so, for instance, I made my first consciously alerted acquaintance with the term Baroque, which because of the periods and styles that they favoured, lay outside their required vocabulary.

We were fortunate to have grown up in a period when so many of these volumes I have mentioned were readily available. Now the situation is changed. There is no space in even the better type of journal for reviews or essays to appear, which in time could be edited into book form as so many of these were. The proliferation of dealers' galleries in London has made it impossible for the critics to be more than reporters of names and titles with the most succinct of comments or the briskest of snap-judgement. The counterpart, it seems, for those books which fed us are little pocket-sized brochures with, maybe, a dozen pages or so of letterpress and a score or two of reproductions in unhappy colour, on some such topic as Chagall or Cubism.

It was to Jack that I owe my introduction to Lewis Mumford's *Technics and Civilisation* almost as soon as it came out; to my mind a much more useful book than the far better known *Culture of Cities*; for, although it had little to do directly with art, Mumford's schematization of the developing phases into Eotechnic, Paleotechnic, and

Neotechnic, gave a clarity to the technological past which made much easier the placing of any given culture. The richness and variety of its hoard of facts made coherent and brought into clear relationship with each other by the application of the dialectical process, presented me with a magazine of effective information and a critical implement, tempered later by an extended reading in the duller but more orthodox texts of Marx, Engels, Plekhanov, Lenin, and their British popularizers, which helped me to make what appears like sense, out of some of the swirls and eddies of the particles of my knowledge and experience; and so, Lewis Mumford has, in this and in his later books, an unassailable place among those who markedly shaped my response to my age.

It was not simply our reading which proved in itself so useful. Billy had a cautious, plodding, relentless mind, hardly to be persuaded, never by a slick argument or a snapping epigram, but tenacious as an octopus when he hugged an argument to his mind. Jack too, kept to his own pace, quicker than Billy at seizing an aspect or quality of a thought, but as thorough as he in organizing his own logical construction. It was this grinding thoroughness which most I lacked, which made me at first feel a lightweight in their company. But in due course I was, I believe, able to hold my own, and, although in the twenty years since our conversation subsided my ideas have altered and developed, nevertheless, they still carry the grain of the original mould from which they were extruded.

By no means all our talk spun round aesthetics, or art history. Technical works were just as eagerly studied. So A.H. Church with his classic *Chemistry of Paints and Painting* of which I was lucky enough to pick up a copy second-hand, and A.P. Laurie's books, especially his *New Light on Old Masters* and Max Doerner's *Materials of the Artist* became basic material in the dedicated search by my friends for permanence: the chiming name of Cennino Cennini, with *The Book of the Art*, as our translation had it, ringing through the discussion of the more prosaic tabulations and analyses with a friendly peal.

Naturally, this kind of knowledge had to be applied almost as soon as grasped, and so, from the demonstrations of my friends, I grew into some awareness of the skills of priming canvas or panel, the various stages of under-painting, of the significance of glaze and scumble, impasto, *alla prima*, and of the comparative values of mastic and dammar resins, of sun-thickened oil, of gesso; a range of knowledge which now seems irrelevant to an appreciation of practically all contemporary painting, which, nevertheless, has enriched my experience, over the years, of the great masters of the past.

One of Billy's chief enthusiasms was for Vernon Blake, a name which, to our deprivation, we never hear nowadays. He led us to Blake's books on drawing and to that magnificent chapter on the primitive mind in art, in R.S. Rattray's *Religion and Art in Ashanti* which has remained the best exposition of the subject known to me. But Vernon Blake meant much more than this to Billy, for he had also invented the cantilever brake for bicycles, which device was explained and expounded to us at length and in exhaustive detail on many occasions, although, lacking any mechanical comprehension whatsoever, I still have no idea of the principle involved or the logic of its application.

It was not in any appreciable measure due to their economic circumstance that my friends were frugal, abstemious and celibate. In our protracted debates and disputations our reason was never clouded nor our wits given a factitious brilliance by alcohol; and I was the only serious smoker in the company. Yet both were men of strongly individual humour in what might be considered unsophisticated styles. To watch Jack's acrobatics as he held a skein of wool for Roberta to wind was to enjoy an uproarious display of nimble contortions.

Billy was a snail's pace worker, but I still take delight in his fine watercolour *Sawmills* which cost me two pounds, an industrial composition in clean washes, influenced in choice of subject by Sir Charles Holmes whose *Notes on the Science of Picture Making* was also one of our important books. John Luke, at the Slade, had passed through an academic period recorded by a small self-portrait in the Orpen manner: and as the Orpen-John tradition lingered, he had become an excellent draughtsman of figure and head; and among his trophies he brought back the plaster cast of a well modelled woman's head taken from Laura Knight's favourite subject. At home, he went into a brief Cezanne phase, and it was exciting to see familiar corners of our walks, a dip and turn in a twisty road, or copper beeches crouching over a weir, translated into an unaccustomed idiom. There is a certain aspect of the northwest flank of the Cavehill which, when I see it, makes me imagine a Cezanne landscape, for, in those days, Jack talked of painting it in his manner of that moment. Then his thought turned to tempera, so I searched around for some way to encourage this. Finally, I persuaded my mother to let me have the handsome black frame of a romantic reproduction which she had bought a year or two before in a flash of extravagance, and then I commissioned Jack to design and carry out a composition to fill its rather unusual proportions for the frame was more than twice as wide as it was high. For this, without demur, he accepted my meagre three guineas; and I watched it grow from the smooth gesso of the panel to the bright colours of an imagined landscape.

When we were married, Roberta took to my friends without hesitation, and they became our most consistent frequenters. Missing the last tram meant nothing to either, for they were indefatigable walkers, not only for economy's sake, but for the physical and moral benefits. After a prolonged exploration of quills and reed-pens and Not Pressed paper and Whatman boards and the relative permanence of pigments and lengthy comparisons of the various wares of Winsor and Newton, Rowney's, Robersons, the colourmen, Billy's interest slipped over into oil painting. So, to give him practice, it was agreed that I should sit for my portrait, Roberta, at the same time, sitting for Jack. Every Sunday for nearly two years, barring holidays, the two artists arrived, unpacking their bags and setting up their easels while we hurried through breakfast. Then the painting began and continued until the light from the high windows failed. Ultimately Jack scrapped his masonite panel of Roberta, dissatisfied – we still have the finished drawing – but Billy plodded on with his half length of me, every touch meditated, and resolved. As he was still unemployed, when it was finished, he went down town with Roberta, who helped him choose a sports coat, grey flannels, and a shirt, to recompense him for his labour, since, as a painfully conscientious person, he would have felt compelled to report any extra Cash earnings to the National Insurance people.

Through my association with Jack I gained a valuable experience. Sir Stephen Tallents had been an admirer of his work in the London days, and when the chance of a mural commission came up, he enquired if Jack would be interested. In the event, would it be possible for the Director of the — Gallery to see some of his recent work, as the final decision rested with him? So, as Roberta and I were passing through London on our way to Paris, we proposed to take over a couple of unframed paintings which we could show to the Director, and then deposit with the Left Luggage at Euston to bide our return. An appointment was made, and, at the hour agreed, I called at the Gallery, and was led to the Director's room. I introduced myself, stating my business, and while I unbundled the paintings, he worked briskly through his mail. When the paintings were unsheathed, I set them up on chairs. The Director rose to his feet for first time, left his letters and came over. A swift glance told him all he wanted to know; so with not more than six words, in fifteen seconds flat, he was back among his letters; and I was left to parcel the paintings again, put the chairs back, and take my departure without even a glance in my direction from the great man. Had I indeed been the artist I should not have been able to hold my tongue.

As I stood in the passage outside the shut door with my roped bundle, I made a firm resolution that, when, in future, anyone brought pictures for me to see professionally, I should discover that person's relationship to the work or works, and then, in considered phrases, give my frank opinion. I should listen to anything my visitor had to say, open the door for him, shake his hand, thank him for calling and wish him well. This has proved, over the years, a time-consuming discipline, but I hope that I have left no uncomfortable memories for my callers to take away; for, who knows, one of them may, someday write his autobiography.

10

Welwyn 1933

The summer before we were married Roberta and I went over the water to the Summer School of the Independent Labour Party, held that year at Welwyn Garden City. Remembering that old Bruce Wallace, saint and childhood hero, had been one of Ebenezer Howard's lieutenants in pioneering the Garden City movement, the place had a certain aura of respect. In the event, we saw little of it, and now I can only recollect some resemblance to Port Sunlight, that other typically English housing experiment, in the absence of hedges and railings round the gardens. Most of our time was spent at the big conference house in the Digswell woods where I had my first acquaintance with the tame and orderly English countryside.

If there were any lectures I have forgotten them. What I best remember had to do with people, meeting the stout bland Chinese, Shelley Wang, his English not of the clearest, who was later to become our friend; meeting old Fred Jowett, a small paunchy man with a shock of white hair, in a crumpled navy blue suit. I got more from him then, than from Wang. He was, of course, the great Bradford socialist, where, so long ago, school milk had been introduced by a wildly revolutionary City Council. He had been in MacDonald's first Labour Cabinet, but refusing to deck himself out in court-dress on the ritual occasions, he was dropped from the second. Surprisingly, he recalled and told me of a visit he had paid to Belfast in January 1900, for the formation of the Labour Representative Council, the seed of the British Labour Party, and of walking over the Cavehill in a snow shower with William Walker, perhaps the first and certainly one of the earliest effective socialists in my native town. A mellow, diffident old man, full of political fire when roused, I set Fred Jowett in my mind as an unspoiled man, the

visionary who kept his visions well-earthed, whose face had not stiff-
ened into a public mask. Fenner Brockway, then in his forties, was
there too, a lean lantern-jawed man with rimless glasses, and, it
seemed, the perpetual scowl of the reformer on his face. He then
looked to me like a caricature of the socialist intellectual, but was
later to establish himself as the bravest fighter in the House of
Commons for the emergent peoples of Africa. He also wrote a good
fat biography of Jowett. We were not to see him again until a quar-
ter of a century later, when he welcomed the Aldermaston marchers
to Slough and found us a Church building where we could wring out
our soaking clothes on that dismal heartening Saturday when barely
a hundred had started out in sleet and snow from Hounslow that
morning.

There were others, lively likeable comrades, and several likeable
cranks; the old man with the rosy cheeks and shoulder length white
hair, in shorts and open-necked cricket shirt, who walked barefoot in
the morning dew before breakfast; the nearly naked sinewy young
man who subsisted entirely on green apples and had cycled from the
far north. But most impressive of all was James Maxton, in that hot
faraway summer usually clad only in grey flannels with a red ban-
dana round his head like a pirate chief. Not long widowed, there was
often a sadness about him, but this was broken by good amusing talk
at table or on deckchairs outside. He and Campbell Stephen, that
other Clydeside musketeer, could sustain an easy flow of fun laced
throughout with an innate socialist philosophy. It was from them
that I learned that no one needs a sense of humour more urgently
than the serious social reformer. One evening we were all marched
into town for a propaganda meeting at which Maxton was the prin-
cipal speaker; and having heard him also in the Ulster Hall at home
on several occasions, I put him at the summit of public utterance,
hardly at all below Saklatvala that other great agitator, now forgot-
ten, though he was at one time Communist MP for Battersea. Once
during that week a pair of young Germans arrived and a space was
cleared in the programme for them to talk to us. Both very blond,
brown with the sun – the girl to my shocked surprise, with tufts of
golden hair in her oxters – they looked excessively Nordic. They
spoke of a man called Hitler and how his party was taking over in

Germany, and the danger of it all. But at that date our imaginations failed us, we listened courteously and applauded politely. Only Jennie Lee, a girl in a white frock, not yet married to Aneurin Bevan, spoke with any answering seriousness.

I am reminded too of the stout young beautiful Dutch girl with the great full breasts and her wiry black-haired German lover, who steadfastly refused to have his photograph taken in that endless snap-shotting, for he was going back over the Dutch frontier. The single women had little rooms in a wing of the old house. The single men slept in a hutted dormitory; and once I had to wait at the foot of the fire escape while Smidt climbed down the creeper-tangled rungs in the moonlight.

This total experience now comes to me most vividly in Auden's lines from 'Look, Stranger' (1936); the perpetual summer, the cropped lawns, the light sky above the black trees, the lounging, the good talk, the cricket, the crankiness, the chatter at the long bare tables:

> Equal with comrades in a ring
> I sit on each calm evening
> Enchanted as the flowers ...
>
> Nor ask what doubtful act allows
> Our freedom in this English house,
> Our picnics in the sun.

11

The First Year

We were married on the 7th May 1934 at the registrar's office in Great Victoria Street, our witnesses being Roberta's stepfather and my father.

After the declaration we walked home to our flat on the Malone Road, about a mile away.

We did not go off for a holiday until September, when we went over to Paris. Roberta, not then conditioned to my strenuous gallery going, found it a strain attempting to deal with the intensive experience. In the Louvre we lost ourselves, and it seemed impossible that we should ever escape from those vast Rubens royal canvasses which confronted us at every turn.

One morning we were awakened very early by a strange forlorn piping, the oddest sound I have ever heard in any city. Roberta, first to rise, opened the shutters, stepped on to the minute balcony and called me to join her. In the bright morning light, in the narrow street below, a young man in country clothes, his hat over his eyes, and fingering a tin whistle, wandered along in a drift of eight or ten shaggy goats, and with his wavering plaintive tune, turned the corner out of sight, a strayed Apollo. And of all our memories of Paris that year, the paintings, the sculptures, the museums, the bookshops, the boulevards, the bridges, this remains the most significant, the stuff of a poem which I have never dared to write, a Joycean epiphany.

In those days we travelled third-class rail and steerage boat, arriving back home with just enough money to pay-off the taxi, and to buy a loaf of bread, half a pound of butter and a bottle of milk, for the next day was Sunday and we could have dinner at my parents'. My salary cheque was waiting for me at the Gallery on Monday.

Very soon we became involved in the Peace Movement, starting with others, Theo Moody, Maurice Boyd, Jack McCracken, our own organization, The Peace League, handing out leaflets, canvassing from door to door, publishing a pamphlet on Poison Gas, holding conferences, arguing with gate-crashing Blackshirts. I too had my debates with followers of Major C.H. Douglas, for at that time Social Credit with its jargon of the A+B Theorem and the National Dividend, made a brief appeal to young executives in the Irish Linen Trade, men of conscience and decency irked by Capitalist blundering but afraid of the Socialist answer. Since grappling with them and their theories, I have learned to consider every political party in greater or lesser degree vitiated by uncritical acceptance of orthodox finance. I do not believe in the sanctity of interest. I believe that money like any other tool must inevitably wear out.

Roberta began her twenty years' devotion to the Nursery School movement, acting as unpaid cook in temporary premises, secretary to a voluntary committee, one of a small band of dedicated women, holding tenaciously to the highest standards, till a tardy education authority took over the responsibility and made the Edenderry Nursery School part of its approved system, whereupon the women moved over and started another in a room at the Friends' Meeting House.

Then, although the twelve months was over, our first year was somehow rounded off with a holiday on Rathlin Island in June.

Rathlin, Raghery, Rachlin of the Ships in the old sagas, where Bruce watched his spider, a place of refuge and massacre in Tudor days, the only inhabited island round the Antrim coast, in our time, and maybe long after, not often visited by mainlanders and those mostly birdwatchers and broadcasters or day-trippers, is approached by motorboat from Ballycastle, traditionally run by the Coyles family.

It was the father, Johnny Coyles, we had, with his roaring stories of the wild silver foxes on the island, and the race of midgets living in caves, descendants of a wrecked circus, all the while with a knuckle at the corner of a watery eye. We had booked a room in a house in the row where the Post Office was, and with that as our base for eight days we tramped and climbed and talked to people over the stone dykes or lolled on the cliff tops, the only aliens there.

We walked south to Ushet Point starting rabbits all around, and watching a fight between a gull and a sparrow hawk. We clambered up the mound of sods and peered into the gloom of 'a sweat house', a primitive sort of Turkish bath no longer used. We saw a low white cloud come over towards us from Ireland, and then when it was half way across the strait, turn at right angles and sail off to the west to Sheep Island, a hump there, and Inishowen a guessed-at smudge. We met an island boy called James McQuilken, hired to a good farmer, earning ten pounds for his six months. He told us of the hiring fairs at Ballycastle, the boys and the girls going over to stand at the Diamond and wait for the farmers to choose.

An old woman came in one night and talked excellent folklore, of the gruagach, for these people in some way think of themselves as of the Western Isles; in Ireland, that would have been the banshee. When she was a girl working in the Big House, she heard the gruagach herself 'coughin' and riddin' its throat'; and that night Mrs Gage died.

Roberta found an oystercatcher's nest on the low rocks of Islandcarragh, where the mother-bird flew round us in widening circles to draw us off. Round the little Protestant Church all are buried, Protestant and Catholic alike. One imposing headstone is inscribed to Prince Albrecht of Waldstein, who was accidentally shot while a guest of the Gages, squires of the island; but the Big House is empty now.

Here we saw a grave opened for an old woman just dead, a brown skull set on top of the peaty raised earth. They would put it on top of the coffin tomorrow, for it was the skull of her man, dead forty years.

We stepped out the five long miles to the West Light across empty moorland, skirting past a little lough covered with a thousand gulls, roused in a hurricane by clapping; gaped at the tall stacks at the cliff bottom, black with birds; descended a hundred stone steps to the cliff foot, puffins and guillemots flashing and flapping past our faces.

We found the house untenanted, a teapot and cups resting on a spread newspaper; the keepers were inside the light polishing the glasses for the Commissioners' visit next week. On the way back a single heron stood beside the gull-deserted lough, rising with offended dignity and flying off towards Scotland.

One evening we visited McQuilkin's master, and saw the stallion we had watched two days ago being hauled up with ropes over the sea wall, out of the rocking boat, to serve the Island mares, as McCurdy led him round the yard in the summer twilight, a slight figure beneath that great lifted head, a piebald engine of power, feather footed yet fearsome.

We learned the place names, first of the little loughs of the Lower End, Ally, Ushet, Mullyroger, then the great historic names, Lagavistavohr, the hollow of the great defeat, and Crocknascreidlin, the rock of the screaming, where the women stood to watch their men go down. I learned to call charlock *prasha*, its name to me forever since: I have to stop and think back to 'charlock'. I had what I took for a sprained hand, and dipped it three times in the Holy Well at McQuilkin's bidding. When the swelling did not go down, James remarked that the well must be no good for sprains. In fact, it turned out to be blood poisoning, lanced, under an anaesthetic in Belfast, when I shot out into space, racing for, and hitting the sun and shattering it into a thousand golden pieces. So I shall never really know about that well.

Rathlin was a microcosm of the Irish past, a folk museum without turnstiles and tickets. It was the Island that everyone dreams of and believes in, Pitcairn and Iona, R.M. Ballantine and Long John Silver. It had its place in clarifying and consolidating my identity: and we have never gone back.

12

My Generation

Looking back now it seems as if no generation was ever so well informed on international politics as ours of the Thirties. The *News Chronicle*, popular daily for [this] kind of people, with A.J. Cummings and Vernon Bartlett, the strident *Penguin Specials* by Edgar Mowrer and Genevieve Tabouis, John Gunther's enormous *Inside* volumes, even, for those who were in the semi-secret, Claud Cockburn's *The Week* that spluttering squib of a newssheet, picked out of the embassy keyholes of half the world, fusilladed us with facts and forecasts. And the consolidating, the focussing instrument was, of course, the Left Book Club.

Here Davie's shop provided the obvious channel for us. At its peak the Club had something like 550 members registered with him, pledged to carry home the orange linen and, later, red cardboard bound volumes every month. And in the L.B.C. we found a new array of faces, as like was drawn to like, iron filings to the magnet, for none of us realized that what seemed personal choice was simply the mass moving of a generation, just as inevitably to be dispersed before the decade was out; but playing its part in creating the mood which gave Britain the Labour Government of 1945. I can recall as somehow a symbolical figure, George Hill the quiet newspaper-man, with the authority of Ulster's only war-novel behind him; still distinct, but without that authority, his henchman, the sporting journalist, and their friend, the red nosed linotype operator who tapped out surrealist poems on long galley strips, and the stout young biochemist and his large beaked dominant wife, and, less and less distinct, the Jewish law student or students (were there two of them?), the bank clerks, the school masters. And, lasting firmly till this day, the survivors of that company, the friendship stronger, the faith invincible, the Stewarts, Jim and Sophie: Sophie, sister of Dorothy Livesay the Canadian poet, an artist herself, her native drawl at times declaring itself, thin, pretty, with deep socketed, amused eyes; Jim, medium build, soldier-straight, his sandy hair receding, headmaster of a technical school in a country town, expert economist, excellent dancer, unshakeable democrat, clinging to his plain accent with clenched teeth.

What else remains? The dwindling pictures and dramas of our meetings: the public debate with the Oxford Group when mill owner and mill girl snuffled over the wrongs they had done to one another, the study circle gnawing through Strachey's *Coming Struggle for Power*, chapter by evening; the Russian films, *General Line*, *Potemkin*, *The Road to Life*, as the slow tractor waddled up the long cornfield, and the smiling brawny girl stood among the socialist apples hanging as heavy as her breasts from the bent branches; the haphazard production of *Where's that Bomb?* and aid for China and aid for Spain, and the ship impounded from Bilbao and the sailors with their red-faced captain; and the visit of the Basque children's choir, Laura and Aurora staying with us, when I had to take Josefa to mass in St Patrick's for, without it, he refused to perform that Sunday night; and when it came to making banners and posters, of all the committed or sympathetic artists, only the reliable John Luke and Sophie Stewart arriving equipped to do the practical work.

The meetings: with mild Tom Wintringham recruiting for the Red Cross in Spain; burly Wilfred Roberts, last of the Liberals, exposing Fascism; solemn Alick West, thorough in his socialist realism; James Bertram, boyish, talking of the Eighth Route Army and the long march; twinkling Professor Levy, dextrous with the dialectic: the first later simply to die; the second to be blown to bits training the Home Guard; the third, to become Professor of English at a Hungarian university; the fourth to be held by the Japanese and afterwards make a good book out of his experience; the last, to discover Anti-Semitism in Soviet Russia and resign from the party – We spoke with him at Reading on the Sunday of the first Aldermaston.

And through the years there were the municipal and parliamentary elections, for which our contemporaries in the L.B.C. did little, leaving them to the workers and the workless. Roberta was active, canvassing, addressing envelopes, folding circulars, supporting the candidate, struck in the back once with a stone thrown in Sandy Row as she stood up in the motor lorry. As a Local Government Officer, I could take no part, so I addressed the envelopes and folded the leaflets, and, once, for an election address, cobbled a few couplets.

It was early in 1937 that I was asked to go to *The Brown Horse*, a public house in Library Street, to discuss a literary project. It was all very confidential and conspiratorial; but when I arrived I found a small party of three, in a snug, waiting. I had come to know these men through the Left Book Club and as frequenters of the Progressive Bookshop, and had accepted the view, without any clear evidence for it, that they were very likely fellow travellers, if not card-carrying members of the Communist Party.

The project was to launch a monthly political journal, to be called *The Irish Democrat*, which would supply effective comment on and analysis of national affairs, while bringing these into proper relation with world events. I was asked to be literary editor, to look after book reviews, and, if any verse or competent fiction should come our way, to look after this too. As all contributors were to be anonymous or pseudonymous, I chose the name Richard Telford; Richard after my uncle, and Telford which was my father's second Christian name.

As, unfortunately, we could not carry on our editorial work in the snug of *The Brown Horse*, a little office was found up a stairway near the Great Northern Railway Station, and to this address I was committed to having my monthly budget delivered on time. I wrote my inaugural manifesto, bidding the proletarian writers of Ireland to unite and deluge us with the stories, the verses, the reportage (a vogue word then) born out of their immediate class and national struggle. I also reviewed George Orwell's *The Road to Wigan Pier*. When I had these typed, I decided against posting in the normal way, for it was accepted that the mails in Northern Ireland were under continual surveillance by the authorities. So, rather than inform the authorities if they did not already know, that Richard Telford was in fact John Hewitt, I took my envelope downtown to *The Democrat* office. I knocked on the door, but got no reply; so I dropped my stuff through the letterbox. Something prompted me to try the door handle. It opened straight away. I went in and saw my envelope lying at an angle in the wire-mesh catcher. This seemed a most insecure way of doing business, so I took out my envelope, stuck it in my pocket and went home, delivering it later by another method.

I was certainly not impressed by this casual attitude, but *The Democrat* came out alright, and continued to come out so long as I was associated with it. Sometime later two of its sponsors left to work in England, and it seemed sensible that the editorial work should be carried on across the water. In these circumstances I wrote less and less for it, my final contribution being an appreciation of Jack B. Yeats, based on a review of Tom MacGreevy's little book.

By means I have never been able to understand, *The Democrat* became the monthly organ of the Connolly Club, a Communist-inspired Irish Association in London, and continues to this day. It seems to me now an altogether deplorable production, its pages well padded with the words of sentimental Irish songs which most Irishmen anyway know by heart and ear. Wildly wrong in its inter-pretation of Irish affairs, foolishly supporting the reactionary I.R.A., lacking in frankness, blatantly opportunist, it has nothing to do with what we intended. Yet when, on the fringes of an open-air meeting in an English city, a young man with a thick brogue invites me to buy a copy, I always experience a momentary thrill of emotion for those far away days of the 'Left Book Club', 'The Popular Front', 'Aid for Spain', the snug in *The Brown Horse*, and take my copy and, turning its pages, rage at the betrayal of our dream.

13

The Henrys

It must have been in the first year of my marriage that I met Grace Henry, wife of Paul Henry the popular landscape painter and herself an artist. Indeed, there were those who maintained that she was better than Paul, but this is due to a misunderstanding. Because of his once ubiquitous railway posters and the reproductions everywhere of his Connemara landscapes with the blatantly blue pyramidal mountains, the billowing cumulus, the turf stacks and thatched cottages, his work seemed restricted to this easy personal convention and hackneyed by its tedious repetitions and by the prolific canvasses of his imitators.

I can remember the pleasurable shock of surprise I experienced, when, visiting a house in North Antrim, to inspect some old pictures offered as a gift, I saw my first Paul Henry outside the canon; a small panel of a dry-stone wall with a wind-twisted thorn-bush atop of it, an exciting and swiftly handled study in greys. Much later when I had seen a wide range of his smaller non-posterized works, I realized that he was the best Irish landscapist of the half-century, capable when occasion demanded, of fine Daumieresque figure compositions, and that Gauguin and Pont-Aven too were influences he used to great advantage in his paintings of the bright shawled women and shirtsleeved men of the west.

His place is with Peploe, Fergusson, Leslie Hunter, the Scottish colourists, as a pioneer in these islands of Post-Impressionism; and it should be remembered that, before his taking-over of Achill and Connemara as his own region, he had been included by Frank Rutter in the first London Salon of the Allied Artists in 1908, with Gilman, Ginner and Bevan, which fixes his period with precision. But the collapse of his reputation in his last years and since, is a signal demonstration of the law of diminishing utility as it operates in the sphere of reproductions, or, if you like, of the Marxist dialect, when popularity, surfeiting, inevitably turns into its opposite. But that is all the more reason why an effort should be made to understand and establish the right way of it.

I met him once in his old age when he was near blind, at a private view in *Waddington's Gallery* in Dublin, a man of about my own height and build, with a round pink soft face, and a black hat which I coveted. But shortly before this I had been asked to take part in a symposium in his honour, broadcast from Radio Eireann, and he had been good enough to send me a note of gratitude.

In my script, I spoke of how important Paul Henry's return to Ireland had been to the whole course, and direction of painting in that island, bringing over the air and ideas of the ateliers by the Seine, clipping a great length out of the time-lag which we had so seriously suffered. I went on:

> I have never met Paul Henry. But his importance for me has not been in his physical presence. I pass his birthplace every day on my way to work. I pass, too, within sight of his old school, which was also mine. I remember reproductions of his work in the long stone flagged corridor – what a generation that was at the Methodist College in the middle eighties! 'George A. Birmingham', born two doors from Paul, was there. Alice Milligan was there. So too was MacNeile Dixon, and, of course, Paul's brother Robert Mitchell Henry. And I have talked with and interrogated elderly men who were with him at the old Government School of Art under the gentle rule of the soft bearded George Trobridge.
>
> For me and for my generation in Belfast, Paul Henry's was the first name we learned in Irish landscape painting. He impressed, almost imposed, his personal vision upon us. His work, unfortunately mostly known through coloured reproductions, seen against the background of steel engravings, purple watercolours of the Mourne Mountains, and oil paintings of baskets of fruit by our mothers, represented our first vivid experience of modern art. And if, in the years since then,

the engravings and the watercolours and the baskets of fruit have been banished from our walls it was Paul Henry who started the aesthetic spring-cleaning.

Then I told how the other day I had 'slipped into the Queen's University, quiet in vacation, with only a few porters and an earnest research worker or two walking urgently across the quad, and in the Great Hall, high roofed and silent, I looked round the portraits hanging on the dark panelled walls, at the Laverys, the de Lászlós, the Gunns, of bearded old professors, benign vice-chancellors and grim diplomats in bright scarlet or glittering braid; and there above the platform was Paul Henry's quiet study of R.M., his brother, compelling in the authority of its silence amid the colour and the flashy rhetoric.'

R.M. Henry naturally bulked much larger in my world, with his sharply pointed bald head and its long back fringe of white, when he uncovered, his monocle and his Inverness cape. He was a great figure as he came down the Malone Road with his short dancing step. There is a place on that Road where it runs between two public houses. Scylla and Charybdis, the only taverns to be found in this highly respectable thoroughfare; and it is told how, one Twelfth of July morning, a tipsy Orangeman stood on the kerb outside one of these giving a bit of a tune on his large drum, when Professor Henry came prancing past. The drummer seeing the impressive figure approach, changed his tune to something more solemn and digni-fied, so, catching the different beat, the Professor stopped courte-ously and listened; then, when the drummer had finished, he raised his hat and proceeded on his way.

I did not attend his lectures – he was Professor of Latin, – but in the University besides his physical presence we also had the legend of his intellectual independence. It was no sort of a way for an Ulster Protestant to hope to achieve social success or popular acclaim by writing a book on *The Evolution of Sinn Fein*, and so the man who overtopped all his contemporaries never became Vice-Chancellor; of course, his other handicap was that he was a Belfast man. Which is partly an expression of the ruling clique's inferiority complex, forever shuffling, cap in hand, to the Ministries in Whitehall, begging for the alms of a battle cruiser or a flying boat.

When Henry left Queen's at the retiring age of sixty-five he was eagerly grabbed by St Andrew's for another five years to reach their limit, ending his days taking classes at Trinity College, Dublin. Before Douglas Hyde was elected President of the Republic of Ireland, Henry's name came up repeatedly in the talk. Now there can be few at his old university who can recall that honourable career of independent thought and action in a context of compromise, expediency and obscurantism.

It is sociologically a tragedy that his voice was never recorded for the archives, for he was the premier exponent of the best Ulster accent of the early century and, I have been told, of the last century also, an accent with its shortened vowels and precise diction giving every consonant its value, which has disappeared and must be forgotten before this century closes. I remember once when we were at supper in the Union with Lord Dunsany after an exhilarating lecture by that versatile man of letters, and somehow the talk turned to an eccentric student not long before consigned to the mental asylum, Henry explaining to our visitor that the student had been prepared to shoot —, a member of the staff of the Classics Department, adding, in his dry way, I can hear the clipped words still, 'but someone ill advisedly dissuaded him.'

I saw most of R.M. for a short period in, I think, 1935, when a small local committee was set up to make preliminary investigations for an enquiry by the National Council for Civil Liberties, into the working of the Special Powers Act of the Northern Ireland Government. Our meetings, at which he presided, were held in a little room at the top of an old office building down town, and when our business finished each evening and we came away, there was a scattering of plainclothes men on the lower treads, in the hallway and at the street door. My wife who acted as a sort of secretary had, for a few weeks, some amusement taking her plainclothes man for long and complicated rambles, when she was doing her shopping, reporting with glee every time she was able to lose him, a dapper little man, rather like a third-rate dancing teacher off duty.

This Act designed by the Government for the control and suppression of the Irish Republic terrorists, is in fact a useful manual for counter-revolution; but although we had no sort of sympathy with the gunman, some of us considered that there were provisions in the Act which diverged a long way from sound democratic practice, as, for instance, the authority to dispense with inquests in any given area, and that the normal processes of the law were adequate in the circumstances.

When we interviewed people who had had first-hand experience of the Act in operation, Henry's penetrating questions demonstrated the sharp clarity of his mind, in a welter of rumour, confusion, prejudice, an object lesson in uncompromizing honesty of purpose, in objectivity, which has given me an ideal to be cherished, an exemplary attitude of mind to be striven for, if seldom attained.

But his sister-in-law, Grace, was a very different person. The Curator had been asked to allow her, since she lived in Dublin, to bring a number of her paintings to the Gallery, so that, on an appointed day, the Marchioness of Londonderry should be able to see them in bulk and in comfort, as she had somewhere at some time expressed the wish to buy one of Mrs Henry's pictures. This was the great lady generally believed to have tattooed legs, one of those current fragments of information or legend like Queen Alexandra's enamel face, King Edward's Louis heels, and George the Fifth's side creases which added an esoteric interest to the upper reaches of society.

The paintings arrived, mostly flower pieces handled with a colourful freedom, and the day for the visit was fixed. The Curator was, for some reason, absent – he must have been ill or else he shouldn't have missed the opportunity of the aristocratic hand – and I had to stand by the artist, a little woman with cherries in her hat, flustered and flapping because of the occasion. We took advantage of the Curator's absence and placed canvasses and boards on every ledge or shelf within reach, and waited. At four o'clock we telephoned Mount Stewart, the Londonderrys' home. Her ladyship had been detained but was just on the point of leaving. Time ticked past. The building closed at six o'clock, so I arranged with the watchman to leave the front door on the latch, and we waited. By seven the Marchioness had not arrived. We telephoned again. No, she would not be coming today. Her secretary would write to Mrs Henry to fix up another time. There was no word of apology.

The little artist seemed to have become smaller and sadder among her pictures which appeared to have increased in number and size. As no lover of the hereditary principle, I was tempted to rage at aristocratic insolence; Grace Henry becoming the symbol for all humiliated artists, standing or sitting – she was sitting in the Curator's swivel-chair – at the doors of the great; and I thought of Sam Johnson's letter to Chesterfield.

So feeling deeply sorry for her, I promised to tidy away the pictures and store them in a safe place until required, and took her home for a meal. We lived within a hundred yards of the Gallery, so it was not inconvenient. My wife never allowing herself to be seen to be surprised or embarrassed, assembled an effective meal, and among the books and pictures Grace quickly shed her chagrin or thrust it under cover, and started on a flow of reminiscence which carried us beyond the vexations of the afternoon. She had spent a good deal of time in Paris and knew the Joyces well. The shelf of books about the Master had not at that date filled up. I knew little more than 'Examination round a Factification' and the texts themselves, having brought back *Ulysses* in its blue paper covers, tied to my braces and hanging in the seat of my plus fours, through the British Customs a few years before. Consequently any personal report was exciting to us. Joyce's prudishness shocked us, when she told how she had to plead with him to allow her to take Lucia to the cinema, just to give her some interest outside the house. When she had beaten down his opposition, the permission was laced and latched with admonitions that the girl was not to be left one instant alone, or in any way whatever left vulnerable to the brutish approaches of lecherous males. Grace Henry liked Lucia, thought her a pleasant and simple lass, rather retarded by the weight of her father's concern. Sisley Huddleston, Grace's best friend in Paris, had also been eager to liberate the girl's bonds a little, and Grace and he had conspired gently to that end.

It was some time after Grace Henry had gone for her train that I realized that Paul Henry's name had not floated up somewhere in the talk. I myself had not raised it, although I had no reason to know how things were between them. Years later I heard from Lennox Robinson that when Paul heard that Grace was nearing Dublin he took to the Wicklow Hills. He also told me a couple of amusing stories about Grace; one of which had to do with a wrist broken by a fall in the guest room of a friend's house, was rather on the lines of *The Man Who Came to Dinner*; the other of a solicitor asking her the date of her marriage, her reply that Paul and she were artists and could not be expected to remember or bother about such bourgeois formalities; but when told that upon the information would depend certain financial advantages, she straightaway reeled off the year, month, day, hour and place of the happy event in a business-like manner.

14

Ulster Unit

Of the earlier exhibitions I handled none was more influential on my thinking than that of the now forgotten Unit One. This was a momentary banding-together of a handful of English painters, sculptors and architects. Paul Nash, John Armstrong, Edward Burra, Ben Nicholson, Henry Moore, Barbara Hepworth, Wells Coates, and another architect whose name escapes me. The group had mobilized an explanatory volume of manifestoes and personal explanations. Their aims and ideals seemed very much in line with the principles enunciated in Wilenski's *Modern Movement*, and, as it were, provided, for us, the evidence for and the proof of these. Easy enough to take in the reading, the actual presence, the physicality of these objects was more difficult to confront and experience. Ben Nicholson's then rather crude abstract constructions (Lavatory seats, we called them) set the stiffest hurdles of all. Paul Nash's paintings, his previous landscapes and still lifes already accepted, were readily taken as part of his growth. And, for the sculpture, the vigorously promulgated dogma of truth to the nature of the material, the woodiness of wood, the stoniness of stone, secured our immediate approval.

This kind of puritanism in art was sympathetic to my nature. Conditioned by the nonconformist intransigence, my aesthetics would not admit the obviously sensual, the lazily graceful: art was a discipline, not an indulgence, logic was all, nonsense or fun impermissible. The result has been that it has taken me a quarter of a century to acknowledge the power of the Baroque; and I still find that I do not readily think of Rubens among the great masters, and am positive that Renoir is grossly overestimated.

This exhibition had a quick impact on our local artists. For the more progressive it demonstrated more clearly than ever before how

77

far out of step with the time's drift elsewhere was the work venerated and practised by their exhibiting contemporaries. The best of these, James Humbert Craig, Frank McKelvey and Hans Iten, were seen to be caught in the trough of an exhausted and now academic impressionism. A new generation of artists had grown up in Ireland. And with us of the north, this was partly due to the emergence of our area as a constitutional and legislative entity. Under the newly established Ministry of Education, an Art Inspector for the first time had been at work. This was John F. Hunter, still known with his military prefix, Captain. A fine wood-engraver and a lively decorative watercolourist, as part of his general campaign to raise the level of art-teaching in the Six Counties, he promoted the interests of senior students in obtaining broader, more expert and more responsibly based training in London, at the Royal College of Art and the Slade School. So, in due course, young men and women stepped down the gangway at Queens Quay, their portfolios and heads full of new ideas. There were two who did not return, of this generation: F.E. McWilliam and William Scott, both from country towns. I have, now and then, wondered if some equally talented, at the very least, who did return, have not, once in a while, had their flashes of regret.

In 1933 a partial crystallization of revolt took place, and a loose group was gathered, including several older artists, such as William Conor the painter and Morris Harding who had come over after the war to carve the capitals in the new Belfast Cathedral. This fell apart after one show, but the next year, a closer knot was tied, a title proposed, The Ulster Unit, a lay secretary found, myself, and plans laid for an exhibition.

It was symptomatic of the lack of enterprise or concern for sincere local activity on the part of the Art Gallery's committee and curator that the exhibition was not held there but down town, in rented premises, the Locksley Hall, a dark panelled room used for receptions and small dances, an adjunct to a well-known Belfast teashop and now destroyed by enemy action. So just before and after Christmas 1934, seventeen exhibitors displayed paintings, watercolours, prints, sculpture, ceramic figurines and pots and architectural designs, for we too had our modern architect, Denis O'D. Hanna. John Hunter, W.R. Gordon and Lady Mabel Annesley represented the senior stratum and the younger artists included my friends John Luke, Colin Middleton, and George MacCann. The catalogue contained brief summaries of their aims by most of the contributors and a foreword by myself, my first essay in a long series of prefaces:

> It is apparent that these artists do not accept the mere imitation of appearance as being adequate motive for their activity. They are conscious of an order and an existence transcending visual phenomena ... they take as their problem the abstraction of some portion of that order from the complicated bundle of their physical and sensory experiences. The second thesis they postulate is the supreme value of the individual expression of this order not found in the expression of subjective caprice or free fancy, but is grounded upon an external responsibility to the nature of plastic media.

A fair enough statement of our basic ideas at the time, strictly in line with the commandments of the most influential art critics of the day; but no better or worse than they in its complete failure to forecast, or, at least, foreshadow the changes that the succeeding decades should bring. For art critics, and literary critics, are, as a rule, poor at prophecy. To fill up a spare half-page, I made up a set of *Notes on the Art of Picture Buying*, and it was these rather than the symposium or the foreword which provoked the strongest reaction from visitors to the exhibition. Hoots of derision, and, in one instance, abuse from a very bad painter who sported a monocle and a stock, seemed a disproportionate response to my very mild remarks, some of which, I believe, have not lost all relevance. 'Avoid the derivative repetitive artist. If he's not perpetually enriching his own experience, he can't possibly enrich yours'. That still goes for the flocks of imitators of Jackson Pollock, David Bomberg and Francis Bacon that now are nosing their way into nearly every local society in the United Kingdom. 'Reproductions are referential data for students'. This is still my belief, confirmed by a glance into the window of any furniture shop.

The exhibits were modestly priced from five to twenty pounds, but, in spite of that, total sales failed to reach the twenty pound mark, only prints and pots proving in any way popular. The only completely non-representational work was by Colin Middleton, whose three canvasses were something in the manner of Klee, while George MacCann's *Stone Mask* with the flat nose and the bulging eyeballs was in Moore's, whose pupil George had been at the Royal College. As our resources were drawn from members of the Unit at thirty shillings each we finished without a deficit. But although we had several further meetings we never mustered enough resolution to mount a second offensive.

The catalogue was decorated with a wood engraving by Colin Middleton. He brought the little block of it to the flat one evening, and that was the first time I really met him. A quiet girl with a fringe of hair over her forehead accompanied him: she was Mae McLean, a painter herself, but I do not remember if they were yet married.

Below medium height, his round head a tangle of dark curls, his eyes large and expressive, his mouth wide, he is one of the very few people whom I have felt, on first meeting, to be exceptional, even, perhaps, a genius. About three years younger than myself, he had been at the local Art School, had been on the Continent once or twice, and had been looking forward to a spell of study in London or farther afield, when his father died, and Colin had to drop his plans, postponing his ambitions to take over his father's business and support his widowed mother.

His father, Charles Middleton, had been a damask designer working freelance for the industry, and painting Impressionist pictures, most successfully, of the sea. About a decade later when Colin had his first Dublin exhibition, in interview he rather suggested that his father had been the North's Impressionist pioneer; but I am clear in my own mind that he shares that distinction with one John McBurney, a rich personality with a ripe Rabelaisian humour who promised much as a painter but died young, and with Stoupe and Taylor to whom I have previously referred in writing of the staff of the Art School.

At any rate Colin had to harness himself to the regular day of the drawing board and the office, giving his hours to maintaining and extending his father's connections with the linen manufacturers, keeping the weekends jealously for his free expression. But while this

drudgery must at times have seemed murderous, it is incontrovert-
ible that the minute work of providing designs consistent with the
loom's necessities, must have given him the discipline, which, allied
to his abundant native ability, made him the most versatile and
accomplished draughtsman I have ever known. I do not now bring
into the reckoning the amazing fecundity of his invention or his
wide ranging control of the brush and the graver.

Once, leafing through the illustrated catalogue of The Great
Exhibition of 1851, which I had found in the Museum Library, and
indicating many of the plates which reached a rare level of mis-
guided ingenuity in the torturing of materials to irrelevant ends, I
received a shock when Colin stopped my fingers turning, to draw
my attention to an elaborate Irish damask, which, only the week
before, he had been engaged on re-presenting on the squared paper,
for a well-known local firm; a circumstance to give me pause to
think hard of the awareness of twentieth century linen manufactur-
ers of the progressive demands of their industry, and their intelli-
gence in employing the skill of a first-rate creative artist on the
copying of a design so antiquated, which, even when it had been up
to date, was still thoroughly bad. Another example of the failure in
alertness of the same people was brought home to me some time
later when I met a Middle European refugee who had designed the
table linen for the *Bremen*, and, in Belfast, had hawked his samples
round the mill offices in vain, and, when I met him, was reduced to
mending sewing machines.

Just before the outbreak of the War, when we, for a while, gave
up flat dwelling and rented a brick semidetached house on the lower
slopes of the Cavehill, we became neighbours, within ten minutes
walk of the avenue where Colin lived. By this time Mae and he were
certainly married and staying with his mother. This gaunt woman
with wild glaring eyes I always felt to be something demoniac. Her
slightest word was heavy with portent. The house with its Victorian
and Edwardian furnishings and hung with Charles' paintings, was, I
believe, as he left it, not to be disturbed by the importunate notions
of the newly married. But outside in the garden, down the side of
the house, Colin had his hut, a large stout wooden affair with steps
up to the door and a knocker. Inside was a spacious drawing bench

facing the window, the painter's heavy easel, and, behind ringed curtains, the stacks of canvasses, painted and virgin. It was here that the four of us, Mae and Colin, Roberta and I, spent many long evenings of smoky talk, once in a while to be joined by some unexpected and, to me, improbable acquaintance, an angler maybe. And out of that hut I carried the first painting of Colin's that we bought, a small abstract in thin tempera, secured for five pounds, to be paid in five monthly instalments. When the deal was closed with the initial clinching pound note, I can remember him, in his rather husky voice, saying 'Corn in Egypt'. The panel is dated 1938.

15

The Art Critic

In my last years at Queen's I had become a member of a tiny group interested in poetry and leftwing politics. Of these Ralph, son of the Professor of Economics, was doing science, Paddy was a medical student, and Graeme the most sophisticated and best informed of us not at the University at all, but an assistant in the Public Library where his *bête noir* was a tiny senior librarian known as Tim, whose claim to fame was that he got a brief mention in Forrest Reid's autobiography *Apostate*, yet, in spite of this, was an addict to the paperbacks of Nat Gould.

During these years I was writing both verse and prose very deliberately and in large quantities. In prose I played the sedulous ape, with interior monologues in the Joyce manner, short stories after Liam O'Flaherty; and general, descriptive work influenced by Richard Jeffries, 'Michael Fairless', his once famous *Roadmender* a prime favourite, only superseded by Wilde's *De Profundis*, and William Morris' *Dream of John Ball*. I wrote parables and allegories in a pseudo-biblical style, and fragments of fiction imitative of T.F. Powys whose *Mr Weston's Good Wine* seemed to our clique one of the great books of the age. But when I took up gallery work and turned to reading Clive Bell, Roger Fry and Frank Rutter, I soon discovered that my revered models had little relevance to the kind of experience I now attempted to describe.

As the Museum was only a short distance from the University, a strip of the Botanic Gardens with the Scots firs and rhododendron bushes and the statue of Lord Kelvin lying between, I held on to my close association, lunched every day in the Students' Union, forgathering with my friends, and continued contributing to the University magazine *The Northman*. In the winter issue for 1931 I

83

made a critique of the annual exhibition of the leading local society of artists. In those days, the art criticism in the four local daily newspapers was the merest hackwork at best; once, before the opening of a similar exhibition, a reporter came to me with a list of names and asked me to point out the associated items. When, in one instance, I said that the pictures were poor and not worth mentioning, he replied that this might well be, but their perpetrator belonged to a family-business which advertised liberally in his paper and so the editor had specifically demanded some notice be provided. So, in an effort to apply firm standards, I belaboured the low quality of the exhibits and insisting on how out of touch the artists were with modern trends, I continued, in my article, to drag in references to Cezanne, Van Gogh, Modigliani, Derain, Braque, Picabia, Metzinger, Miro, Paul Nash and Edward Wadsworth. In mustering the names of sculptors, Bourdelle, Maillol, Milles, Manship, Archipenko, I went somewhat beyond my own visual experience, and drew upon my reading of Kineton Parkes' book. In this connection I made a slighting comment on 'the confections' of Miss S. Rosamond Praeger, the well-known and well-loved sculptor of *The Fairy Fountain* and *The Philosopher* and a large family of small plaster infants in sentimental poses or situations. From Miss Praeger whom I had not then met I received a happy little pen and ink sketch of myself as she conceived me and herself as I thought of her: a young man with long hair and a long neck and a loose collar confronting a maiden with sloping shoulders, coiled plaits of hair over her ears, simpering and dropping large tears. This I treasured for years, for it seemed to me a neat riposte, but somehow it got mislaid, or, I fancy, stolen. Later I met the lady, learned to respect her and to enjoy her conversation of her days at the Slade with Professor Lanteri in the last century, but there was always the tip of irony on her tongue; and when in 1951 I made a survey for *The Arts in Ulster* in which I paid her something of a tribute for her sincerity and skill, I received a firm rebuke for having made no mention of Wilhelmina Geddes, the stained-glass pioneer, in her opinion the greatest creative artist the province had yet produced.

I did not review this society's exhibitions again until 1934. I reiterated my views on the weakness of the selection and the general flabbiness of local written comment. Sir John Lavery was then

President of the society, a figure of enormous prestige. And of him I wrote 'The people he paints get exactly the painting they deserve. The Lonsdale portrait looks as if it had been painted by a coachman'. This was particularly rough, for little Sir John, with his tailcoat and sideburns, always reminded me of such a person. 'The shoddy reach-me-down handling, the badly realized crossed legs, the bungled distribution of weight, the clipped-off cigar, all cry shame on the hand that gave us the subtle *Logue* and the cavalier *Cunningham Graham*'.

My concluding paragraph ran: 'A last word of protest. Why must maiden ladies paint flowers? A flower is a naked thing, a shameless thing, a wanton thing, flaunting its sexual capacities, soliciting the lascivious air. Let strong men and women who love and know, master them, distilling their colour and strength in the limbec of the heart. But why, O why, must maiden ladies paint flowers?'

The comment on Lavery I still think fair, and from his own very honest *Life of a Painter* (1940), I can argue that he would have agreed with me, since he wrote:

> I have always admired the courage of Sargent, Orpen and John, for the way they chose to please themselves in painting a portrait, and in doing so, to please posterity. I, on the other hand, have too often tried to please the sitter, and like the man, the donkey, and the bridge, ended by pleasing nobody. I have felt ashamed of having spent my life trying to please sitters and made friends instead of telling the truth and making enemies.

But, unfortunately, my remarks were premature. I had not then the support of the artist himself. When, in 1946, a new edition of the Gallery's Lavery Catalogue was called for, I recast the whole thing and inserted a page of critical Estimates and Comments, taking care to include the master's own words.

While my concluding paragraph carries more than a whiff of the Laurentian approach, and, dare I say, flaunts its immaturity, it does ask a question which I have never seen asked elsewhere.

The first hint of looming trouble that I was made aware of, came in an oddly unpleasant way. Shortly after the magazine came out, I

was told by both Alfred and Harold that the Curator had been call-
ing them in, one at a time, to enquire if I habitually used bad lan-
guage or told dirty stories. All this because I had dared to write the
word sexual. Then the row started. At the next meeting of the
Committee, a councillor rose in rage and demanded my dismissal. I
had insulted Sir John Lavery who was one of the city's greatest sons
and a principal benefactor of the Gallery. I had used improper lan-
guage about a very respectable section of the community, the maiden
ladies. I was clearly irresponsible and unfit to be employed by the
Belfast Corporation.

My friend W.R. Gordon who was a co-opted member of the
Committee told me that he had felt sick when the Curator, with no
sense of loyalty to his staff, no feeling for the rights of free expression,
failed to speak up on my behalf. W.R. modestly did not tell me of his
own outburst on my behalf. But the temper of the councillors ran
high, and the best that he could do was to propose that the matter
which had not been on the agenda be deferred until the next meeting.

When, in a fortnight's time, this was held, tempers had cooled;
even some pressure from outside had warned the members not to
make asses of themselves, so it was decided that I be interviewed by
two senior members of the Committee in the presence of the Curator
and asked to explain my remarks. On the appointed day I was called
before my judge, Alderman McCurdy, a heavily built moustached
trades union official of the traditional type, who gave me a patient
hearing, and, at the end, asked me to give an undertaking not to
repeat my offence, or, as he put it, 'not to go so far the next time.'

My undertaking was reported back, and then the incident closed.
It had been disturbing while it lasted for, had I still been single, the
threat of dismissal would not have been so alarming, but having a
wife now, seemed to increase my vulnerability, My real offence, of
course, had not been what I said about Sir John, and only, in a small
way, what I had said about the flower-painters; my main crime had
been in my general attack on the low standards of the members'
work. The instigators, one of whom I could name, were stung by my
strictures but realizing that the general position could not be easily
defended without provoking public ridicule, they fastened, on my
remarks about Sir John and the spinsters as points of attack.

During the days when this business was in the air, my chief feeling was of isolation. Apart from W.R. Gordon, no Committee member approached me, and apart from Alfred and Harold, no one made any reference to my predicament. I went about my normal duties, frequently conversing with the Curator and his deputy, but neither made the slightest allusion to the affair, although I knew from my two friends, that they talked of little else when I was not there.

Lavery I met a year or two later: the first time at the annual dinner of the society of which he was President, when our conversation was brief and his handshake limp; but neither then nor on the second occasion did he give any hint that he had heard of my critical opinions. Our second meeting occurred when he unexpectedly called in at the Gallery on a day when both the Curator and his deputy were absent, otherwise I should not have had the opportunity of spending so much time in his company.

He was a very small man, clean shaven, with long dark strands of thinning hair brushed back over a long oval skull, with a long sharp nose and two of the tiniest eyes that I have ever seen, deep in little red pits, like a pig's. He wore a very high collar, a pepper and salt stock, with a black cut-away coat, grey trousers and spats, the only living person I ever spoke to, so attired. But talk with him was easy, when we went upstairs to his roomful of paintings. There was, dominating the collection, the tall portrait of *Hazel in Green and Gold*, of that American lady whose face as an Irish colleen decorates the currency notes of the Irish Free State, who was so much taller than Sir John, that, when they were photographed in front of their house in Cromwell Place, Kensington, she always stood a couple of steps down in front of him. At first, I felt that I should leave him to his memories for, by this date, both Hazel, his second wife, and Eileen his daughter who had been the subject of the little *Communion Dress*, were dead; but, after brushing an eye with a knuckle, he brightened, and soon we were deep in discussion. There were odd points, here and there, in the paintings which, as a gallery man, I wanted cleared up. And he was brisk and forthcoming in his replies. Yes, there had been a statuette of the Blessed Virgin on the window-ledge of *The Daylight Raid* which he had painted out – I had surmised this from the pintimento, when the canvas was viewed in a raking light – but it had been for reasons of composition, not in deference to Belfast's sectarian bias. The girl on the bed holding up the infant in *The Mother* was a composite figure of Eileen and a professional model. There had been an apocryphal story in some Dubliner's memoirs that Belfast had refused to show this picture once until the artist painted a wedding ring on the girl's proper finger. I had taken this as a crack at Northern puritanism, and I was correct. That was Steve Donoghue there, in *The Weighing Room*.

I pointed out the older pictures which showed surface deterioration. The answer shocked me. In his early years, Alfred East, his friend, had made it a practice to go over the surfaces of his finished paintings with a hot iron, to give them an Old Master patina, and Sir John had followed his advice for a while. One painting in particular, *Summer*, of Hazel holding a parasol and reclining in a hammock, had vast cracks in certain areas, rivers a quarter of an inch wide, where it looked as if large islands of pigment had floated apart. This, it turned out, had not been ironed. It had been painted in 1906 or '07, the face, that of Kathleen, Lavery's first wife. Put away in the studio for years, he brought it out again in 1923 and changed the face to that of Hazel, and otherwise altered details in it. As there seemed no possible way of restoring this, he bluntly enquired if there were a local man competent enough to make a copy of it. I could not recommend anyone, so he asked me to have it packed up and sent over to him in London. We did this, and, about a year later, *Summer* returned, a painting on a new canvas with the dates 1907–1923–1936 written on the back. It differed in a few small details of drapery from the original; but whether the copy was made by Sir John or someone else we shall never know: after all, he was about eighty at the time and it was a big picture.

For the Festival of Britain in 1951, I gathered in a representative exhibition of his work, from his grandchildren, from Dublin, from Glasgow where some of his best paintings are. On the return journey the crate containing one of his notable House of Commons interiors fell on the quayside from the docker's sling and was smashed. Among the other Glasgow pictures, one, picked up somewhere by Dr Tom Honeyman, was easily my favourite, a small girl in a pinafore wearing a paddy hat and a woman's boots, unlaced,

whitewashing a cottage wall. I had never seen anything so sponta-
neous and vigorous from his brush. And in the Belgrade National
Museum I was surprised to see a cottage-interior with Irish country
folk, a couple of them, seated at the open hearth, and a small girl
whitewashing the wall to the right. But whether the Glasgow paint-
ing which was slightly larger and a vertical rectangle instead of a
horizontal, was a sketch for the Belgrade work or an enlarged study
of the figure in it I shall never know.

16

The Fair at Kilrea

One day I was called into the Curator's office to meet some visitors: they proved to be the widow, the daughter and the son of Hugh Thomson the well-known illustrator. Thomson (1860–1920) had been born in Coleraine, and had been apprenticed, with the firm of Marcus Ward, which, under the direction of John Vinycomb, used the talents of many young Ulstermen in the production of calendars, Christmas cards (for these they were famous), and, less often, illustrated books. Vinycomb, an Englishman, and who, as something of an expert in heraldry, designed coats of arms for several boroughs and families in the North, was a legend, in my early years, of inspiration and discipline. I even met one old man who had worked under him. Because of these strong local associations, the purpose of the Thomson family's visit was to suggest that an exhibition should be held of the artist's work in his native province. We were offered the loan of a selection of his own favourite watercolours and drawings still in the possession of the widow or her children. We were also given the names of collectors who would also be prepared to lend works for such an event. At that time, the Gallery did not own a single drawing by one of Ulster's best known artists.

Out of the drift and tangle of the talk, I can remember the son, a tall, clean-shaven, well built man, making mention of his superior in the Fisheries Department, Austin Dobson. At once I was able to make the obvious linkage. Hugh Thomson had been a close friend of Austin Dobson, the accomplished Victorian writer of light verse, and his illustrations to his friend's *Ballad of Beau Brocade* were among his most celebrated drawings. Austin Dobson had been at the Board of Trade, as Max Beerbohm's famous cartoon reminds us. He must have found a job for his son in the Civil Service, or, at any rate, done nothing to divert his attention from it, and, later, another niche was found for the son of his friend; a tie-up as natural as breathing. We were told also of a sister of the artist who was still post-mistress at Kilrea, a village just over the County Derry border, on the far side of the Bann, and who possessed a large number of his watercolours.

In art gallery and museum work, one of the aspects which give it its interesting variety over other desk or institutional jobs, especially as you grow older, is that there can be a fair amount of travelling, of dodging in and out for short or long periods; visits to auctions, sales, private collections, or the inspection of material offered for purchase, donation or bequest. With us these had inevitably fallen to the Curator, or, less often, to his deputy. No junior was, in those days, trusted out of doors on official business. We had to be content with rumours of what had been seen or missed. Only when long afterwards packing cases or furniture vans arrived at the goods entrance, could we judge whether the journeys had been worthwhile.

How it happened in this Thomson business I do not know. Maybe the weather was unpromising, or Kilrea too remote – curators could not afford cars then – or else a postmistress, even if an artist's sister, did not rate the courtesy of a curatorial visitation. Anyhow, I was instructed to make the journey, inspect the pictures, and report back.

Because it was my first mission, my first adventure of this kind, I can recall a multiplicity of details about it. An early morning bus jolted me through the growing light to Ballymena, then west to Portglenone and the crossing of the Bann, 'the fishy fruitful Bann', as Spenser called it, then almost due north along that river valley, to Kilrea itself where I stepped down about eleven in the forenoon. The broad street and the square were thick with stirring shapes of beasts and men: I could see at once that it was a Fair Day. Along both sides of the street heifers and cows heaved and shouldered, their rumps against the Bank and the houses, their dung spattered along the sidewalks, and, in some places, on the low window-sills, while men with sticks marched up and down, or hovered in little clusters with loud voices and the smacking of palms, for this was the ritual and the routine of the luck-penny closing the bargain.

The square was bulged with market-stalls, old clothes, confectionary, harness and farm equipment. Stepping cat-careful through the throng, I asked and edged my way to the Post Office, announced my business to the girl behind the counter, and, after a brief wait, was brought in behind the shop to meet Miss Thomson, a stout elderly lady in black with a friendly but not effusive manner. Her suggestion was that I should take a walk through the fair until lunchtime, return about one o'clock and have a bite with her, and then see the pictures at my leisure. This suited me admirably, for there was much that I had not yet seen, and any fair, even the meanest straggle of calves and carts, fascinates any Irishman.

So back I plunged into the noise and turmoil, taking time now, time I was merrily filching from the Belfast Corporation, a comfortable truancy, to halt and hover on the rim of every huddle of bargaining, to admire the piglets that slithered and thumped and clattered, staccato-footed, on and off the rush mats that carpeted the tilted carts, to pity the cowering calves and the sad-eyed horses as their owners held their heads and dealers pawed over them. Then on, irresistible to the stalls; stalls with phalanxed bottles of lemonade, with hillocks of lozenges and liquorice, or with penny Paris-buns and cakes of the more garish varieties, with copper dishes for weighing-out and little fleets of paper bags to put them in, already blown or being blown open for easy access. Women were examining old overcoats and holding up bright cotton dresses, and men were trying the fit of caps that cost eight pence or a shilling for the best.

The prince of the fair was undoubtedly the man who sold harness. He stood on a box or a chair to be seen by all. One stubborn customer he tried with saddles, reins, metal bits, straps and whips, suggesting in feigned frustration and despair 'Ye'll be wantin' a whip for sixpence, wi' a whistle tied till it, that ye can blow all the road home'. His cascades of patter and country wit gripped the largest audience of all with a skill that would have been the envy of many a music hall comedian. Even when he stopped for breath, infrequently, the grimaces of his silence were sufficient oratory.

There were other lesser performers; the man who swigged paraffin from a lemonade bottle and belched flame, above the island of cloth caps; the lumbering strongman whose limited round of tricks, the simplest, was to draw attention to the wonder embrocation which he was trying to sell to reluctant lads and young men – this fellow I recognized, after a while, and after consultation which confirmed it, with a grating-voiced man in a decent suit, as an ex-prize fighter, once a Belfast policeman, now coarsened and battered and gone to fat. And, tacking through the crush, the thick shawls, brown arms and baskets of the tinker women promising luck, and, above the hubbub and the bellowing of beasts, an anxious old man with a clean, pale face, standing on a stool, heard, if at all, only by a ring of children, and a tramp in a long overcoat, offering salvation to the unheeding, if they but turn from their wickedness.

This was the Ireland of William Carleton, of William Allingham, and I was fortunate to savour and indulge my appetite for it, before it vanished down the years. Not a fair like that of The Moy or Castledawson, famous for their horses, mounts for half the cavalries of Europe; not a half-carnival, Tourist Board attraction like the Lammas Fair at Ballycastle, with its song and its dulse and its 'yellow-man' toffee, with its busloads of visitors with blazers and cameras, with the steep little side street of the Diamond where the grey donkeys from Donegal wait for the snapshots: but the normal and necessary peak of the rural rhythm, the coming-together and the kindling of the folk from the misty hills and cold fields of their daily drudgery. Marketing Boards, Fat Stock Markets, motor lorries and men in leggings and white coats and all the apparatus of grading and subsidy, have cleaned the streets and emptied the hearts of the little Irish towns and villages. And the same faces that swum or mooned round the old fairs, or faces indistinguishable from them, down to the last long upper lip, now bob and float with the multitude, among faces of many hues and a clashing of many accents, in the supermarkets of a Midland Saturday afternoon.

When I threaded my way back to the Post Office, lunch was ready, not, this time, pink ham and red tomatoes with a green lettuce leaf, but floury potatoes, splitting their sides, and brown beef and gravy. Upstairs in the drawing room, full of furniture, I saw at once the framed watercolours of my quest on the walls, and, round the skirting board and the piano legs, a reef of gold frames and picture cord of the added numbers taken down and brought in from the rest of the house. Most, in a strange way, seemed familiar. Miss Thomson explained. Her brother had given her many of the earlier smaller versions of the illustrations he had made for the *de luxe* editions, *Quality Street*, *The Admirable Crichton* and so on. And these, I thought, had a freshness and a delicacy which somehow got lost in the finished states. She had too, several Irish landscapes, a kind of subject of which few coloured reproductions appear in Thomson's topographical work, four only I know of in *The Fair Hills of Ireland* to Stephen Gwynn's text. There are no coloured plates in the more popular *Highways and Byways in Donegal and Antrim*.

So, with an impressive list and a quickened interest in Thomson and his work, I stepped through the ebb of the fair, the acetylene flares shining on the puddles and last faces, as the stalls were being dismembered, to the bus stop, with memories to last me a lifetime.

Twenty-five years later, in a Coventry Irish Club, when I met Father Arthur Diamond, and knew by his quiet voice that he haled from somewhere in my province, I asked him where. 'From a wee village called Kilrea. You'll hardly have heard of it', he answered. And when I discovered that he remembered Miss Thomson the Postmistress, the clashing contrast of that Fair and the still room with the delicate watercolours in it, flashed across my mind. And now Kilrea, its Fair, and Miss Thomson and Father Diamond are inextricably mingled and fixed in a strange image of my native country in all its heart warming, heart breaking complexities.

17

The Taste of Mayors

My childhood had its calendar of street spectacles; beyond the more customary balloon man with his handcart dragging its flotilla of coloured spheres, and the knifegrinder with the swiftly creaking treadle, the bright sparks spraying from his broad thumb, there were organ grinders with sadfaced monkeys, or with green parrots that beaked your fortune-card out of a rack, there were dancing bears and German bands, and, one tremendous evening, the brassy fire-engine clanging past, drawn by great galloping chargers and tufted with a backblown plume of fiery smoke. We had too, in the days before the War, the mustering of Ulster Volunteers with bandoliers and wooden rifles, and every July, the route-march of the Orangemen with dancing banners and enormous drums; but the first official occasion I can remember was the civic funeral of a Lord Mayor who had died in office. His name I cannot recall, but the flag-covered coffin on the high slowly turning wheels, the trotting and nodding horses and the silent ranks of the young men in grey uniforms are still a sharp picture, moving-off from the City Hall. The grey uniforms were of the then recently established and short-lived Young Citizen Volunteers, a local variant of Territorials, to be changed for khaki later and shipped off for France, part of the Ulster Division. A framed document inaugurating this body, with a long list of sponsors, among them my Uncle Sam Martin, used to be displayed in a glass case in the Museum, with a badly stuffed headless figure wearing the uniform with the dark blue facings.

When Belfast was first chartered as a borough by James I, the chief citizen was known as The Sovereign, but that is not the kind of history my people most care for, and so, like any English city, it has a Lord Mayor. During much of my school and working life the

Mayoralty was largely shared between Sir Crawford McCullagh, Bart and Sir William Turner. The latter had a chain of fruit shops and was therefore known as The Banana King. He once sold the city a large plot of land for a proposed civic airport which never got beyond the proposal and the sale. He was not generally considered a dishonest man. McCullagh, Lord Mayor for sixteen years in all, had wide business interests, largely, I believe, in real estate, and, during his epoch, there were several governmental inquiries into various municipal activities. A redfaced man of medium build, he had no distinction of manner or affectation of utterance, but he must have had some talent for business and personal relations to maintain his secure eminence for so long. In an interview which he gave the *Daily Express*, he referred nostalgically to his humble origins and regretted that his early poverty had made impossible the realization of his ambition to become a clergyman, a remark which, on its pub-lication, provoked some surprise and comment. Deaf in his last years, when a deputation waited upon him to thank him for his long and devoted service to the public interest, and to suggest, out of sheer kindness, that a younger man might take over the burden, whether he heard or not, he thanked them and accepted the renewed nomination. He is now commemorated by the worst stained glass window I have ever seen, fortunately it is quite small. His long tenure of office brought about something of a revolt; it was felt that the honour and responsibility might be more fairly shared, and since then, each Lord Mayor is elected for two consecutive years only. Among Sir Crawford's successors have been three estate agents, a calling which in Belfast has shown a heartfelt dedication to unpaid public service in local government out of all proportion to its numerical strength in the community.

By tradition the Lord Mayor is always a wealthy man, and at the end of his term he is always knighted. Sir Crawford was for so long paramount that he secured a baronetcy. Since the Conservative party has always held a vast majority of council seats and since the Lord Mayor invariably belongs to that party, this means, in effect, that the regular knighthood is conferred by the local caucus, the Royal Confirmation being never withheld, which plays havoc with the naive theory that the Crown is the Fount of Honour. But since no party in these islands has for so long been so emphatic in its declarations of loyalty to the Crown, the circumstance may be considered in the light of identity of interests and so seem not at all out of line or other than highly appropriate.

Apart from appearing on the platform at the opening of an occasional exhibition, the Lord Mayors in my experience played little part in the Gallery's activities. Only one instance to the contrary stands out. In April 1936 the North West Museums Federation held a short conference in Belfast. At the first meeting the delegates were welcomed by Sir Crawford. He struck a note of topicality by referring to the recent exhibition of Chinese Art at Burlington House, which the *Times* had designated as 'one of the great imaginative experiences of our age'. Sturdily in his role as the plain, ordinary man, he continued 'As we were comin' down the steps I turned to the wife and said "There's nothin' in there I'd give houseroom to". And she replied "No Crawford, there's nothing"'. The delegates laughed uproariously and unrestrainedly applauded the honest man.

Belfast Castle, a copy-book essay in Scots Baronial, built in 1870, was handed over to the city by its owner, the Earl of Shaftesbury. As it stands on a plateau with the well wooded Cavehill behind and the Lough spread before it in the distance, a very pleasant situation, it was decided by a triumph of municipal imagination to turn it into a sort of super cafe, catering for wedding receptions and dances. A couple of days before its official opening the Gallery was called-in to supply pictures for the lounge. We had nothing in hand very suitable; with an uncertain future, good pictures could not fairly be risked, and old canvasses from store would not match the new furnishings. So we were left with a number of large bright wellframed reproductions of some of the Impressionists and Van Gogh and Signac.

I went up with the van to distribute these as effectively as possible. Just when the last cord was knotted and the last frame slung in place, Sir Crawford arrived with attendant officials to give the apartments his final approval. When his rather expressionless eyes fastened on the pictures, he roared 'Where did that rubbish come from? Get them out of here; they're disgusting'. The officials fluttered and nodded. No one referred to me. In an embarrassed silence the workmen removed the offensive objects, Van Gogh's yellow

Portrait of a Young Man, Monet's blue *Yachts at Argeneuil*, Signac's pink *Paris* and the rest. Now, I am no enthusiast for coloured reproductions of any kind, basically on the grounds that they only remotely resemble their originals. The Lord Mayor's dislike sprang from the fact that they resembled them too closely.

There was another, later, Lord Mayor, in my experience, who approved only of pictures in black frames. His Lady went a little further in preferring 'pictures with distance in them'. Especially for hospital patients.

In Sir Crawford's day the Lady Mayoress' Parlour in the City Hall, besides the inscribed photographs of royal personages, was decorated with large oil paintings by William Shayer a Victorian derivative in the Morland tradition, and an artist – I fancy there were two of him, Senior and Junior – who, to this day, maintains a steady position in the mysterious undergrowth of *nouveau riche* appreciation, a position he shares with Birket Poster and E.M. Wimperis. A Shayer of, say, *Woodcutters in the Forest*, will still fetch a couple of hundred pounds in the auction rooms, for the dealers know their men.

When the McCullaghs left the City Hall, the Gallery was given the responsibility of filling the bare but ornately papered walls. In this, benefitting by experience, I used for the purpose several watercolours by Foster from a collection of them, bequeathed – the bequest also included a stormy Wimperis fenland – by a knighted draper. These gave the utmost satisfaction, particularly since I had primed the Lord Mayor's batman with their current market prices, until a youngish Lord Mayor arrived whose Lady herself painted; all the while the supply of appositely inscribed photographs continued to signalize the more recent royal visits to the borough. It was, of course, about Manchester and Liverpool that George Moore wrote his once celebrated essay, 'The Alderman in Art', sixty or more years ago.

It was at this conference of the North Western Federation that I gave an address on *Aesthetics in the Museum and Art Gallery*. This marks for me an interesting stage in the development of my own aesthetics, demonstrating my drift away from Clive Bell's 'significant form', and indulging in exercises in the Marxist dialectic. Among the examples of the latter I used Courbet as the Thesis, the Impressionists as the Antithesis, and Cezanne as the Synthesis, a dialectical sequence which still seems to me amusing. There is, however, this to be said, that I did not claim that the dialectic could offer us any more than a social or technical explanation; it could go no way towards a qualitative assessment. My argument was that paintings should not be divorced from their physical and social context, that it was a gross over simplification to pluck them out of their environment and exhibit them simply as pictures unrelated to anything else but other pictures, that the tone and style of a society can only be grasped from the experience of a wide sample of its artefacts in a number of media.

In the discussion which followed, one curator rebuked me, declaring that I should find that 'Clive Bell had a few more shots in his locker'. I have not found this: indeed, on re-reading his book *Art* when it came out as a paperback in 1961, I could not help wondering why I had ever been influenced or impressed by it; the author's thin wit was so oppressive and his attitude so self-conscious that I could only with difficulty get through it.

When, months later, the substance of my talk had been reduced to writing, it was published in *The Museums Journal*, and I was flattered to receive a note of congratulation from one of the leading Art Directors of the day. But when, at the next Annual Conference, the same person incorporated many of its ideas with no acknowledgement whatsoever, I was less pleased. From that occasion dates my pedantic interest in the footnote, the reference, the bibliography; and that interest has given me a handy method for ascertaining whether any volume of apparent scholarship in the areas in which I am concerned, is worth my attention.

The Chinese Exhibition which Sir Crawford dismissed so abruptly, was, as it must have been for thousands, a deep and compelling experience. T'ang and Sung became for me periods of human achievement of equal significance with the great ages of European art. The still inevitability of the pot shapes, the humour and gentleness of the ceramic creatures, the pleasure of the glaze-colour in drip and run and texture, the compact life-full postures of the sleeve-dancers, the planes, edges and surfaces of the carved jade, the gestures of the charged brush, the stain and blot on the grain of silk, the absorbance of rice-paper awoke responses in me which till then I did not know existed.

Besides the astonishing riches of the display, the crowding gazers also had their odd fascination: the political figures known from newspaper photographs still public faces in the teeming lobby; St John Ervine and his wife trudging along obviously not enjoying their experience; Aldous Huxley with thick glasses and white socks, the first I had ever seen since childhood or off the cricket field, hunkering down to peer in a trance of concentration at a low case of small objects with, yes, a fat volume under his oxter, entitled, for I crept close enough to read, *The Yogi Religions*.

Just before this, Huxley had been, with Lawrence, the most admired of English writers for my generation, but I had never completely succumbed to his spell, and was frequently at a loss to keep my end up, when the conversation of my friends was threaded with allusions to *Crome Yellow* and *Antic Hay*. Now, although his work is full of urgent and important ideas, and we neglect him at our peril, he has somehow receded from the field of modern literature, and I seldom find myself taking him into account.

When over for the Exhibition, we were caught up in the general uneasiness about the Hoare-Laval Pact, and found ourselves attending an anti-colonial meeting in the Livingstone Hall, hearing George Padmore, the stocky grey haired West Indian, later to be adviser to Nkrumah, and the taller, leaner Jomo Kenyatta. I spoke up in the discussion afterwards and, overcome by emotion, gave a poundnote to the collection, being just as deeply stirred when, on going out, a very black man said 'Goodnight, comrade, and thanks'. The audience mustered outside and marched to Westminster to make our protest, but we were headed-off and scattered by the police. When Roberta and I, our excitement not all dissipated, found our way to Charing Cross, I bought a copy of the *Daily Worker* dated for the next day, and read in it an inexact account of the meeting we had just attended and the demonstration which had fizzled out. This was one of those little things which, all through the agitations of the Thirties, kept us out of the Communist Party. I have always believed that, in the long run, the smart alecks are caught out and only that which is achieved by honesty is worth attempting, that defeat is never so overwhelming when your hands are clean.

From Chinese art to Chinese literature was an inevitable step; and here for me Arthur Waley's *170 Chinese Poems* became an influential book. Exactly how much my own verse owes to it would be hard to define. Certainly the quiet, undramatic tone, the even texture, the significant abstraction from experience of natural phenomena, the awareness of landscape, and man-in-landscape, these were qualities which I admired and which I must half-consciously have attempted to reproduce. My friend Wang insisted to my surprise that while Waley's 'translations' might be very good English poems in their own way, by ignoring the original rhythms and metrical patterns and by failing to incorporate the elements of wit and word-play, they could scarcely give a hint of the Chinese poets' intentions.

I remember Wang sitting by the hearth and beating out the bold rhythm of one Chinese ballad with a poker for want of a baton. My wife and I had met him when we attended the I.L.P. Summer School at Welwyn, but had hardly got beyond a nod or a smile. His English, when I sat at the edge of the cluster round his straw-chair in the Conservatory, had not been clear enough to draw me any closer or to fix me where I squatted. But when he came to Belfast to speak at a public meeting on Aid for China, and we were asked to put him up, we did not hesitate.

He remained with us a bare ten days before going off to his next engagement in Dublin, but that span of days was one of those brief intense periods which, in life, suggest that time has depth and breadth as well as simple duration, has thickness too as well as length. He did not assert but exemplified stillness, tolerance and single-mindedness. On the platform at the big meeting he spoke for over an hour and never shifted a heel. When she had come to make-up his bed for a couple of mornings, my wife found the hot water-bottle apparently where she had placed it the evening before, so, as a quiet joke, she put it in various corners of the bed, and, each morning, sure enough, it was where she had left it.

One evening when some friends were in, we had a long and tangled discussion until the last bus had gone. One of our friends, a bankclerk, had missed his train, so we offered him the other single bed in Wang's room. By this time the talk had swung over to Irish history and lasted until we went to bed about 2 a.m. Our friend George, later declared that while undressing and even when already in bed Wang had continued his questions. Weary, George answered the last as briefly as courtesy allowed and then abruptly said Goodnight and pulled the clothes about his ears; and in the morning when he awoke, Wang, already dressed, was sitting on the other bed facing him, and when George stirred, he was asked, 'And then what did the Citizens' Army do?', as if the night's sleep had vanished in a blink.

His name was Wang Li Hsi; but by a gesture common enough among his countrymen, he gave it a Western look by reversing the name-order, putting the family cognomen last; and because the other syllables sounded like the name of the English poet, he anglicized them into Shelley: so it was as Shelley Wang that he was known in Britain.

One day when I was too busy to be with him, my brother-in-law, Norman Todhunter took him for a drive in the County Down to glimpse the countryside; and on the way back, while having tea in a cafe, Wang wrote a poem on the inside of a cigarette packet. It was about the Mourne Mountains, already famous, although he could not have known that, in popular song. A few evenings later with Wang's assistance I englished it and some months after had it published in the *New Statesman*:

> The Mourne Mountains like a team of bears
> tumbling into the sea,
> the embroidered fields like a monk's patched cloak
> spreading their skirts to every door,
> the peasants leisurely allowing
> the chickens and dogs to wander at will
> the bare trees standing silent
> entangle the stranger's dream.

The cigarette packet was of the Kensitas brand which, in those days, gave two bonus fags with every ten. For Wang was poor. There was a hole in the sole of each shoe, but he never complained or alluded to the fact. He had so much to explain about his country, its past, its arts, its problems, that there was no time for personal trivia. With untroubled courtesy and patience he would demonstrate the holding of the writing brush and the brisk stroking of the characters, explaining the parts and the meaning thereof; Tree is growing-thing-with-roots; Evening is Sun-in-the-grass …

Taking him round the Art Gallery and Museum one morning, we found ourselves in front of the long glass case propagating the notion of the Evolution of Man. The display was in three parts; a diagrammatic geological column lettered with the mysterious names, as of Goth or Visigoth dynasties, Jurassic, Triassic, Ordovician … but not to scale; the centre and principal extent of the case was taken up with a large and sprawling tree shape looking as if it had been made of bitumen and old rope, this set out the skulls of antiquity, Java, Neanderthal, Piltdown, but not Peking; for the last had been discovered too late for inclusion in the textbook from which the tree had been transplanted; then at the far end of the case, symmetrically balancing the geological column, was another, much smaller tree of similar texture; this showed the skulls of the living races of mankind in progressive order. As I stood beside my friend looking, I suddenly realized, for the first time, that at the tip of the treetop sat the White Man's skull, with the Mongolian and the Negro a good way down one on each side, with the Australian a bad fourth. Wang said not a word, but I knew that he had noticed it and my veins ran shame instead of blood. Here was I, beside a good even a great man, a man wiser and richer in experience than I should ever be, a man who in the past days had been giving me largesse of his people's wealth of philosophy, folklore, art, history, literature, of a range and a depth far outreaching that of my own people; and yet as we stood together, inside the glass case mocking us the skull of his race was set below the skull of mine without comment or explanation. That instant for all my shame I believe that I really became a man, not merely an Irishman or a European. And from that time I face all value-judgements on race with a cheerful scepticism, free of all *herrenvolkery*, be it Nazi, Afrikaans, English, Irish, Jewish, or Negro.

After that I could never pass that exhibition case without a mental blush, but it remained in its place until the man responsible for it retired, and, although it was not my business, I rejoiced when the Keeper of Natural History demolished that place of skulls and substituted his own conception of the Natural History of Ireland.

When the day of his departure had come we went with Wang to the Railway Station, and, on the platform taking my leave, I knew that I should never see him again, yet no one had so rapidly become a friend of my heart. I could not speak, and, as I waved to that pale moon face over the carriage door, my eyes were full of tears.

He sent me several poems and ballads in the form of literal translations and asked me to put metre on them. Then, from Chungking, I received a booklet of verses, page for page Chinese and English, in the latter my tidyings of his English. Then, sometime later, early in 1939, a paragraph in *The Daily Worker*, reported that Shelley Wang had died behind the Japanese lines, in Honan, involved in the cultural-guerrilla warfare of which he had told us. The book he had been working on for Gollancz never appeared, possibly never got finished. And, of all the men I have met I place Shelley Wang first, in essential humanity, in every quality by which any man dare be great; a poor man in thick glasses who smoked cheap cigarettes. Later I made my elegy, or rather it emerged in a long discursive poem about the world of that time, about the Basque sailors, and the German refugees, and thirty lines of it found their way into *The New Statesman*, the last ten of them run so:

> a gentle poet, even of our hills
> making a lovely stanza as he passed,
> disliking our coarse literal arts' conceit
> and setting style and reason against despair.
>
> For all his greatness life could offer him
> only a little death in a vast campaign
> a manuscript unpublished and a book
> of badly printed verse on wartime paper.
> Yet I do not think he would have understood
> that sick word failure. There are other words ...

18

Adelphi Centre

I had been reading *The Adelphi* for a good while, beginning, I rather fancy, with a bundle of back numbers, when the paper was thicker, although the covers always remained yellow, which someone gave my father, for it was hardly his kind of magazine, for his interests were more pedagogical than literary. Off and on, from 1932 I had had verses published in it, when Richard Rees was editor. The authority of John Middleton Murry was still pervasive and predominant, and I was a devoted enthusiast for his literary criticism. So, although our Laurentian phase, never so marked with Roberta and me as with some of our friends, had receded, we were sufficiently excited to cross over to the Summer School in August 1936 at Langham, near Colchester, where the Adelphi Centre had just been established. This promised to be more than just another summer school, for Murry, in setting up the Centre, had declared that it would be a training centre for making socialist – 'but real socialists not socialist politicians ... No such socialist centre can be really living until each member, or guest, takes as an obvious duty his full share, according to his capacity, of the actual work of the place; nor can it be truly healthy until it becomes largely self-supporting in the simple necessities of life'.

With the morning bell at 7.15 and lights out by a quarter to twelve, easy with a simple framework, we did our share of the work, some days bedmaking, some in the kitchen, some in the garden, once, romantic, traipsing through the nearby woods picking up sticks and meeting in a pool of sunlight S.L. Bensusan, who owned them, a great genial bear of a man with a slashing billhook in his hand for keeping the narrow tracks open. I remember being impressed with the functional planning of the vegetable plots in the garden; the plants growing up and coming on as they were needed, or as we were needed to eat them. This organization had been devised by N.A. Holdaway, a shock-headed schoolmaster in shorts, who was, in debate and in thinking on his feet, the best dialectician of them all. So too I recall seeing with surprise Professor John MacMurray, the philosopher, sweeping up the fag ends and dusting the chairs in the large room the morning after he had given a brilliant lecture there, a gesture of deep and lasting significance to me, for I had grown up with a house-proud and hardworking mother who would never have contemplated any male interfering with her domestic prerogatives, any man who dared would promptly have been designated 'an oul' jinny jo'. Herbert Read came too and lectured, but I do not recollect his sweeping the floor. In a grey flannel suit; with that earnest head of his, the shape of a seagull's egg, Roberta, at first glance, christened him the Grey Egg, a nickname, which, for me, had validity for more than his simple appearance. But he did not stay at Langham for long. Eric Blair, better known as George Orwell, stayed all the time and took his full share of the duties and the chores. I can remember sharing the potato-peeling with him and listening to some excellent talk. At that period, he respected Somerset Maugham as a literary craftsman and contended his close study of the prose of Swift, not merely reading but trying to re-create the cadences. Eric Blair was really the first man of the Left in my acquaintance who could have fairly been called Anti-Soviet. With many of us, I guess, the position was that while, from time to time, we learned things about the Russian regime which disturbed us, in so much it seemed on the right side, that we felt public criticism was letting the side down, playing into the capitalists' hands. We thought that we were choosing not the lesser evil, but the speckled good. It was not until reports came back from Spain about the behaviour of the Communists to the POUM Trotskyists or Anarchists, that our attitude became more objective. One of Eric Blair's cracks, I remember, was that shortly the Soviet leaders would claim to have established 'The largest aspirin factory in the world', an image which has remained with me as the most telling expression of the materialist's dream; bigger headaches with vaster means of curing them, rather than a simplification of life which would attack the cause. I can remember my disappointment when it was announced as an achievement of Communism that white bread had replaced the more wholesome traditional food.

In July, before the Summer School had assembled, civil war had broken out in Spain, but this caused little or no comment among us. Yet, ironically, it was this war which later played an important part in the development of two of the most impressive leading men at Langham. Eric Blair was, of course, one, with his fine book *Homage to Catalonia* ahead of him, and that bullet in the throat which, I believe, shortened his life. I had come upon his name in *The Adelphi* as a versewriter of some power, his tramp-poems being rather like the grimmer lines of W.H. Davies; but that remains an aspect of his work which has received little attention. He was not robustly built, with a clipped moustache, a middle parting in his hair, and a long jaw. The other man who became involved in Spain was Richard Rees, a tall thin fair-to-sandy man, clean-shaven with little hair and a corrugated brow. Although he took small part in discussion, and seemed closer to Eric Blair than anyone else, he moved, not at all pompously, but with a sense of responsibility among the more bizarre personalities, the bearded, the sandalled.

John Middleton Murry was below average height, with a slightly bowlegged, lop-sided stance. His hair was black and wiry on wrists and fingers. The tonsure of baldness made his identification with Burlap in Aldous Huxley's *Point Counter Point* abundantly clear. But Huxley's was a name that never came up in anybody's talk. Murry seemed to have his nostrils twitched and his lips set in a kind of per-manent smirk. His skin was dry and yellow ... Altogether an unpleasant looking fellow, with sometimes a devilish expression.

I found it visually difficult to connect him with the fine body of critical work which I so admired, with the sensitive perceptions of his studies of Smart, Clare, Hopkins, Edward Thomas and the light-hearted puncturing of Churchill's flatulent prose in that masterly little squib 'Beauty Hunting' in *Countries of the Mind*, yet, interven-ing in discussions and in his own formal addresses, more than a hint of the imaginative warmth and spiritual authority came through. When Murry quoted something from Keats or Shakespeare and added 'that is one of the large imaginative utterances by which I live', almost as a throwaway, it did not sound as pretentious as it looks on the page. Indeed, that morning, when he took his text from that marvellous serial-letter which John Keats in the spring of 1819 wrote to his brother in America, and moved with affectionate and illuminating ease among its images and clarified its conclusion and bade us follow its directive, I had no sense that this was anything other than a passionate search and a triumphant revelation. This is one of those very rare moments of which my memory is sensorily rounded; I can still hear the speaking voice. The result has been that 'the creature hath a purpose and its eyes are bright with it', and 'there is continually some birth of new heroism. The pity is, that we must continually wonder at it as we should at finding a pearl in rubbish', have remained since then among the large imaginative utterances by which I live myself.

This was about the period when, having gone beyond Lawrence to his own brand of Communism, he was approaching Pacifism; later to box the compass and end up as a Red-baiting Fascist Messiah, the Godhead of his little Community-dictatorship. For me, it remains one of the minor enigmas of my experience that so sensitive a literary critic could prove to be such an unprincipled rascal or so completely the uncritical dupe of his vanity. One evening while she was dancing with him, to make conversation, Roberta rather innocently asked him how long it had taken him to write his book on Shakespeare, which, out earlier that year, had excited my interest. He replied smiling and with a faraway look in his eyes 'A lifetime, my dear, a lifetime'.

Publicly the nasty side of Murry's nature broke surface once when, for some trivial matter such as being late for a lecture – forgetting the time and staying too long on the river – he attacked Rayner Heppenstall with malicious energy. During the outburst and onslaught, we all gasped and thought 'this is too much. Has the great man no sense of proportion?' It was a Judas-trick, for Rayner had written a very good study of Murry only a short while before, and at that moment, I suspect, depended upon the hospitality of the Centre. After Langham we were not to meet Rayner again until during the war he clumped into the Art Gallery in those army boots which he hated so much.

After the war Colin Middleton and Kathleen decided to join Murry's communal farm in Norfolk. As gently as we could we told them what we thought of Murry. But realizing that their hearts were set on the venture we wasted no more breath. One side of that story saw print in *Community Farm* in which Murry writes of the Middletons as a Scottish artist and his wife, and I hope that the correcting narrative will one day appear, for the sake of the record. When Colin and Kathleen returned, what they had to tell bore out every dread we had thought of, but even so we could hardly conceive of the satanic lunacy of the creature, so grounded upon the most calculating business sense, that a rundown farm should be turned into a highly efficient undertaking, while the pacifists and earnest goodlifers who broke the stubborn earth and brought it back to fertility by sweat, ache and blister, should, one by one, be expelled from the presence, until, in the end, Murry had an A1 farm and no pacifists.

Although Roberta and I were short-term visitors only, for two weeks out of the school's three, we became aware of a vast web of intrigue, backbiting, swift shuttling of conversation when the company changed. And of the residents, those whose home the Centre was, not a few, each time in strict confidence, assured one or other of us that he was the sheet anchor of the whole edifice, one bearded fellow asserting that he had 'the bee-keeper's skill', a phrase which I have been happy to use since. There were some congenial folk around, Francis Andrews, editor of the Postal Workers' magazine, and a pleasant poet in the Georgian vein; E.C. Large, a tall, bulky man with a black Nietzsche moustache and a great mop of black hair at the back of a high bald forehead. Either before or after this, he wrote a very good novel, *Sugar in the Air;* an industrial-scientific satire. Then old Mrs. Hicks, over eighty, a nurse and midwife all her days, who lost her evangelical Christianity assisting childbirth in the slums, but kept an innocent sweetness; it had been her admiration for Katharine Mansfield that brought her under *The Adelphi* influence. She was looking forward wide-eyed, to a visit to Australia where the descendants of some of her kin lived. And I remember how we thought that such optimism at eighty, such youthfulness of interest in so frail a body, was an affirmation to be marvelled at and saluted.

Langham is, of course, in the Constable country, and we spent as much time as we could manage walking there around. The familiar names became known places, East Bergholt, Dedham, Willy Lott's House, Flatford Mill, where the lazy Stour drew its slow wandering line between Essex and Suffolk, as our eyes and visual memories made the connexions and adjustments between view and canvas, and canvas and view. It seemed odd, one day, to peep over a hedge to see a little pink man, naked except for khaki shorts, and sitting under a broad parasol, driving a tractor across a very large, flat and dusty field, for nothing further from the Constable canon could easily be imagined. This was indeed our first glimpse of the age of mechanized agriculture.

In the Holly Trees Museum in Colchester among the multitude of bygones, I noticed an engraving of Sir Thomas Smyth, undertaker of one of the Elizabethan plantations at home, and wondered if, by any chance, Hewitts among his henchmen had taken our surname across the Irish Sea, for I have, off and on, had a gust of curiosity about where my folk had started from. In the Castle there were Constable portraits of his parents and pencil studies in that kind, none of much quality.

But this submersion in his atmosphere had its proper coincidental rounding off, when in London we saw the big exhibition of his work at the Victoria and Albert Museum. So Constable entered my hierarchy, with that interlocking of place, person and work, which, for me, gives art its most palpable value and meaning. It was the fashion then to admire his sketches, and this I had done years before with the landscapes in the Royal Academy Diploma Gallery; but more than his small sketches, it was held self evident that his hand and eye were best assessed in the full scale versions before he carried out the finished paintings, which betrayed a loss of feeling, a timidity, or so Wilenski persuaded us to believe. And in this belief the years passed, till in the UNESCO Exhibition of Romantic Art in the Tate Gallery 1959, I found to my surprise, when I saw the two versions of *The Leaping Horse*, of *Salisbury Cathedral from the Meadows*, that the later form, in pigment control and more successfully arranged composition, was the better work. In front of them I stood and fought, or paced about like a referee, weighing stroke for stroke and blow for blow, reluctant to allow my fancy to flinch before the steady onset of its more mature and better organized rival.

In the end, I found my mind changed for me, another long-enjoyed idea gone, preferring instead of the exploratory piece, the finished canvas as the painter had planned it.

In Colchester Castle too we saw some stone sculpture, the Tombstone of Longinus, a Roman cavalryman, particularly, and a Sphinx of the First Century, which brought Eric Gill irresistible to mind, for I had been reading him at home. So, in London that time, we made the journey to Westminster Cathedral to see his then highly commended *Stations of the Cross*, being, I recollect, a little disappointed that their impact was restrained.

In spite of the disturbed atmosphere at the Centre, Roberta always easier and more skilful with people than I, became quietly popular, and a pleasant middle-aged woman discovering that we were going to London for a week, offered us the use of her ground floor flat in Hampstead Garden Suburb for our sojourn there; and a gentle, oldish man who wore knickerbockers or plus-fours, one of the Centre's Trustees, I believe, when he found out that we were on the point of leaving, drew me aside and, greatly to my amazement, thanked us for our being there together, and so effectively demonstrating that marriage was still a valid sacrament; while all the time we had, as it were, stood shoulder to shoulder among so many strangers.

In the community there was one proletarian, something of a professional at that, and because of his uniqueness he was fussed over, listened to more attentively than he deserved, forgiven his failure consistently to co-operate where any manual work was required, walked with slowly along the gravel paths, and played bowls with by Murry. To my eye, conditioned by familiarity with Labour Party supporters, many of them unemployed in the depression years, this man looked about as typically proletarian as a discharged waiter from a medium-sized hotel, or a cashiered police sergeant; but in a group for the most part drawn from a wide range of the middleclass, from schoolmaster to baronet, and all emphatically literate, this fellow stood out as something different. I remember well, one evening, when resting from culture and Keats, we gave ourselves up rather selfconsciously to games and dancing – though not so absurdly as that other evening when we marched into the local pub in a body to drink beer and play darts and drove the half dozen natives into silent corners – that Murry spent most of his time and attention on a blond young authoress who wore purple stockings and shook monstrous earrings. When, finally, we got to our room, the night being warm we left the window wide-open, and suddenly we heard the voice of our proletarian in his room talking to his wife, their window open and directly below ours; and the vocabulary in which he analysed Murry's interest in the girl was unmistakably that of the industrial working class male.

A trivial incident, but important in my subsequent thinking on the problem of community living, relevant in its implications for any consideration we may be compelled to give to counteract the impoverished isolation of the small family unit in our epoch and the next. In retrospect, there was far more of the warmth and affection of fellowship and neighbourliness with the I.L.P. at Welwyn, among the devoted political workers, from Jimmy Maxton to the lad who ate the green apples, than at Langham, in that steaming fish tank of supercharged egos, where the words service, religion, purpose, imagination, integration, were as 'frequent as the bad puns and canny Scots jokes of the other place'.

19

Diploma for the Straw Man

In the early Thirties the Council of the Museums Association, the organization representing members of the museum and gallery profession and the institutions wherein they were employed, became concerned about vocational standards, about the absence of recognized qualifications. Up till then, the provincial galleries and museums had been staffed without system. Delicate lads whose hobby was collecting butterflies, obsessed antiquarians who were never young, serious minded men not quite able to break into the regular professions, by drift of circumstance, or sometimes by laying-on of hands, men and women, somehow, found places in which to follow their eccentric concerns. The pay was generally poor, so there was little competition. And for historical reasons the close meshing in with the public library service, the museum being frequently the room about the library, kept the gallery and museum workers in a subordinate position. That much was accomplished was largely due to the activities of a few inspired librarians with interests beyond catalogue-system and statistics of book issues. But, although in the past, the absence of any fitness test permitted the entrance into the gallery world of quite unsuitable persons, the low salaries often ensured that utterly unmercenary individuals were able to establish themselves and by degrees give the authority of their independence and honesty to what had been, before, a haphazard, amateur pursuit.

So a trial course in basic training was attempted in Manchester, both the civic authorities and the University collaborating in the organization. Alfred and I obtained leave to attend and we managed to recoup part of our expenses from the Carnegie Trust. We had lectures and talks on practical tips for restoration and conservation. One tall blonde boy whose name I have forgotten described in detail how, by the method of electrolysis, he completely destroyed a Roman shield-boss. But it was the visit to the Whitworth Institute, then an independent institution, which had the most telling effect, for its director G.P. Dudley Wallis, a lean alert man with a, tight wrinkled mouth and sparking eyes behind large owl-round glasses, was an infectious enthusiast. He invited three of us to his home one evening, Ian Finlay was, I think, the third, and for the first time I saw a real collector in his lair. His basement was hung with great smouldering nudes by Matthew Smith, but its chief treasure was the large Sickert derived from a newspaper photograph of Belgian infantrymen set against the great arc of a gun carriage wheel. When I admired a small sculpture by Gertrude Hermes, Wallis deplored the bad habit of women artists marrying and ceasing to be artists. He talked volubly and effectively, leaping into ready argument, to which, since he proved to be a convert to Catholicism, I was not backward in joining issue. Mishearing my surname as Hewart, we found ourselves sparring round Lord Hewart's then much discussed book *The New Despotism*. All the while, a little old man in a tasselled smoking cap padded round the perimeter of our debate, introduced, at intervals, by Wallis as his father. Sometime after this, Wallis left the Whitworth for picture dealing, and I never encountered him again; but he was a true enthusiast, with a fierce passion for modern art, loving what he liked, damning what he disliked.

The Association folk considering this Manchester venture a success or, at least, a pointer to success, thereafter drew up a scheme and organized courses. I went to Liverpool, but all that I remember now are Dr Hay Murray, a genial midget, lecturing to us from the vast tableland of a laboratory bench, utterly unembarrassed as he toddled from one end to the other stabbing questions at his gaping ring of listeners, all eyes wide in hope and dread that he would suddenly throw a cartwheel or attempt a hand stand, this, also the inventor of *Murrayite* a once popular fixative or adhesive; and Trevor Thomas, sandy-haired, gay, deaf, courageous with colour, an *avant garde* interior decorator let loose in a Waxworks Show, making a ballet of West African basketry and a drama of Chinese embroidery; and a dark young man called Rimmer who skinned a rabbit in thirty seconds or so it seemed, I goggled at his sleight of hand, but some of my fellow students were critical in the finer points. These positive persons and little more, except the crowded violence of Martini's panel, *Christ Carrying his Cross* from the remarkable Roscoe Collection in the Walker Gallery, are all that survives of Course One, Liverpool.

The next course was at Bristol in 1935; this bore richer fruit, for afterwards I used the experience in a long blank verse poem. We were taken on an excursion to visit the archaeological site of Meare Lake Village, a milestone in my imaginative journey, for there, I underwent some sort of mystical conversion, a true turning towards, and away from; not to be expressed in orthodox religious terms, but rather, an upspringing of self realization:

> At Meare, in a wind-whipped field as flat as bog,
> (My Antrim eye had noted; so it proved)
> there had been dug a magic hole through time,
> revealing a crisscross raft of oak and alder
> and silver birch with the bark not rotted yet,
> where men had wrought and sung before Christ's birth:
> the nail-scored pot, bonecomb, smooth ring of jet,
> the blade now shattered, and the amber beads
> the baked clay hearth and the bars of hammered iron.

I had been away alone before this. But Paris, London, Liverpool are cities, autonomous, their meaning contained within themselves. Bristol was the Wills Tower at the University and Burke's statue where the trams spun round, and St Mary's Radcliffe and Chatterton and the bridge slung high and the Severn Sea: it was, in a way, a microcosm of England, the first England to salute me in street, road, tree, hill, and not by the smeared fragments of these drawn across the window of the train. When I returned to my own country, I noticed the difference, the change in my thought and feeling, and so *The Return* came out of it.

In something like two hundred lines I summarized the year past, plucking out the emotive images from my experience. The first complete year of married life – it was, in its way, leaving my wife for the first time which emphasized the aloneness of my Bristol journey

– in which we had together spent a holiday on Rathlin Island, another allegory there, had become deeply involved in the Peace movement, in that work for the Council of Civil Liberties: it was also the year of Mussolini's assault on Abyssinia, when we saw the match struck and the fuse began to spark and splutter toward the inevitable. Yet Meare with its moral of man's persistence in the things his hands had made, and Rathlin with its momentary crystal-lization of human life in a naturally circumscribed context, offered me points to spin my threads between, so that I achieved a sort of humanist aesthetic:

> Man has gone on, endured the incidence
> of Rome and Caesar, lived to see the end
> of woad and crucifixion, Thor and Zeus:
> if not men individual with these faces,
> jaws set so, brows this angle, eyes this colour,
> man has gone on, essential man, the Maker,
> the double man, destroyer in his blood,
> charring the wood and heaping the hills of slag,
> smearing a plain with slums and firing the whin;
> Yet out of his nature making something lovely,
> a bronze blade meant to kill, but leaf-precise,
> Always the touch of immortality
> upon the things of death –

and, with that, an imaginative grasp of my calling and destiny; 'pre-server of the shards, keeper of names,/ lackey of time, ostler of the Apocalypse'.

On the other level I learned something of the Bristol water-colourists, finding a high place for W.J. Muller, and interested that our old George Petrie and James O'Connor had come this way and stopped awhile, heard a brilliant lecture on the application of Gestalt to the arrangement of museum specimens from a clever man called Codrington, watched a shaggy old man in knickerbockers reline old canvasses, was wakened to the cherry-stone art of drafting specimen labels by little Dr. P.J. North, the kindly geologist, and, beyond these, observed first, with shock, then, with amusement, the harsh interplay of jangling personalities, the bland, successful, hollow man, the frustrated-but-controlled, growing smaller and chiller in the process, the frustrated and malicious, in that malice finding release. Two of these I encountered years after, and the hollow man had become so hollow that he tinkled, while the controlled man sat immobile in a corner.

The third course was delayed until the spring of 1938: the others had been general; my fellow students had been bird-watchers, pot-holers, philatelists, numismatists, ruin-fanciers, taxidermists, each with that folding lens in his vest pocket: this, pivoted on the National Gallery in Edinburgh, was to be more specialized. For me professionally it was by far the most nourishing and memorable; yet, on the other hand, no poem came out of it. The Director of the Gallery, Stanley Cursiter, although not in the front rank of the Scottish painters of his generation, was an intelligent artist, with good reason for everything he did, painterly most when his brush stroked the light on some silver object or flecked a rose with texture. Above all he knew his techniques thoroughly and rounded and enriched the media-education I had received from Billy and Jack. It was as if the conversation had continued. He knew his Raeburn from priming to varnish and back again, indicating the square stroke and the timing of the darks. Taking us to the workshop where the MacLeod portraits by Allan Ramsay were being cleaned for the Empire Exhibition in Glasgow later in the year, he expounded and demonstrated the processes with a craftsman's sensitivity. Then round his galleries he explained and discussed the elements of good hanging and intelligent arrangement. All these, embellished with brief but memorable snatches of general information, giving background to what was before us; as, for instance, the true story of the origin of the Kilt. From him I gained some appreciation of the Scottish painters of Jamesone, of Thomson of Duddingston, of Raeburn, Geddes, Dyce, and David Scott, and of McTaggart's lonely pioneering, which has helped me to see the English and the artists of my own country's past in clear perspective. And when I crossed to Glasgow with my father in August to see the Exhibition I felt equipped for the experience.

In my career as a keeper of art, the greatest single debt I owe is to that lean keen Orcadian in the blue double-breasted suit, with the grey curly hair, for he showed me how much there was to learn and how I might begin, with gentleness and humility.

After this there was a day's trip to Manchester, to the Art Gallery, for the practical tests, hanging a wall of paintings, arranging pots in a case, under the friendly eye of a curator who read Greek for fun, and played the fiddle in the Halle Orchestra. Then, a written examination, the papers posted to Belfast, the invigilator a member of the staff of the Technical College where Alfred and I sat and wrote. That day was memorable for another reason: for only on my return home in the evening did I discover that Roberta was seriously ill. She had gritted her teeth, and got me out well-breakfasted in good time, without a wince or word to worry me.

The courses attended, the practical tests and the written examination disposed of, there remained The Thesis. I had chosen for my subject 'The Problems of a Provincial Gallery' prophetic surely, for these problems have always been with me. The reading for, the thinking about, and the writing of that have served me well, for although I have since read more widely, thought more broadly, and learned to write more simply it keeps its place in the course my ideas have taken. And so, with about six or seven others, Alfred among them, I was in the first batch ever to be awarded the Diploma of the Museums Association.

20

Griffin

In my early years, largely at my wife's urging, I made two or three attempts to leave Belfast. Several years in Canada and the United States had given her a breath of air outside: even in a most literal sense, the dry continental air of North America had proved much more comfortable than the damp airs of home. She had experienced an emotional release from the constrictions of conservative insularity, in the context of a more vigorous and buoyant society, which even the hazards of the Great Depression did not seem to offset. And so, it has been that she always sat more lightly to what I deemed my obligations and loyalties than I, was not without a word of warning that my judgement had been known to fail before, having been out much farther and much longer, had, perhaps, a better sense of scale than I.

I was on a short list for Norwich. A museum man, a naturalist or an archaeologist was what was wanted. The first advertisement had found no takers. I had seen it, without interest. Then the retiring Curator wrote to Arthur Deane to ask him to think of somebody, anybody, who might remotely do. So I applied for the sake of the journey. Well worthwhile it was, for all expenses were paid, not only to see the museum's then handsome dioramas of wild life, of gulls and terns by an estuary, but for the feel of the place, an English Castle bulked above a busy cattle market, rough stone to the handpalms, dung tang in the air. And most certainly, for the chance to see the Colman Collection of Watercolours, the Norwich School in their own place. Yet it is Colman's lovely little oil of the backend of a covered wagon jolting over a hump which remains an item in my ideal gallery.

Because of the distance, I stayed overnight in London on the way back, and before train time I saw Frank Woolley playing his last game at the Oval in the morning, and Leonid Massine making his last appearance with the De Basil Ballet in the afternoon: Woolley driving Gover, with Sandham in the outfield; and Massine leaping about in the *Povlotsvian Dances*, a gluttony of a sort, but with a good taste lasting after.

I was on a short list for secretaryship of a cultural institute in the West Indies, interviewed in London at the Victoria and Albert Museum, by the sallow high collared Sir Eric MacLagan, the rubicund Governor General of the island, ahead of him a fatal seizure there six months further on, and a table length of unremembered faces. But neither I nor A.G. Sewter was appointed. Who it was I have forgotten, but although I have not met Sewter since, I have saluted his name under poems and over articles with a friendly nod of recognition as one should say I knew your father years ago. Another short list took me to Liverpool, when Charles Carter left for Plymouth, but a well connected young man took the votes.

Then the war came and peacetime possibilities were packed away. By the time the ports were open again I was deep in my concern of the stirring situation in the province, for writers and artists were among us, and I was busy with the recently established C.E.M.A., with courses of lectures in Belfast and talks in country towns, with membership of the B.B.C. Northern Ireland Regional Advisory Panel, with my private campaign for Ulster Regionalism, with my reading and research in the Ulster Poets of the past, with making my own verses still, though not so many as before.

Naturally in the small community I had become quite well known, and it seemed fairly likely that, when the time came, I would have a good chance of being appointed Director at Stranmillis, poor Alfred, my senior, having been thrust aside by the tragic onset of ill health; so I carried on with my interests, took my Master's degree by thesis – there had been no one to supervise my studies, the field being outside all academic attention heretofore. I heard of one professor visiting the Linen Hall Library to see for himself if the books I had listed and commented on did, in fact, exist – wrote my reviews for *Tribune* and *The Bell*, my articles for *The Studio* and the local miscellanies, my letters to *The New Statesman*, the *TLS*, the Belfast press, when I felt strongly that a word was needed.

So it was in 1945 that F.L. Green's *Odd Man Out* appeared with a character in it, a minor character called Griffin, an art dealer:

> Tall, thin, and of an incisive temperament, humorous, kindly, he was an established authority not only on painting, but on literature, the drama, religion, politics, and many other diversions by which the public sought an outlet for energies which were hemmed in by the sea which divides them from England and by their temperament which separates them from the outer world. There was hardly a platform which he could prevent himself from taking, and from which he theorized in a robust, crisp fashion. There was scarcely a stranger to the city who, coming to the North for information regarding its history, literature, drama, painting, politics, commerce, hopes, was not swiftly and adroitly contacted by Griffin and as swiftly loaded with facts. And similarly, when a new artist or novelist, poet, politician, playwright appeared from amongst the population, Griffin was there to study him from some vantage point and thereafter applaud him or dismiss him in a few theorizing remarks.
>
> It did not occur to Griffin that, in the past, he had sometimes exalted fools or made little mistakes regarding men of talent. What mattered to him was the fact that he had to safeguard certain principles and defend the gateways of art from charlatans.

This 'tall, thin' nonsense – I am five feet nine and was then something over thirteen stones in weight – was a palpable diversion; for, a few pages farther on, Green forgot this, and, with me in his mind's eye wrote 'Griffin laughed heartily from relief. Tucking his wreathed chin against his chest he emitted a shattering guffaw'. My wife frequently rebuked me for the loudness and coarseness of my laugh. An obvious trick of self assertion, I suspect that it has, of late years, become moderated, although the older I grow, I cannot affirm that there is less to laugh about. That other novelist Benedict Kiely in a Radio Éireann broadcast once referred to me as 'a quiet, scholarly man', an image which, in my mind, I fondle, to offset the rather brash Griffin.

The Sour Laugh

When Sean O'Faolain's book *An Irish Journey* came out in 1940, although I found his general reactions to Belfast bracingly provocative, and his phrasing of them now and then, memorable, I was greatly annoyed and properly indignant at his reference to the Museum:

> One might well visit the Museum and Art Gallery if one wants a sour laugh. Most of it is enough to make one believe that the Ulsterman has no sense of humour. For it is largely devoted to such things as Waterford glass, Viking ornaments, the inauguration chair of the O'Neills, reproductions of ancient Irish ornaments, a skeleton of the extinct Irish elk, a plaster-cast of a cross from Monasterboice, and such like things, every one of which mocks at modern Belfast and the Six Counties with foreign jaws. So, one likewise will see there a statue of Wellington who lived in and was educated in County Meath. The paintings in the art gallery make a pleasant collection, including a fine Paul Henry. Then come a dreary pile of casts.

Although, in my first decade, I had found plenty to cavil at in my place of work, I did not welcome the savage comment of an outsider. I had achieved sufficient identification with it immediately to leap to its defence. There was, however, nothing that I could do. My superiors, as Englishmen, could never feel so involved; and, very likely, had they read the words and understood them, would have taken it as commendation, for who, in his senses, looks for a sense of humour in a museum?

At least, Sean O'Faolain had observed more than H.V. Morton had, in 'that happy afternoon in the new Belfast Museum' which he mentioned in his *In Search of Ireland* (1930); for all that the latter noticed for praise were the watercolours of Old Belfast, the Lavery paintings and the very reproductions which the former deplored. In fact, the only evidence of any acute observation on Morton's part was his reference to the tiny glazed Chinese seals so oddly discovered in various parts of the County Down in the middle of last century.

With O'Faolain at first I sought pleasurable relief in his gaffes. There are, so far as I know, very few Viking ornaments in any Irish museum. There are none in Belfast; but it would be no harm if there were, for Carlingford and Strangford still keep syllables of their talk on our tongues. They came to the northern part of Ireland a long time before Mr O'Faolain and proved themselves even less friendly than he during their sojourn. The stone seat of the O'Neills belonged to a sept of that clan which was once powerful in the Castlereagh Hills, across the Lagan valley, where this rough hewn boulder was found. Where else than here should it now repose? We do not now speak of the Irish elk, that is a relic of nineteenth century antiquarianism when they called a dolmen a cromlech and spoke of the Firbolgs. Mr. O'Faolain could hardly be expected to know that in the entrance hall of almost every big house in the North the antlers of a great Irish deer dug out of an adjacent bog will hang opposite the halflength portrait of King William from the Kneller factory: by the first totem the family is making its assertion of Irishry, by the second of its membership of the Protestant Ascendancy. Besides, if he had scrutinized the Stranmillis skeleton, he might have observed that strips of leather have eked out any deficiency of rib. Further, by the same token, what right has the Royal College of Surgeons to the skeleton of the Irish Giant so proudly displayed in the Hunterian Museum?

But other barbs stuck stubbornly: as, for instance, that enormous cast of Muireadach's Cross, its intricate Romanesque reliefs well clogged with repeated coats of paint, as much a relic of nineteenth century antiquarianism as Mr. O'Faolain's elk. I had never liked it since the first time I saw it in the Grainger Room in the Free

Library. That and the reproductions of Celtic metal craft, the Ardagh Chalice, the Tara Brooch, St. Patrick's Shrine, and the Cross of Cong (if it is Celtic) always seemed to me out of place, for I have long had my strong antipathy to copies and imitations and facsimiles. Nor with Waterford glass was I very happy, but for another reason altogether. Indeed, when Arthur Deane retired, I changed the display of this, clapped on it the more honest title of Irish Glass and with explicit labelling left no excuse for the old nonsense. In its best period the glass was made in Ireland by a fiscal accident, when the duties on the raw materials levied in Great Britain made it temporarily profitable for the English manufacturers to transfer men and plant across the water.

Something else which bothered me, he did not mention. Actually in 1940 it was not so evident, but under Deane's successor an active policy was developed for buying pieces of Irish Silver, often with handsome grants by the National Art Collections Fund of London. Certainly, in my time, more was spent on silver than on paintings. To acquire Irish glass was shaky enough, but there had been a Belfast manufactory of it early in the last century, so it could be argued that the other specimens from Waterford, Cork or Dublin had value in comparative study. But with silver this did not obtain. Irish silver is Dublin Silver. Silver is expensive and can be expensive looking; you can demonstrate to the Committee that they are getting value for their money. Silver is usually wellmarked, thus permitting the manipulation of the pocket lens as you purposefully peer at the rim or examine the base. The symbols and date letter you can check from the table at the back of your diary. And if you consider buying something in a London saleroom, you can always ask the man from the Victoria and Albert to vet it for you. Silver is not likely to depreciate. It is the timid museum man's temptation.

Enough of O'Faolain's strictures had point. And I was compelled to meditate more deeply and analytically on what the purpose and scope of our museum and art gallery should be, in the context of a split nation and divided allegiance. It was, to begin with, the Municipal Museum and Art Gallery sustained by the ratepayers of the city, a large majority of them Ulster Unionists and therefore, anti-National in their views. Was it then our business to present the city to itself, and as much of the world as we could interpret, to our-selves. But with no other effective institution in the hinterland, should we not also concern ourselves with the statutory Six Counties? And what then of the three lost counties of the historic nine counties province? And what should be our relationship to the other fragment of our country? To Geology, Natural History, Archaeology, the Border was irrelevant. Should we claim to repre-sent, as adequately as our material allowed, what belonged to the whole country up to the date when Partition broke off the story and another story began, and then represent the new story, our story? Had ethnography any place? If not, what of the Singhalese Dancing Masks, the Solomon Islanders' war canoe, the Royal Feather Cloak, the Easter Island wood sculptures, the Maori carved panels, the tapa-cloth figure which the British Museum once wanted to buy? Could anyone arrange these in an informative sequence or order? Or should more specimens be sought to provide contexts for these, necessitating the building of a new wing to house the lot? Or should these not be retained as explorers' loot, soldiers' booty, missionar-ies' keepsakes or traders' plunder, part of the intricate social history of Victorian Imperialism, important in themselves and in how they got here?

When, after the risk of air raids had passed, we re-organized the art gallery, Boehm's plaster Wellington was not brought back and the roomful of classical casts, where I had met my Waterloo with the Juvenile Trainees, was turned into a useful store, the contents having been offered to and taken by the Headmaster of the College of Art. So Wilenski's brilliant, but, by vested interests blatantly evaded exposure of the Myth of Greek Sculpture had, with us, at least, one minute ripple of response. On the museum floor, to the long and exceedingly monotonous array of spinning wheels and textile appli-ances in the Homer Collection, I added a meagre halfcase illustrat-ing the Social Life of the Handloom Weaver, to the contemporary engravings and the inscribed utensils adding the tattered remnants of one old weaver's book of verse, in an effort to suggest that these wooden machines had been handled by folk not unlike ourselves and not so far back in our geneology. This last small gesture, of course, tied-in with my exploration of the work and the lives of my

Rhyming Weavers, which in its own positive way had to do, as my re-assessment of the museum and art gallery's function made its contribution, to the development of the notion of Regionalism then taking over my thought and imagination.

22

The War Years I

A few days after war had been declared Harold and I went down to the recruiting office. We found a crowd before us, mostly, by their appearance, young unemployed men. But, although there was no conscription in Northern Ireland, – the Catholic population would have resisted it as they did all over Ireland over twenty years before, – and of the rest, not even the hyperloyal Orange Order suggested it – we were told that as we were both Local Government Officers we were in a reserved occupation, and could not be taken unless we resigned and became unemployed, which seemed a silly sort of thing to do, since we had assumed that our salaries would have been made-up by the Local Authority for the maintenance of our dependents. Our patriotism was rather more provisional than headlong. This ruling seemed, later, somewhat anomalous when Douglas Deane our colleague, not many years younger, joined the R.A.F. as a photographer. Later, a press notice asked for graduates to be considered for commissions; but when it was understood that I had no O.T.C. experience I was sent home.

Maybe eighteen months later, feeling rather guilty at my earlier status, with Patrick Maybin in the R.A.M.C., Cecil Cree in the R.A.F. and George MacCann somewhere in Burma with the Enniskillen Fusiliers, I started negotiations to join the Camouflage people, went to the Northern Ireland H.Q. at Lisburn for interview, and after a couple of drinks, it was agreed that I should have to wait till a Colonel Beddington, then in Malta, arrived, for a final decision. I still have the note on my files, but I never heard from the Colonel. And so, though I tried, admittedly not hard enough to hurt, I was not able to take any part in what I realized must have been the greatest imaginative experience of my generation; and maybe in that loss

I have suffered a serious deprivation which has left me perhaps less adult than my years require.

There was enough to do in the Gallery. The top floor was completely cleared of exhibits, and a bed of loose sand poured over it, for the roof above, being practically all glass, was particularly vulnerable. The paintings were stored in a Masonic Hall in a small village about ten miles from town.

About the time of the fall of France when Roberta had gone to the country with the evacuated children from the nursery school, there was talk that our building should be turned into a hospital, and repeatedly R.A.M.C. teams came round with notebooks and tape measures, but nothing came of it. Being at some distance from the city centre, it was not, like museums in many other towns, made headquarters for the Ministry of Food, or of Civil Defence. So, apart from the siren on the roof, it remained outside the war machine.

During this period the Deputy Curator was a happy man, involved in Civil Defence, in the elaborate organization of weekend exercises, bustling with memoranda and never for long parted from his tin hat. The Curator, simply awaiting the day of his retirement, spent his time cataloguing lantern-slides. The rest of us, in our respective home districts, took part in Civil Defence also. And when, in 1940, we moved to Mount Charles, we came under the Deputy Curator's surveillance, and Roberta and I joined the district control centre staff, where F.L. Green was one of our associates. After the first small raid on the docks, we went out with the motor canteen, the most vivid memories being of dog-tired fire-fighters hosing great mounds of smouldering grain-sacks, of an hysterical young sailor shouting like a mad prophet in the midst of a little crowd, and of people trickling back, with shocked faces, to discover if their little houses still stood.

There were two serious raids on the city after this, and nearly a thousand people were killed, a number not generally appreciated across the water where the accepted story is that the whole of Ireland had been immune from attack. Then the war seemed to move away from us, and as the risk of air raids diminished, the sand was swept up from the Gallery floors; and we launched in 1943 our first One Man Exhibition of a local artist's work. It was a good beginning, for in Colin Middleton we had a phenomenally prolific painter, able to provide one hundred and ten works in an astonishing variety of styles. It was, I think, the most exciting display of an Irishman's work that I have seen, and certainly confirmed me in my opinion that Middleton is, of his generation the most remarkable and talented painter in that country. An immediate reaction to that first show was that the artist was hypersensitive to influence; from one point of view the run of painting and drawings looked like a comprehensive anthology of modern art, Picasso, Chagall, Kandinsky, Klee, to name only four disparate forces, having here and there a finger in it. But there was enough, particularly in the lovely sequence *The Poet's Garden*, most unfortunately dispersed, to show that Middleton had his own song to sing.

His next exhibition was sponsored by C.E.M.A. in 1945, and thereafter he was taken up by Victor Waddington and shown in Dublin and abroad. In these years Colin and Kathleen, his second wife, set out on their rather restless career with residences of varying duration round the coast of County Down and, later, Antrim. But before the Waddington period they entered elated and returned disillusioned from John Middleton Murry's Community Farm at Thelnetham. In his book, Murry masks them as a Scottish painter and his wife, and tells a story which does not agree with theirs, for they had come within his orbit when his mental instability had become a matter for alarm.

Colin Middleton, for me, epitomizes the puzzle and the problem of the artist now. In any other epoch or place, when style was an established thing, when a man worked wholeheartedly within a tradition, maintaining or extending it according to his painterly strength, Colin would, I believe, have been a formidable master, for there would have been no skills in the armoury which he could not have made his own. Now, in this fragmented age, when all our confusions and contradictions, our centrifugal specializations, have shattered the old mould and mode, and we have not yet achieved the necessary conceptual synthesis, he must inevitably fail to make the coherent impact, which his innate ability promised. Too honest, too open-minded, he has refused to drive or goad his genius along any single avenue among the oneway thorough fares of contemporary convention, and so his paintings, when exhibited in Bond Street, have never attracted any attention comparable to that secured by others less well equipped technically, less original in thought, less dynamic in temperament, but far more single-mindedly directed to social and economic success than he.

This One Man show was a new venture, the first in the Gallery's history, and, thereafter, the usage was kept up until, just before I left Belfast in March 1957, the large retrospective exhibition of William Conor's work, for me worthily completed the sequence. I had always believed that charity begins at home. There were, of course other exhibitions in those years; the Collection of paintings and water colours belonging to the English Arts Council (then C.E.M.A.), among the artists then included, hardly a name with fashionable resonance now, save perhaps Victor Pasmore, Rodrigo Moynihan and Kenneth Martin, and, at that time, these were figurative in manner; Zoltan Frankl's own collection giving the local public a good chance to experience Jack B. Yeats and Feliks Topolski, in most instances, for the first time; four Polish War Artists, one of them Aleksander Zyw then applying a Goyaesque approach to another war's disasters, when I met him in Edinburgh later, a pioneer, I now realize, of abstract expressionism, proud to have his name the very last in the Edinburgh Telephone Directory, chagrined when, in the Paris book, he lost his place to an Arab whose name began with double 'Z'; most important, the Czechoslovak Exhibition of painting and sculpture, when Jan Masaryk had time to dodge the platform party to talk of poetry in a corner.

This last exhibition which included a self portrait by Kokoschka, not to be seen again until 1962, in the great exhibition at the Tate, was memorable to me as the occasion of a rare delight. During the weeks of the showing I conducted many parties of school children round the exhibits. One painting by Fulla, a Slovak, was a rural scene, in drawing, though not in colour, related to Chagall, with farm houses, barns, a church, a well, sacks, sheep, cattle, peasants, and, at the back, a ripple of low hills from side to side, and, in the sky above this, an elongated shepherd lay or floated, blowing a long horn. Examining this picture with one group, I got them, as was my practice, to explain each part, each detail. This was working well: the sacks, I was told, probably contained 'pig-meal'; one little girl showed us how to carry water from a well, her left arm at an angle to her little body. Words and gestures were found for everything except for the recumbent shepherd. Over and over again everything else, till we met again this abrupt obstacle. I made no suggestions, that would have been cheating.

Then, after a long time when hope was guttering, a small boy, who had not spoken hitherto, cried out excitedly 'Please sir, he's playing the tune of it!', and I blessed him in my heart. It was one of those moments when I suddenly knew that my care for art is no idle struggle with the pedantries of art history or the momentary jargon of fashionable response. I was even more gratified when the teacher told me that he was one of the dull.

Not being in uniform, not being conscripted salted my ease with a recurring sense of guilt. So, as some sort of gesture of requital, I took to lecturing to the troops for the extra mural department of the University. So once, twice, sometimes thrice a week I was whisked away in fast cars or in draughty jeeps, carrying culture to camps and gunposts over the Six Counties in my slide container. I spoke from a boxing ring in a gymnasium. Once, after my talk, I was taken to the little station with that lovely name Trew and Moy, and, as it was a frosty night, I sat high up in the signal box till my late train came.

Then, when Hitler attacked the Soviet Union, and talks on our new, approved ally were in demand, since qualified speakers were scarce – only my friend J.U. Stewart had any authority, as an economist who had visited Russia – the Director of Extra Mural Studies roped me in, because he knew my Leftwing but non-Communist opinions. And so the Marxist Dialectic was wafted from Ballymoney to Newry.

When the war ended and men in barracks waited for demobilization I was drawn in to entertain them among their fretting calculations. No point then in being pedagogic, I showed them slides of landscape, and quizzed until they located and named the country and the season; of genre, till they told me the place and the period or invented stories to explain the figures. These repeated weekly with changing groups, taught me a great deal about catching and holding the ordinary men's interest in art. Aesthetics might shudder, but we enjoyed ourselves.

Of service men we saw more than in barracks or camp. The flat at Mountcharles was easy to find, and a varied company shared our hearth and often enough our breakfast. Rayner Heppenstall whom we had met in the Adelphi School days, came, and every Sunday for months, threatened to desert over the Border, for he hated battle-dress and army boots. Paul Potts, that wistful Canadian poet, was a frequenter. Borrowing clothes from this one and that one, he shed his uniform and spent a weekend in Dublin, forbidden to the armed forces. He came back roaring 'these boots are crucifying me'. There had been a strike of the gas workers on in Dublin, so he had taken a package of candles to give out at the church steps. Another evening he rose to leave before midnight. As he usually stayed much later I asked him why so early. 'Oh John – you see, I'm confined to barracks this week'. John Manifold, the Australian poet, came and cheered us with his rhyming couplets against literary pretensions, and his happy ballading. But there were others of no reputation; the Cockney despatch rider who, at home, was a neighbour of Harry Pollitt, or so he claimed, while we wondered who had planted him on us; the R.A.F. officer who borrowed and never returned my copy of *Poetics* by E.S. Dallas, a rare book, more interesting to me than his better known *The Gay Science*; the young sailorboy shaken by his Murmansk voyages and the dead bodies on the Archangel quayside; the little American lieutenant who worshipped Roosevelt; ex-school-masters, ex-journalists, ex-art students, eager for talk of books and paintings. Some of them have come back across the years, married now with teenage daughters, as friendly as if there had been no gap in time.

23

The War Years II

With the war Billy enrolled in Civil Defence, the ambulance side of it; and that was really an end to his painting, for, with his punctilious regard for timekeeping and scrupulous attention to the commas and semi-colons of his duties and obligations, his days and nights became so strangulatingly organized that he had little opportunity for loose-box leisure. Another man in the same service, though, none of us knew him then, was Brian Moore, who in his early novels *Judith Hearne* and *The Feast of Lupercal* evoked aspects of the city's life with rare intensity. The first was set very much in our neighbourhood; the second was his bitter verdict on our leading Catholic boys' school where David Kennedy was on the staff. The reverend head-man of it is reported to have said, 'I see young Moore has bitten the hand that flogged him'.

For the duration of the war and for some years after as he continued with the Ambulances, Billy enjoyed an economic blossoming unimaginable in the harsh days of depression. He flourished most generously a handsome cigarette case and was swift with the attendant flame from an efficient lighter. He bought himself useful books, one of Klee's among them. But his good fortune could not endure. The ambulance section to which he was attached was based on a Fire Station. One afternoon, coming off duty he paused at the door to talk to an incoming colleague. A length of metal gutter fell from on high and split his skull. The Ambulance people rejected responsibility as he had not been on duty, and anyhow, the defective gutter was none of their property. The Fire Service likewise, refused to admit liability for one who was no employee of theirs. So it went on; a human being caught between clauses, tangled among the small print of bureaucracy. I bombarded Dame Debra Parker, then the responsible Minister but she was manacled by her permanent officials. Roy McFadden, as a solicitor, sent in his letters. Finally, Andrew Millar, my brother-in-law, an active member of the Hospitals Authority, used his tact and determination, so that, in the fullness of time, Billy received an *ex-gratia* lump sum, and presented me with a copy of the Phaidon edition of Berenson's *Italian Painters of the Renaissance*, Roberta with a powder compact, and Andy with a fountain pen. This long drawn out dispute and my previous extended argument over that tubercular attendant from the Art Gallery and his right to mercy as well as justice, have kept me an uncharitable and savage antagonist of those enemies of life, the grey men with asterisks for eyes and footnotes for feet.

John Luke having no interest in the war, an unrecognized fraction of the civilization which was being fought for, kept well away from the ramifying machine, and, disliking air raids as he lived with his mother in a vulnerable area, cleared off with her to the country, finding a cottage on the farm at Knappagh in County Armagh belonging to the solid Major Paul Terriss, a Frenchman who spoke English with an Armagh accent. Here, with some regular teaching in an evacuated girls' school near at hand, to pay the rent, he indulged his vegetarian habit in proper composting for the first time. The story of his search for and finding the seed-potatoes his orthodoxy demanded should one day be given its record.

War or Peace made so little difference to him that he lengthened his stay from early in 1942 until late in 1950, when, having accepted the City Hall Mural commission, he was compelled to come back to town permanently.

During those years his visits to Belfast were infrequent, Major Terriss coming up for cattle sales proving a cheerful errand boy for him. But although previously very much a man of the slowly spoken word he developed a fine epistolary skill, and in the fat bundle of over forty letters, some running to twenty packed pages, I still find myself closer to his mind and spirit than at any time before or since. Little of the every day business of his existence seemed worth communicating. But his observations on books or magazines which came his way, perspicacious comments on verses or articles of mine which appeared in these, his attention to atmospheric effects throughout the sequence of seasonal changes around him, his intensifying commitment to certain painterly techniques, his concern with accuracy of vision, were all reported with clarity and exactitude. I still remember with gratitude the hard thinking and unencumbered prose of that passage on composition, rhythm, scale and focus, for Jack always considered visible things in visual terms; not for him the slovenly jargons of grammar and syntax which slip so glibly through the black beards of the young painters now.

But it was the long meditated and long awaited letter dated simply January-February 1945 which gave me the deepest and most lasting delight; when he described the frosty landscape and its trees, for Knappagh is in a magnificently wooded part of the county, and pointed out that the effect is that of 'heightening with white', as when on a dark ground the painter defines and models his forms with white pigment, before the other colours are superimposed. The most memorable section of the same letter was centred on the problem of the blueness or otherwise of the sky.

> I carried out a small experiment here with the aid of a small mirror and coloured papers, by putting the mirror on to the middle of each sheet of paper, with the so-called blue sky reflected in it. The reflected sky was compared with middle grey, bright blue, blue green, violet, green, yellow green, yellow, orange, red and scarlet; and, believe it or not, the so-called blue sky was neutral to *all* colours except grey; it differed from grey only in that it appeared as light, the paper remaining as a dull pigment.
>
> So the next time you see what you think is a very blue sky, *luke* carefully at the surrounding nature; near and distant, including clouds, you will notice that they are warm in colour. It is the earthly contrast with the ethereal background that makes the grey sky (grey light) appear blue.
>
> Summed up simply, the sky is part of the white light from the sun caught by our atmosphere, beyond which is black space; in other words, it is the effect of black seen through white light or light over darkness. In still other words, a scumble; the so-called blue sky is just a vast scumble of white over black, but what a scumble, and how beautifully done …

And since reading this and making the required observations, I have never seen a blue sky. For, in this, as in everything else, we see what we expect to see; our seeing is no more objective than our thinking.

It was the same thoroughness which led him before the war to examine Ostwald's theories with care, to test the then celebrated Colour Circle and to decide that while likely of value for fabric design or interior decoration, it had nothing to offer the painter. So too he had been led to look at Goethe's Colour Theory, the fact that this had been evaded or ignored by the academic physicists stimulating his sympathetic attention.

In my experience no one has been so committed to the necessity for driving to the fundamentals of a problem or process, whether it be in aesthetics, dietetics, or philosophies of living. When the chance occurred of an acceptable commission in stone-carving, he betook himself to a mason's yard, watched and talked with the men at work, under the guidance of the oldest made and tempered his own tools and tried out his hand with a head in relief and a head in the round. The commission did not come his way, but years later this all proved indispensable when he designed and cut the plaque of Lord Wakefield's coat of arms for Government House at Hillsborough.

The years of withdrawal to Knappagh and the opportunity which they afforded for continued and uninterrupted concentration on his individual lines of thought and practice, and the almost complete isolation from the example of and rivalry with his contemporaries served, in reality, only to intensify and confirm his idiosyncratic attitude; and so he has remained an artist for whom the great bulk of present day painting might well not exist, a belated Florentine, he has never found any need to finger farther than the landscape, still life, human figure – gamut.

Alfred Janes the Welsh painter, friend and portraitist of Dylan Thomas and Vernon Watkins, in his earlier phases had something of the same tightness of handling and deliberation of technique, though always with a heavier hand; but he too made a sudden leap through a kind of decorative analytical cubism to the abandon of abstract expressionism, which landed him squarely in the splash and eddy of the international movement of the fifties. John Luke, and it is surely

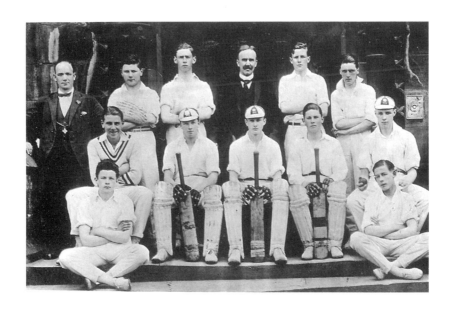

1. John Hewitt (first pupil standing on the left, back row), Methodist College Belfast 1st XI, 1923

2. John Hewitt, *c.* 1927–8

8. John and Roberta Hewitt, with May Morton,
P.E.N. conference, Vienna, 1955

9. John Hewitt, *c.*1960

10. John Hewitt with Peter Peri, Coventry, *c.*1963

11. John and Roberta Hewitt, Kennelwoutl, *c.*1964

too late now to expect it, has never given a hair's breadth hint of deviation from his own road.

In 1949, believing that some form of permanent demonstration of the technique of underpainting, heightening with white and final glazing should be secured for the Art Gallery, to provide for the future information of students and, perhaps, antiquarians of the twenty-first and subsequent centuries, when so much other work of our time should have inevitably perished, I managed to have him commissioned for the project, the subject, proposed and accepted, being a group of circus performers out of doors. To this end I greatly enjoyed myself drawing up a contract with exact material specifications, having on *my* side the authority of antiquity and fair dealing, and making my little protest against the accidental and unconsidered so generally accepted as of the essence of art in our time. This commission took the most of a year, and we were then able to mount and display on a double sided screen, a selection of the preliminary drawings, first sketches for the composition, enlarged and developed studies for several of the figures – which, incidentally, John Luke designed in the nude and then clothed – the complete under- painting, and then, on an identical panel with the same design, the finished work.

But in the carrying out of this project, Jack, human after all, began to find the exigencies of the craft involved somewhat frustrating, feeling the need for a speedier method, as these were the largest of the panels he had ever attempted, and, even more arduous, in duplicate up to the most elaborate of the stages in his method. On one of his infrequent visits to town, at a momentary pause in his undertaking, he talked of this and of his difficulty. Thinking over this and meditating on my response to his most recent work, after he had gone back to Knappagh, I felt compelled to write him a long letter, setting out my considered views. I had always admired his landscapes, but had sensed that, with the introduction of human figures as the principal elements in his themes, an overcomplication of rhythm and a corresponding emphasis on the figures as components of this, had not been compensated by an equal enrichment of feeling. I had also come to think that an unrelieved interest in technical matters had, in a measure, made the emotional content less urgent to its maker, and while never demanding in content a propagandist or politically charged message, the absolute lack of any comment, direct or indirect, on social relationships, had disappointed me. In political theory, in the austerity and rectitude of his attitude to commercial values or considerations, and in his comprehensive critique of capitalist materialism and the profit motive as it debased or vitiated the textures of human life, Jack was a sound socialist; but his paintings bore the same relationship to his political thought as the verse romances and fabrics of William Morris did to his. Both were producers of magnificently designed and executed luxury goods. I was waiting hopefully for the breakthrough, the life-enhancing interpenetration which had ultimately failed the poetic-upholsterer. So I argued that technical excellence was not all. 'William Blake', I wrote,

> playing tricks with media, with glue, with fugitive pigments, can, even in the shattered ghosts of pictures which are all that survive, still call on me "to change my life". Permanence is not in itself a good. We must always ask ourselves, good for what? Good to recover a lost tradition of craftsmanship certainly; but not just to clarify and hand on methods and recipes. Good emphatically in providing men who have something compelling to say to us, or to people a hundred years hence, that life has had and will have certain significances, certain basic meanings, in providing these men with the best methods of expressing or communicating their responses to these meanings and significances. I am afraid your tremendous concentration on technical problems, your years of almost religious devotion to the disciplines of the means, have gradually, imperceptibly to yourself, lured you away from your first responsibility as Artist, which is to further the ends of life in yourself and in us. You have been as it were led up a high mountain and offered the Kingdom of Virtuosity, have been persuaded to try to make stones into bread ...

> 'So when you turn to a speedier medium, you must, if you are to fulfil your proper destiny, also turn to life. You must grapple with reality, exterior or interior, and commit yourself to it, making some utterance, some comment on being. I

know well enough the times are difficult. Picasso twists tricy-
cles and crustaceans into horrid obscenities. Men swither here
and there in a malaise of doubt. The artist and society drift
farther and farther apart, and in agonies of frustration cry out
in their dreams for the comfort of Contact ... But life remains
undefeated, more difficult, more complex, more challenging
– but life everlastingly. And because many in this generation
fail and are defeated you need not succumb ...

My long friendship with Jack, my sponsorship of his work, I hon-
estly believed absolved me from any charge of impertinence or con-
trived indignation, but these were certainly hard words and might in
some circumstances have endangered our mutual regard. In three
weeks I had his twenty page reply, courteous, humble, gentle, firm,
realistic. Point by point he dealt with my animadversions. He simply
claimed that, with a nature such as his, 'a very reserved shy and
extremely quiet sort of person, often silent to the point of dumb-
ness', the personality expressed in his work must be of the same
kind, and that so far as he could judge he had expressed himself fairly
completely. He continued 'An artist like Blake was possessed by a
tremendous inner power; he just could not help being on fire about
his subjects or messages. I'm not like that at all, worse luck! I have
sense enough to realize what I am not. Artists like Van Gogh and
Blake are born not made. I'm very much a made artist still in the
process of making ...' Technically, compared to even the minor mas-
ters of the past, he was, he wrote, a novice. As for interior reality,
although he had plenty of them, he had no urge to paint his dreams.
He reminded me very fairly of 'the horrors perpetrated in that
human, warm and comfortable period, the Victorian and late 19th
century, when content ruled the roost.' 'I can't agree to your sug-
gestion that I am just providing technical data or samples. I am only
making use (in my own slow way) of one of a number of slow tech-
niques to bring the picture into full realization of colour and sug-
gested form. The technique does not as you seem to think determine
the subject. Nor the shape, proportion or form of a figure. Nor the
rhythm, style, tones or colour. These are all of my own personal and
deliberate choice irrespective of what technique I use ...'

Most people are by outlook and certainly by training literary-minded. There's nothing wrong with this, but they tend to overlook and even despise manual work, and, as Renoir wrote on painting, 'it is primarily a manual métier, and must be performed like a good workman'. Many literary-minded people feel annoyed and uncomfortable when confronted with technical excellence as they are unhappy with their hands. They can't speak with them. They are so expert at reading the labels and filling in the gaps, voids and mysterious spaces for their own imaginative pleasure that they are content, or very satisfied, with the merest hint or loose suggestion. The looser and vaguer it is, the more and better the spectator can doodle his own thoughts and feelings into it the happier he is; it ministers so much to his own self esteem that he feels it part of him.

So, by a strange coincidence, just when American doodling was about to orbit the Free World, this withdrawn artist, remote from the centres of influence and opinion, hit upon the explanation of the fashionable painting of the next decade.

And when the commission for the large mural in the City Hall came along later that year, a change of medium and a simplification of method enabled him to accomplish the task in a much shorter time than we had anticipated for so large a surface. Incidentally when he received the final payment for this and subsequently made his Income Tax return, the Inland Revenue folk brought him in for investigation for they could not, until he proved it, understand how a human being had lived so frugally for so long.

Another durable correspondent of the war years was Patrick Maybin, absent from us for another reason than Jack's, for he held a commission in the Royal Medical Corps, working with a Blood Transfusion Unit in North Africa and Italy, with one dart across the narrow water to Split to help the Yugoslav partisans, and gaining a mention in despatches. We had come to know him when he was at the University, had sat on the top of a long pair of steps in Ralph Meredith's morality *When Adam Delved*, and was writing fine verse of a very personal kind.

About the time of his father's death, he was involved in his finals, and, although he belonged to a large family of active and interesting habit, it seemed to us that, unconsciously, he found us solid and dependable, a decade older than he and therefore to a young man sufficiently senior to be acceptable: as uncle and aunt figures. From then on he became a frequent caller at the flat. And when his profession inexorably swept him into the war, his regular letters continued the lines of our mutual interests and the unfolding and maturing of a personality and a mind securely lodged in our affections: his abiding love for the Irish landscape contrasted with his present dusty reality, Monte Cassino, Trotters' *Instincts of the Herd*, in *War and Peace*, George Eliot, Rebecca West, the village child brought in when the landmine exploded (Vickers or Krupps, Patrick wondered), the interplay of personalities among his fellow officers, the Indian soldiers' coloured underwear, his ambition on his twenty eighth birthday 'to become a reasonably efficient doctor as free from intolerance and cruelty as human frailty will permit, with a few good friends and an understanding of the society and country in which I live'; all of these observed, realized, grappled with, always in a sharp and unflinching perspective, for, from his father, he had learned that kind of astronomy which keeps a man aware of his place in space and time. So cool-headed and clear-sighted, I never lost his presence in the mounting tally of crabbedly scribbled pages, till he stepped out, unscathed, from the delirium of war to the neurosis of peace.

I have gained much from talking with my friends: I have gained much from Patrick's talk: but the silences between us have been more nourishing than any other human silences I have experienced.

24

Regionalism

Before the war all our holidays were spent across the water; usually intensive bouts of gallery and theatre going, what we most lacked at home. Then with the closure on our sea travel we had perforce to mark time. Consequently with vacations now regularly taken in the Glens of Antrim, I had the opportunity of getting to know one area of the countryside well; and that association with Cushendall and the Glens close till 1956 and still maintained, for good, or ill has had so deep a significance on my thought and feeling, and particularly on my verse, that without it I should have been another kind of person, another kind of poet.

And, twice, during the war, we visited County Donegal. The Six Counties of constitutional Northern Ireland left out three of the original nine counties of the province of Ulster, for the very obvious reason that their inclusion would have put nationalist voters in a majority or so nearly so as to have made the position precarious for the Unionists. So Donegal, Cavan and Monaghan may be thought of as *Ulidia Irridenta*. It was to the Rosses that we went, to the extreme west of the county, and although the landscape was the roughest that I had seen I found that the people by pace and accent were closer to me than Dubliners, were, in fact, fellow provincials, indubitably northerners. As a consequence I now could realize my area as the historical province and not as the politician's convenience. It was very much Peadar O'Donnell's country. He had a house at Dungloe at the water's edge. His pencilled card opened the doors of hospitality for us at Innisfree, and neighbourly officers, on a coastal watch inspection, packed us into Willy Bonar's boat for the island and rock-threading voyage to Aranmore. On our second Donegal holiday we talked with a man who makes *curraghs* at

Dunfanaghy, attended a Gaelic children's concert at Gortahork, saw a tremendous sunset over the Atlantic from Bunbeg, and, walking all of it, found our old room at the Tailor's, in Burtonport, with the chromolithograph of St Teresa over the bed, and the smell of bacon sizzling in the kitchen.

Further, during all the war years, through my visits talking and lecturing at military camps or stations, I covered and grew familiar with great parts of the counties of Antrim, Down, Armagh. I made my first visit to the City of Derry in the snow, a flock of waxwings crouching in a field near the railway station, to select exhibits for a display of arts and crafts by Civil Defence personnel. So that I who had been singularly uninformed about the topography and landscape of my own province, at the same time as my thought was moving inwards to the heart of my relationship with my place in time, was widening my physical and sensory experience of that very place. My journey already mentioned to Kilmore where the Hewitts were first planted in Ireland, was, therefore, something of a symbolical gesture, a rite, and that I spent my first night of the journey at Loughgall where W.R. Rodgers, that fine poet, was Presbyterian Minister, and the next, on the far side of primatial Armagh, at Killylea where John Luke and his mother, fugitives from the Belfast air raids, now lived, seemed to give even more point to my pilgrimage.

I knew my Ulster now from its compass points and in some depth. The places: the road across the broad mountain of heather where the little lake comes up and goes down; the scatter of wooded islets on the long wandering loch; the square stone keep by the narrow water; the reedy river with the long low bridge; the high round tower on the level field; the turf-stacks in the driving mist on the bare slope; the crooked street with the squat cathedral peering down on it from the hill; and the Georgian fanlights winking in the evening sun across the leafy square; the eel-weir pleated with swirling water; the small fresh-water loch among the boulders within hearing of the roaring ocean; and the smoke of the city drifting up the wide river valley. The sounds: the corncrake, the curlew, the heather bleat, the rooks, the skylarks; water tumbling over stones, splashing out of an iron pipe; the fife, the *ceilidhe* band, the hissing gas-jets in the mission-hall, the factory hooters, the ship's sirens at night, the hammering of hulls.

And the smell of retting flax, of turf smoke in the village street, of cut hay, of beanfields in blossom, of rotting apples in a corner of the orchard, of the bright whins in sun, of bracken where a fox has lain. And the salt taste of dulse and yellow butter, and of buttermilk. And St Brigid crosses of plaited rushes, gable paintings of King William, party slogans in thick white paint, black faced mountain yowes, red tramcars, and a stone face over a doorway.

By this time I became aware of the concept of Regionalism, which I found first in Lewis Mumford whose *Culture of Cities* I had left unread until the cheap edition of 1942; the same theme even more explicit in his *A Faith for Living* of the same year. He pointed me back to Patrick Geddes, and in the little volume an *Evolution* which Geddes shared with J. Arthur Thomson, I came upon that application to human ecology which I discovered that I was already involved in: 'Explore our region here … fully, thoroughly, repeatedly, from hill-top to sea-bottom and back again.' It was not obvious to me at that time, but Geddes is clearly the link with Morris, carrying his thinking into a wider field than Gill or Lethaby. My regionalism lay, I now see, somewhere in the rich realm of Socialist Utopias, nearer perhaps the frontier of possibility than many of the more romantic and highly coloured concepts with which that indispensable dreamscape is studded. I laid down no rules, no chart or time-table for its realization, content simply to make propaganda for the idea. I formed no society for its furtherance, enrolled no followers, but by the written and broadcast word and by frequent talks to all sorts of groups from Young Farmers to Rotarians, I let the idea take wings where it would.

There was some opposition voiced. On one occasion, in response to my direct challenge, the then Minister of Education declared with vehemence that the Six Counties area was as much part of Great Britain as Yorkshire. Sir David Keir gave the local Chamber of Trade 'a warning against regionalism', and when I wrote a longish letter to the press, making my points that 'Ulster is neither a colony nor a nation; but in its own right a Region of the British Isles with its own history, traditions and roots in thought and in speech', and that 'Regionalism is the answer of the individual human personality to the vast drift of our days towards anonymity and standardization', not a chirrup came from the eaves of the Vice-Chancellor's lodge.

As has so often happened to me, when the need rose, the book with the answer thrust itself into my hand. I picked up Victor Branford's *Science and Sanity* (1925) twenty years old, in a second-hand bookshop. This, strangely, not to me an easy book to read – something to do with its page proportions, width of margins, and its rather oddly rhetorical prose – nevertheless, by its emphatic presentation of the necessary constellation of Hearth, Workshop, Marketplace, Cloister, as the *foci* for the Good City, has with the compulsions of its grand simplifications, kept me from straying too far from social realities when I air my dreams in public.

But my reading had always to be critical. In attempting to clarify and present my ideas as firmly as possible against easy attack, I had to subject them to a harsher hammering than anyone else might be expected to give them. So it was amusing to find that my first inspirer, Mumford, should have written: 'The movement is sometimes confused with nationalism, but it has a more local and concentrated objective, except in places where the regional and national boundaries coincide, as in Ireland', making the very mistake he warns against, and surely generalizing on insufficient evidence, but, perhaps, by his error compelling me to look more searchingly to the foundations of my argument. For, in the attempt to discover or isolate the group or unit larger than the family, smaller than the nation, which possesses some sort of topographical and economic diversity-in-unity that can be identified and recognized, and folkways, sharing and enjoying a broadly common heritage, the province of Ulster seemed to go a long way towards fulfilling the specifications.

Regionalism must have been in the air – this again has been a common enough experience for me, to find that some idea which I had thought was mine alone, or had dawned on a few of whom I was one, should, suddenly, appear as a widespread fashion or a widely accepted belief. Certainly in Britain there must have been a fair field of folk battering away at the same notion, unknown to and ignorant of the rest of us. In 1947 R.E. Dickinson's *City Region and Regionalism: a geographical contribution to human ecology* was published. A well reasoned, well documented book, it was obviously the enduring work of years, no hurried job to catch the tide. I found, among much else of value, that G.D.H. Cole, a scholar whom I respected but did not delight in, had a crisp description for what I was after, an attempt to define areas which are at once *units of social feeling*, and, as far as possible, also areas of economic life, and suitable to serve as units for the work of administration. For, back of all my arguments stood the conception of a Federation of the British Isles, with home rule for Scotland and Wales and some degree of autonomy for Yorkshire, Lancashire, the Midlands, the West Country and the South East. Two years later, in 1949, Peter Self produced a useful Fabian booklet on the structure of local government which he declared in his preface had 'emerged as the result of a long series of discussions by a small Group of the Society who met to examine the general question of "Regionalism"'. The next year Denys Val Baker wrote his stocktaking *Britain Discovers Herself*. Very likely more aware of what was happening with the growing ends of culture in these islands, he had become known for his series of *Little Reviews Anthologies*, in the 1946 volume of which a poem of mine taken from *Lagan* had appeared. His first chapter is entitled' 'The Regional Renaissance' and begins 'The regional renaissance has developed unostentatiously. Most of the "isms" so popular today require for their stimulation the constant beating of the drum plus a regular flourish of trumpets. Regionalism has slipped into usage quite without premeditation: a trend that has developed, rather, than a force that has been applied'. And in his second chapter on *Literature*, rounding up the perimeter writers, Welsh, Scots and the rest, he remarks on the strong 'crop of important new writers since 1939 – notably Michael McLaverty, John Hewitt, Roy McFadden, Robert Greacen, W.R. Rodgers, which had come out of Ulster'.

It was in the air, and then with so much else the idea got pushed aside or forgotten. Although I have suggested a Utopian element in my own and in perhaps everybody's regionalism, that it is not to imply that I believe the regionalist idea to have been unreal, or irrelevant now. On the contrary, when the economic decay in the north-east and the north-west of England became suddenly apparent towards the end of 1962, as the belts tightened and the shoes wore thin in the drab streets, the national journalists just as suddenly remembered 'The Two Nations' but saw the force to giving them a local habitation and word of the worth of regions began to be heard again. I could not but remember how, twenty years ago, in my plea for decentralization, I was forever quoting the old Frenchman's dictum that the nemesis of modern industrial society must inevitably be paralysis at the extremities and apoplexy at the centre. Yet this is one of those matters upon which one would prefer that one's prophecies had gone astray; the more poignantly so, since, of the now admittedly depressed areas of these islands, no area has suffered so long or so deeply, as paralysis takes over the shipbuilding, the linen industries of Northern Ireland, an area where, since figures were taken, the percentage of unemployed workers has remained stubbornly several times that of the British 'National Average'. So much for the bankers and the practical men of affairs, the political party that has all the experience, since it has been continuously in office from the time the Six Counties State was set up over forty years ago, a stubborn history of decay, more fitting for an oriental satrapy than for a twentieth century European administration.

25

Lagan

My interest in Regionalism was not entirely taken up either with my personal identity problems or the political strategies single handedly to bridge over the crevasses of segregation and partition. The better part of any regional development I conceived as rooted in and burgeoning through the creative arts: and at this time there was so much happening in the North which seemed consistent with such a development.

C.E.M.A had been set up and was showing an unprecedented, if still rudimentary care for our artists. A lively and inventive generation of students was about to graduate from the Belfast College of Art. The Group Theatre having taken over the Ulster Minor Hall after the petering-out of The Little Theatre and its successor company of strolling players, began to discover effective native actors and several acceptable plays by local writers no longer spancelled to the kitchen comedy convention. More individuals seemed to be making better short stories and better verse than we had been generally used to.

In 1942 Peadar O'Donnell, editing the Dublin literary magazine *The Bell*, and always on the watch for new skills, found occasion to gather up his bundle of Northern contributions into a special Ulster Number for its July issue, with enough left over for an overflow parcel the next month. This was, in a way, a signal of recognition that literary activity around and in Belfast was sizeable and strong enough to edge out of the long shadows. For years few of our writers were closely identified with their native province. Robert Lynd and St John Ervine had long been expatriates in Great Britain. Shan F. Bullock had been too, until his death. Lynn Doyle, our chief humorous writer, lived in Dublin, and Forrest Reid, whom I never met, kept to a semi-detached seclusion in a Belfast suburb.

Away back, about 1952 or so, verse of mine appeared beside Michael McLaverty's story, 'The Wild Duck's Nest' in the London *Adelphi*. A schoolmaster the same age as myself, his crystalline observation and his accurate ear for the rural idiom won his success in America too; and his first novel *Call My Brother Back* promised the approach of a major figure in our fiction writing, someone else to measure shoulders with Carleton. But by the next decade he was, though still the best, no longer the only short story writer we had, nor was I the only poet of my generation at home. Sam Hanna Bell had come forward in the first category; W.R. Rodgers had achieved almost instantaneous salute in the second, largely through *Horizon* which Cyril Connolly had quickly made the most powerful opinion forming journal of its day; but both *The Bell* with Geoffrey Taylor as Poetry Editor, and Radio Eireann through Austin Clarke's weekly verse programmes had also played their parts in stimulating and establishing a new exciting and adventurous poet.

While we were staying at Loughgall, where his manse was, in the early months of the war, before he had written any verse, Bertie asked me to lend him some modern books of it. So I sent him a volume of Day Lewis, and, I think, Auden. Consequently, when he later inscribed my copy of his *Awake and Other Poems*, he did so, for 'John Hewitt who first put me in the way of poetry'.

At the University a tiny group of students, four of them, Robert Greacen their leader and driver, his most talented henchman Roy McFadden, at a remove associated with the contemporary English Apocalyptic movement with Henry Treece, Nicholas Moore and Alex Comfort, had taken over or revived *The New Northman* and made it a coterie literary organ, exactly as, more than ten years before, Ralph Meredith, Paddy Fisher and I had done. Then in 1943 they came out with the first of a series of verse broadsheets, *Ulster Voices*; for the fourth and last of these the name was changed to *Irish Voices*.

Simultaneously another cluster was active: John Boyd, a schoolmaster, Sam Hanna Bell, a shipping clerk, and Robert Davidson, a commercial traveller, all in their thirties. With John Boyd as editor they launched and paid for a literary magazine *Lagan*, after the friendly unexciting river which Belfast straddles. Printed on wartime paper and stapled with wire, not stitched with thread, in its first blue

covers it looked like a railway timetable or a country auctioneer's cat-
alogue. Here the emphasis was not on verse alone: short stories, crit-
icism, reportage with local relevance made up eighty-five of its
ninety-nine pages. Among the short stories were items by the three
sponsors, by McLaverty, and by Joseph Tomelty a former house-
painter now emerging as a leading actor at the Group. Of the three
fairly solid prose articles, one was by Denis Ireland, one by David
Kennedy, a schoolmaster and our best drama critic, and one on Irish
painting by myself. To the by now expected team of poets, was added
Patrick Maybin, our only contributor on active service.

It could honestly be claimed that *Lagan* was representative; and
while no editorial attitude to political or social issues had been
defined, the fact that Catholic and Protestant sat side by side was a
notable circumstance. Not for nearly forty years, when *Uladh* ran its
short course, had anything of a like nature been tried.

Lagan somehow hit the mood of the time, got some sensible
reviews, was noticed in Great Britain and speedily started off imita-
tors, such as *Now in Ulster*, and *Northern Harvest*. But only *Lagan* had
the strength to persist.

The appearance of the second *Lagan* coincided with the publica-
tion in Dublin of two anthologies of verse: *Irish Poems of Today* drawn
from the past pages of *The Bell*, and *Poems from Ireland* in the same
way selected from the columns of the *Irish Times*. These marked the
appearance of the Northern poets on the national scene; four or five
of us having a toehold in each book.

Lagan (1944) with the many of its predecessor's contributors, had
a 'North African Retrospect' from Patrick Maybin, by now, splint-
ing and bandaging his way up the Italian leg; and George Buchanan
came in with pages from his notebook, dreaming of what we might
do with our bombed cities. For the next year's issue the organization
was changed a little, the editor John Boyd, being now supported by
associates, David Kennedy, Roy McFadden, Jack Loudon, the
C.E.M.A. organizer and myself. I contributed a long article, 'The
Bitter Gourd', which was a fairly full statement on regionalism and
the arts as relevant to our own area.

Lagan (1946) had a more definitely regionalist tone. The very
cautious editor in his Comment wrote of 'The two political regions

of Ireland', and of 'a regionalist publication like *Lagan*' (although, perhaps he really meant 'regional'); and the equally cautious David Kennedy set out his views on 'The Ulster Region and the Theatre'. My very long couplet poem 'Freehold', stated the position unequivocally:

> My region's Ulster. How can we afford
> to take the shouting politicians word,
> Map-makers' frenzy, who, with crazy line,
> Cut off three counties history marked our own?

But this was the last of *Lagan*. Sales fell catastrophically, largely, we believed, because the hordes of literate servicemen stationed in the Six Counties and hungry for any intelligible print had all gone home and left us with our own reading public. It was arranged for each of the associate editors to give a radio talk, and the whip round which followed, cleared the outstanding bills. Yet the four years of it, with its more than fifty local contributors, makes *Lagan* a landmark in the cultural history of the North; one of the little reviews in a period when, certainly, these proliferated, it has its own nature, its own texture and voice.

Tom Harrisson, author of *Savage Civilisation* which had been an additional Left Book Club choice, and co-founder of Mass-Observation, spent the winter of 1943 and the subsequent spring with the army in Northern Ireland, and reported his findings in articles in the *Cornhill*. *Lagan* and *Northern Harvest* he thought 'full of remarkably even, well done poetry and prose, if much of it is flat and quiet, in the Ulster way afraid to start any strong emotion lest the old sores erupt again. No comparable area of England could do a third as well'.

We were staying at the Coach House in Cushendall behind the high wall of The Cottage, when he came to visit us. Travelling by motorcycle from Ballymena over the wide boglands and down the long glen, he observed everything, could tell, for instance, how many weekly changes of programme you could have at the Moyle Cinema. So I began to appreciate the Mass Observer's skill; and when, while the men were hauling the two ends of the long net, as we walked in the dusk by the shore, he remarked that technologically we could well be in Ceylon, I caught a glimpse of the anthropologists' objectivity.

From his talk, and, later, in his articles, he formulated Ulster's problems as two-fold: those that are stretched tense on the Town-County dichotomy, and those crushed within the Catholic–Protestant collision. Yet for those four years *Lagan* existed, free. Maybe we were timid, avoiding offence – though my 'Freehold' lines:

> Yet we shall ride the waters in their spite,
> who thrash and wallow to the left and right,
> drop gurgling down into the Romish pit,
> or on a melting iceberg scold at it.

seem equally provocative to both sides – But it did present a moment of unity of some kind, a phase of emotional maturity; and if ever an Ulster regional literature takes its place within the broader scope of Irish literature in English, *Lagan* will be the launching pad.

Tom Harrisson mentioned 'the near-pioneer Group Theatre'. There Cecil Cree's comedy *A Title for Buxey* dealing with the hazards of a small boxing promoter's career, and Patricia O'Connor's *Highly Efficient* concerned with the hazards of a school teacher's career and Joseph Tomelty's *All Souls Night*, a near Syngean tragedy of County Down fisherfolk and later his highly popular *Is the Priest at Home?* seemed to be giving us a theatre of some vitality and breadth, although the normal staple was still provided by George Shiels, steadily prolific, and by frequent revivals of St John Ervine's *Boyd's Shop*. George Shiels had of course the widest national reputation, for his plays held the Abbey stage, in David Kennedy's phase 'keeping that theatre open between geniuses'. In the Festival Year Tyrone Guthrie gave his *Passing Day* a multiple set, but the construction and characterization remain stubbornly tied to the three walled stage.

Besides short stories for which Irishmen seem to have a special aptitude, and in which medium McLaverty and Bell were joined by the gentle John O'Connor, novels appeared in some quantity as

McLaverty's good tempered narratives continued, with the businessman Stephen Gilbert, protégé of Forrest Reid, the actor Tomelty, and the women Janet McNeill and Meta Mayne Reid, and, long awaited, Bell's *December Bride*. Widest known, Anne Crone's *Bridie Steen* was perhaps overpraised; but the shelves began filling up creditably.

And, beyond fiction, topography, folklore, history, biography found characteristic and valuable forms. Even humour secured its anthology.

For the poets I take 1948 as a nodal point. That year Maurice Craig's, Robert Greacen's and my own books of verse were published: we all had had our brochures and pamphlets of verse before this, but hard covers seemed to mark our coming of age. The year before Roy McFadden's third book *The Heart's Townland* indicated a clear maturing, a deeper intention to grasp his community in feeling and concept. It was dedicated to John Boyd and me; and it had a pleasant poem on our Lodge in the Glens, a companion piece to the cottage at Ballyorney which belonged to Barbara Hunter and her husband Oliver Edwards. But in the long blank verse 'Calendar' inscribed to me alone the poet's generosity was not so obvious.

> Once you were symbol of the arrogant mind,
> Cold hand that blighted miracle at birth,
> Philosopher of all the noisy blind
> Who flouted those who swore they saw the sun.
> It might have been so once; but though you still
> Assume opinions with your hat and coat
> You have an eye to greet the miracle
> In all well-rooted things, in child and tree:
> in paintings …
>
> But here's the brick wrapped in the compliment
> I've thrown at you; so listen to me now:
> Adopted children remain orphans still;
> Life's no poor poet to be patronised:
> Thoreau, who taught you to be regional,
> Laboured the land you cultivate in verse.

The late Forties too saw anthologies carry our verse as far as we could hope. Kathleen Hoagland's tome, *1,000 years of Irish Poetry* and Devin Garrity's *New Irish Poets* displayed our wares across the Atlantic; but our most handsome representation was naturally in *Contemporary Irish Poetry* (Faber 1949) as this was edited by Robert Greacen and Valentin Iremonger, one for each side of the border.

The Festival year might also be thought of as memorable in that one of the ventures sponsored by C.E.M.A., *The Arts in Ulster* was the first volume devoted to a serious assessment of our Northern attainments. Sam Hanna Bell was editor; Nesca Robb and I were his assistants. Denis Hanna wrote on Architecture, David Kennedy on Drama, John Boyd on Prose, Nelson Browne on Poetry, while I covered Painting and Sculpture. You could have called it our stock-taking.

1948 I return to, as important in another way: for it was in the summer of that year that Roy McFadden and Barbara Hunter, then both living in Lisburn, started *Rann A Quarterly of Ulster Poetry*. *Rann* is a verse form in Gaelic, probably sharing the same root as Rune: there is a traditional story of a Cromwellian trooper throwing an old Irish bard off a cliff with the remark 'Chant your rann now, little man'. By the second number the subtitle was changed to '*An Ulster Quarterly of Poetry*', as if the editors had realized that there might not be enough local verse to keep it running. With the thirteenth number 'and Comment' was added, as room was made for theatre and radio criticism. It persisted for twenty numbers in all, after the first, well printed, and with an original design on the cover each time. At an estimate there were a hundred contributors, and these included English poets like Wain, Amis, Abse; Scots, Maurice Lindsay; Welsh, Vernon Watkins and R. S. Thomas.

Leafing through its pages, I come on the names of George Buchanan and Barbara Hunter more frequently than I had remembered, but the space is well used.

The editors' greatest scoop (through Oliver Edwards' influence with Mrs George Yeats) was the first publication of 'Reprisals', a Civil War poem which Yeats suppressed when he let the others out. So *Rann* now has its own line in the bibliographies.

Then in 1955 when the International P.E.N. Congress was to be held in Dublin with a long day's dart to the North, the Belfast

Centre took up the editors' offer and a specially enlarged number was subsidized, 72 pages of it, for presentation to each visiting delegate. Besides a generous selection of new verse from about a dozen of us, the opportunity was taken to summarize what we had been after in the Theatre, the Novel, Verse, since the beginning of the century; and Howard Sergeant's article on Ulster Regionalism was reprinted, as a statement from someone outside. But most useful of all, a reference section of biographical notes on Ulster writers since 1900 was assembled by the City Library staff, providing the first gathering of such material since D.J. O'Donoghue's monumental *The Poets of Ireland* (1912).

The vast effort proved the end of *Rann*, an appropriate and worthy conclusion, for Number 20 will hold its modest place among reference-sources for writing in the North of Ireland so long as anyone is interested; and it also draws the line for us when any talk of Regionalism in Ulster comes up; for it had to do with the period of surprising activity and fertility which spanned from 1942 to 1953.

26

Council for Encouragement

In 1940, when the war made us serious and high minded but left us with little to do while we waited for Hitler's attack to make sense of the situation, the University Joint Committee for Adult Education, my father being a member through his activities with the Workers' Educational Association, managed to lay hands on £750 from the Pilgrim Trust, to promote 'Music and Art for the People'. As a committee man of the Ulster Academy of Arts, my father had already talked that society into sponsoring art exhibitions at seaside resorts, finding himself inevitably with all the work to do, cataloguing, hanging and supervising. With the organizing of the Loan Exhibition, held in the Art Gallery Lecture Hall, since the floors upstairs were sanded, the committee made a good start, besides Jack Yeats' *Man in a Train Thinking*, it had William Coldstream's portrait of *Stephen Spender*, a classic of the Euston Road School, and a good Vlaminck and a Signac watercolour borrowed from old Sarah Purser in Dublin.

The trust was then persuaded to offer £1,500 a year for two years, if the Northern Government would match pound for pound, and, thereafter, take over the venture completely. So the Council for the Encouragement of Music and the Arts was set up in 1943. My father and I were both asked to join the Art Advisory Sub-Committee, but this came at the time of his stroke, and so, although he had been one of the tracklayers, he was never able to attend.

The first chairman, nominated by the University, a lecturer who had recently written a book on aesthetics, which I never heard of anybody reading, left very shortly to fill a Chair across the water, being succeeded by John F. Hunter, the Ministry's Art Inspector. By 1947 we became the Art Committee, and I was appointed Vice Chairman. Next year, John Hunter retired from the chairmanship, but not the committee, and I took over, to remain in that post for six years and staying on the committee until the autumn of 1956, thirteen years in all.

Set up as a parallel to C.E.M.A. in Great Britain, when that body became The Arts Council, we held to the earlier designation, as the organizations drew their revenues from different sources and cooperated only to a limited extent. For example, we never could lay a finger on any of the big touring exhibitions like the Van Gogh, the Picasso–Matisse which were such popular events in the immediate post-war years, although the Arts Council did help generously with smaller displays. But as their intention was to concentrate on the metropolis and to do little more than supplement activities outside, we were able to cultivate our own garden in our own way. Of course, we regretted being kept outside the touring route of the bigtops, but we took whatever was offered gladly and sought other sources for exhibitions.

Our people had, over the years, a chance to see not only Scottish and Welsh painting and work from the North West of England, but Turkish, Dutch, Australian – Drysdale, Dobell, Nolan; Italian – Chirico, Severini, Carra, Morandi, Campigli –, and in sculpture one expansive show took in Moore, McWilliam, Chadwick, as well as the best of the Irish, north and south.

We also began the tradition of borrowing the annual Living Irish Art Exhibition after its Dublin exposition, so that our artists might realize that they belonged to a nation. We combed the County Down for Old Masters from the big houses with no surprising results, for the descendents of those who had done well out of the various plantations and seizures of the land had seldom acquired much culture or taste in their long tenure of the Ascendancy./ The first gathering of lists of where likely pictures were, had been in the hands of a small committee of noble ladies of large estate; and we were rather shocked when they sent in a bill for postage, amounting to about thirty shillings, if I remember, a sobering demonstration of how to take care of the pence and further evidence to me that the wealthy are perhaps necessarily not to be numbered among the naturally generous or less economical. Another gathering of paintings in Enniskillen, of Fermanagh Old Masters, significantly displayed in the town's Orange Hall, where few Catholic art lovers would care to set foot, indicated that the farther from Dublin the scantier the crop. The poet Thomas Parnell, Pope's friend, had referred to this countryside 'where half an acre yields but half a sheaf', and that was still true for more than corn.

But, though the necessity for exhibitions from outside, of contemporary work, was always in our minds, to provide standards and comparisons against which our artists could fairly measure themselves or be measured by the rest of us, and so be saved from the smugness of parochialism, I for one was ever critical of the smugness of the smallest parish of all, from Bruton Street down to St James' Square, and therefore we sought our measures more frequently from our neighbour Scots as providing a more appropriate door-jamb.

Where we differed most widely from the Arts Council was that we made working artists not modish works our chief concern. We had degrees in our patronage; now and then sponsoring and paying for exhibitions by elderly artists without waiting till they were dead: this utmost degree of complete sponsorship went through the generations to the youngest of whom we could heartily approve. Others less significant in our judgment we helped partially, seeing to the rest of the down-town gallery we used, or paying the printer's bills. And as often as we could we bought paintings and drawings and built up a collection of local work which could be toured throughout the Six Counties. In this way we secured several fine works – we did not look for masterpieces. We also maybe encouraged now and then a few who proved neither responsible nor sincere practitioners; but, at any rate, the money went to those that laid paint on canvas, not to dealers or middlemen or merely confectioners of the fashionable. In this way too, an example was set to the public, so that, in due course, the University Common Room began to buy pictures rather than reproductions, and to put on its own smaller shows. Our assistance was distributed as fairly as we could gauge; and as painting in Northern Ireland in the second quarter of this century came in generations roughly ten years apart, our men were Middleton, Thomas Carr, Luke born around 1910; O'Neill, Dillon, George Campbell born around 1920; and the two distinct strains born around 1930, the first of these rather followers of Daniel O'Neill and his friends, among them Arthur Armstrong and James MacIntyre, the second which came out of the College of Art, Basil Blackshaw, Terence Flanagan, Martin MacKeown. Further, because the North is not well breeched with travel grants for young artists, we started in a very modest way to hand out enough money for a couple of young-sters every year to sniff the soapy air of the metro, or, if no farther, *tabac* on the quayside at Dieppe.

I am not being naive when I say that I do not think that those we helped in any of these ways were grateful. As an organized, official body we were always the target for abuse. Several times I had the experience of hearing the spokesman of some group or other at the opening of an exhibition of theirs which in some way C.E.M.A. was assisting, attack the Art Committee and by not too oblique reference its chairman, for indifference to, and neglect of their welfare. And once, because in a radio discussion of one such show, I had suggested that inflated prices on the part of the young suggested inflated self-esteem, an angry round robin appeared in the evening paper, accus-ing me of taking the bite out of their mouths. Yet no young artists were having so much done on their behalf in any other corner of these islands. It was far from enough, but other bodies elsewhere which could have afforded more did much less. As a poet myself I had long since realized and accepted the fact that society owed me nothing, that I was among the fortunate few in having an art to prac-tise, that hundreds of thousands of my fellows did not possess such good fortune, that I ought to be grateful for whatever gift I had and for the opportunity it gave me to give pleasure or satisfaction to a few of my fellows.

Not so frequently but consistently we helped the younger archi-tects to make public their ideas for town planning and good design. In one exhibition during the war, they made drawings and models for a new layout for the city centre. John Miller Andrews, for a brief period Prime Minister, commenting on one major project, remarked in a sudden flash of realization, 'But that hasn't been blitzed!' And through the Art Committee's support for one of its members, Denis O'D. Hanna, it became possible, for the first time, for our people to focus and appreciate something of their own architectural heritage.

Denis, it was, that voluble propagandist, who isolated and defined for us, those characteristic features in our building styles, *Planter's Gothic*, the *Barn Church*, *Post Regency*. Of course, he earned the pioneer's wage. When, for the British Association Handbook for the Belfast Meeting, an English archaeologist attached to the University was rather oddly engaged to write of our historical heritage, he omitted any reference to Denis' first footing, listing in his bibliography none of the seminal forewords to exhibitions which Denis had brought together, but included in it a review by a Dublin critic of one of these displays. It is, of course, a commonplace that bibliographies provide a good gauge for an author's scholarship.

Denis was then, and, very likely still is, friendly to Moral Rearmament, a Conservative, and an active member of the Church of Ireland, none of these causes close to my heart, but because of his abiding affection for the best in our past, his unquenchable hopes for our cultural future, his restless energy in promulgating his ideas, I count him as one of the most useful Ulstermen of my generation. We were never close friends, but we stood on the same side in our Thirty Years War; and his book, *The Face of Ulster*, for all its joyous inaccuracies, remains one of the sturdiest and warm hearted treatments of its subject.

The Art Committee of C.E.M.A., as I realized later when I was, by the march of the years, promoted to the Standing Committee, was a comfortable, friendly body of decent folk held together by a generous sense of their purpose. Of course, we had our characters. John Hunter, suffering from heart trouble in his last years, was prone to scorching outbursts of rage, but there was always provocation, from myself now and then, or from the civil servant seconded to supervise the Association's administration; an honest, painstaking man, without a matchstick of imagination, an addict to minutes, a devotee of constitutional clauses, a bondslave of precedent where we were making our own, he seemed so irrelevant to our concerns that when he impinged upon them, we were shocked. Zoltan Frankl was never an effective committee man; generous in his lending of pictures from his collections, fussy about the frames when they were returned; enthusiastic for his favourite styles or artists, he easily took affront if a scheme of his were outvoted as impracticable. All in all, there was no audible axe-grinding, no splitting-off into factions, and a serious regard for the necessary discretions.

With the Standing Committee therefore I first became acquainted with a more characteristic sample of the *genus*. It was in many ways the essence of official voluntary committees; for C.E.M.A, by statute and by usage, had its senior civil servants waiting for their C.B.E.s, its University politicians, its B.B.C. officials and its successful business men, all safe people, lacking in intellectual passion, in imaginative gesture, in self-criticism.

The brisk and businesslike but humorous, the ruthlessly efficient, the cocksure but kindly, the ambitious and vulgar, the born intriguer, the cultural snob hugging his limitations, the suave man deft with the newest cliché, the dull but worthy, the dull and empty; I thought in time that I had identified them all, and could remain uncontaminated. But towards the end of my service I found myself manipulated for a base end too late to redeem the situation. I still regret deeply that I allowed myself to be so used, and, worst of all, by someone whom I had instinctively mistrusted. Nevertheless, it was interesting to experience at first hand the masterly summing up, the meaningless compromise, the *fait accompli*, the rigged decision, the tactical reference back, for no one can tell where familiarity with these may not come in handy.

To arrange the festival of 1951 in Northern Ireland, meetings of this body were frequent and lengthy, subcommittees proliferated, reports were voluminous, and yet anything of any permanence which emerged for that occasion came from the steady Art Committee. There is that mural by John Luke in a lunette inside Belfast City Hall. There are two carved reliefs by George MacCann in the Londonderry Guild Hall. There is a memorial plaque on George A. Birmingham's birthplace, designed by James Warwick. There is the book, *The Arts in Ulster*, in which for the first and only time serious and scholarly accounts are rendered of the wayward course of the creative spirit in the province.

There were other useful, if more transient undertakings. As, for example, when Sophie Stewart living in Newtownards, where Jim was now Principal of the Technical School, arranged an exhibition under the C.E.M.A. banner, in the grave Georgian Town Hall. The paintings, appropriately, were in a large measure drawn from the Lewinter-Frankl Collection, since it was in this town that the knitwear factory had been established and was thriving. The opening ceremony was performed by a member of the Londonderry family, the local landlords. When I spoke, in my turn, my remarks on the necessity for the democratization of the arts were considered by some, not, of course, Sophie or Jim, hardly to have been tactfully enough adjusted to the sensitivities of the company, and Frankl, private collector and capitalist as he was, huffily disapproved; he knew my views of old, but thought that there was a time and a place for everything.

When the time came for me to leave C.E.M.A. on my departure for England, I had great fun in resigning from the Board, the Standing Committee, and the Art Committee in proper sequence, and repeating on each occasion my continued distress, at the proportionate allocation of funds to Drama, Music and Art, £10,000 for the first, £5,000 for the second, £1,500 for the last; and by the inerrable operation of Parkinson's Law, £6,000 to administer the spending of just over twice that amount. Never once, in our deliberations in that multitude of meetings, did we pause to consider by what justification, on what basis, and to what end were we engaged in the statutory encouragement of music and the arts.

27

Jack B. Yeats

The first paintings of Jack B. Yeats that I ever saw were *The Liffey Swim* and *The Small Ring*, in the Dublin Municipal Gallery, and while they seemed to me free and fresh in their handling, they were both small scale works of rather restrained colour, and so I did not seriously consider him more important than Sean Keating, or William Conor at his best.

Then, in 1936 or '37, the Haverty Trust bought his *Morning in a City*, specifically for presentation to the Belfast Art Gallery. This trust which became active about 1930, was founded by the bequest of a Thomas Haverty, a painter, I believe, though I have never to my knowledge seen any of his work and have no idea how he came by his fortune. It was to be devoted to the purchase and presentation of paintings by living Irish artists to public galleries and institutions in Ireland; and, although based in Dublin and naturally more generous to the Free State painters than our Northerners, in its benefactions it knew no Border, allocating to Ulster strictly one quarter of the monetary value of its purchases as the proportion due to one of the Four Green Fields of Ireland. We, in Belfast, had already received several works by southern painters, as well as, by some legerdemain on the part of the Curator, who was, *ex officio*, one of the Trust's Advisory Committee, the oddly sited mural, *The Bronze Age in Ireland*, by John F. Hunter and W.R. Gordon, in the Natural History Gallery.

To assist the Belfast Committee in its consideration of the Trust's offer, the Yeats painting was hung in one of the galleries. Largely in black, indigo and prussian blue, rather thinly spread, it represented maybe half a dozen indeterminate figures in a cold dark thoroughfare between tall shadowy buildings. At that time my taste was all for the light, if not indeed the very bright in colour, and for compositions with well articulated architectural structure in the Wilenski sense, so I could make very little of it.

For once I did not feel abashed or frustrated when the Committee rejected the offer and I had to pack it back to Dublin, where it now hangs in the National Gallery of Ireland.

Then, in 1940, when a loan exhibition was arranged by the art committee of a joint body sponsored by the University for Adult Education, of which my father was chairman, to fill the lull that the phoney war had occasioned, among the forty-three paintings, was *Man in a Train Thinking* by Yeats. Having to give daily talks on the pictures I began to grasp, in this, what the artist was about. I recognized the sense of loneliness and mystery, and although in technique and in colour similar to *Morning in a City*, it seemed to me more coherent and concentrated. About the same time too I became aware of his line drawings of the people of the west, by a strange series of coincidences, picking up within the space of a few months the four little paper-backed lesson books in the Irish language which came out early in the Language Revival, and contained his quaint and affectionate illustrations of animals, children and beggar men. Then too I found his black and white and his coloured drawings for Patricia Lynch's children's classic *The Turfcutter's Donkey* which gave me a key to his highly individual kind of folk fantasy.

I was, in fact, beginning at the right end; for after his studies in the Slade under Frederick Brown, he made his living as a draughtsman, contributing to *Punch* above the *nom de guerre* of 'W. Bird'; from 1887 to 1910 working mainly in pen and ink and watercolour. It was not, however, until April 1961 when Victor Waddington exhibited about sixty drawings of this period in his Cork Street gallery, and produced a fine and authoritative catalogue with every item figured, that people of my generation and younger were able to appreciate the full range of his earlier work.

During the war years, when the Free State remained neutral, and in Maurice Craig's phrase Dublin was 'the last lit city', Victor opened his gallery there and very shortly took up Yeats and devoted his superb talents to the task of establishing him as Ireland's national artist. That Victor also brought forward and found a market for a dozen or so of the younger Irish painters, made his gallery the only shop window for modern art in the country. For a decade or more he was the enthusiastic impresario for Middleton, O'Neill, Conolly, Dillon and Campbell, the very practical benefactor to a lively generation.

There were economic and social factors which made this urgent sponsorship amazingly effective. The country being neutral, the Irish manufacturers and the industrialists achieved a high degree of prosperity. Many consumer goods, the possession of which would confer status, were unavailable; so that, when the newly affluent were stimulated, in many instances for the first time, to buy works of art, the local artists met the demand without any outside competition. Further, the old agonies of the Irish War of Independence and the subsequent Civil War were by now abated, their memory serving only to provide the perorations for the professional politicians; and a new set of faces and names had assumed the leadership in law, medicine and the civil service, which for so long had been merely appended to the Dublin Viceregal Court. Just as in any country which has had a successful revolution, has seen the passing of power from one class to another, in this instance, from the Anglo-Irish Protestant Ascendancy of landowners to the Irish Catholic bourgeoisie of industrialists, tariff-cushioned, and cattle-ranchers, the kind of art favoured by the new ruling class will first be in an academic patriotic style – in Soviet Russia, called Socialist Realism – so, in Ireland, the first state-recognized artists were Sean Keating, Leo Whelan, Maurice MacGonigal, with their heroic paintings of guerrilla fighters and portraits of popular leaders, what my friend James White, now Curator of the Dublin Municipal Gallery calls 'the epic themes of the Revolution and the nobility of essentially native figures'. But by 1940 a new, a second generation rose, of the dominant middleclass. This generation had little use for the pistols and bandoliers of their insurgent fathers, and, in their by-now established security, turned from the plays of O'Casey and the novels of O'Flaherty to more pacific, more comfortable fare. Yet they still had a strong sense of nationality, if not of insurrection. So that Jack Yeats provided an admirable answer to their cultural ideological aspirations, a fact which, of course, required the persistent tillage of the small group of those already sincerely convinced of the artist's greatness, before it rooted and blossomed in the public consciousness.

The name Yeats had tremendous prestige and the poet was no longer around to corner it. Jack had, in the Twenties, painted his national tributes, of the mass funerals of martyred leaders, of women waving to Republican prisoners at the gaol windows, of a flowergirl dropping a tribute on the spot in the street where a great fighter was killed. Now most of his works were romantic in the literary, theatrical, show-business, folklore fields, whimsical, with the indubitably national 'smile and the tear'; and most of them were small enough for domestic convenience. Even more, he was, in spite of the vigour of his gentle expressionism, no upstart modern; he had worked and lived in Ireland for a very long time. The years of his lonely poverty and misunderstanding were forgotten, or, to be fair, perhaps not widely appreciated.

By the summer of 1945 the apotheosis was achieved. A Jack B. Yeats National Loan Exhibition was held in the Dublin College of Art under state patronage. The sponsoring committee ran to about fifty names including two Ministers, a senator, a titled lady, several senior clergy, with a good representation of laymen of culture like Con Curran, Joyce's friend, the irrepressible Eoin O'Mahony, Tom MacGreevy whose little book on the artist had just come out bearing the Waddington imprint, and Ernie O'Malley, guerrilla leader turned aesthete by his exile in Mexico. The cover of the catalogue and the preface were printed in Irish, the latter signed by the Reverend Father Senan, O.F.M. Cap., who acted as Chairman of the Committee. In all, the mustering of such a volume of authoritative support and the effective blending and balancing of interests, represented a first rate organizational achievement, which may well remain unique in Irish social history.

This chance to see a full scale display of the accepted master was not to be missed, so Roberta and I dutifully went to the Mountain. With its 179 works, covering nearly half a century, the exhibition proved rather overwhelming to me with my hitherto meagre acquaintance with the artist's range. And, perhaps irrationally, in the face of this massive assertion of his importance, I resented the fact that nowhere was the artist's age disclosed or the record of his birth in London set out. I know now that painters can be as shy as women about their age. When I wanted to put the date of old Andrew

Foyer's birth in a catalogue once that charming primitive very gently excused himself from divulging it. But, as in my own way a historian of the arts of my country, I have maybe an over-developed belief in the importance and the plain recording of such facts. That Jack Yeats was born in Fitzroy Street, London, on the 29th August 1871, I do not hold against him. Good men have been born in the Great Wen, and will be again. Yet, somehow, the apparent lack of frankness in this, set against the heavy implication that Sligo was his native place and the strong assertion of his claim to be nominated The National Artist, kept my grip on my enthusiasm very tight indeed.

And in the great throng of visitors the heightened mood of the occasion was evident. Fashion and culture joined hands or at least touched gloves. After a few snatches of talk with folk she knew already or had just been introduced to, Roberta came back to report 'You'd no more dare to say a word against J.B.Y. than against the B.V.M.' I was led to Father Senan himself, a fat bearded man in the brown Capuchin habit and sandals, and his first salutation was 'Ah, John Hewitt. The man that doesn't like Yeats'. This, before I had offered any quotable opinion, since maybe 1937. We Irish have long memories and long ears.

I found when I took the pictures carefully, that I could go with them up to about 1935 or thereabouts. But the last period, the later paintings seemed so disorganized, so messy in their handling, so careless of the physical soundness of the medium, so blatantly literary in their titles *The Man in the Moon has Patience*, *Farewell to the Sea*, *Homage to Bret Harte*, that they stood, on every count, outside my frame of reference. I had been schooled to reject sentimentality, to respect craftsmanship, to look for the significance of a work of art in itself only. And I had a frantic dislike of bandwagons which keeps me isolated to this day.

Tom MacGreevy, whose long and patient loyalty to the artist absolves him from any stricture, did his fluent best, by drawing my attention to many passages in the execution which he thought masterly, but without penetrating my carapace of scepticism. Kindly Ernie O'Malley, who had written the rather exuberant introduction in the catalogue, gave up after a long and painstaking discussion, remarking sadly 'It's alright, John. I can see your difficulty. It's because you are not a Kelt'. And I was so taken aback that I had not the wit to inquire if Jack Yeats were any more Keltic than I.

It may have been that autumn or early in the spring of 1946 that when we went again to Dublin, Oliver Edwards, most generous of helpers, then living at Enniskerry, took us on a guided tour round houses where Yeats' paintings were to be seen. His method of procedure was this: he called at our hotel, named the first house that we were to visit, led us to the appropriate bus stop, wheeling his bicycle the while, then, when we were aboard, sped off, overtaking, dropping behind, and again overtaking our bus with a wave of the hand in passing. When we got off at the appointed place and knocked on the right door, Oliver was there to open it and to introduce us to our host or hostess. Then when we had talked a while and seen the paintings, he would take his leave after naming our next rendezvous. It may have been that he had planned our itinerary with great care, or that the Yeats' owners known to him lived in the same district. Most of these were academic people of either of Dublin's two universities; and I remember remarking that the staff of my own university up north would be unable to make any sort of a competitive showing. It may, of course, have been that possession of a Yeats painting was a social diploma. I did notice that the sizes and numbers of the pictures bore some sort of relation to the general well being of the house holders. At home I had observed that folk in medicine normally had a Dorothea Sharp painting of children at play on the seashore and/or a flower-piece by Hans Iten, a Swiss who had lived in Belfast for many years. Prosperous specialists frequently had two of each. One more humble general practitioner had, for want of better, a colour print by Miss Sharp. But none had the ardour of identification with their pictures that was so evident as in Dublin. There our round terminated with Mrs George Yeats, the poet's widow, that great hearted woman who also showed us the impressive half length self-portrait of John B. Yeats who had been variously reported as claiming that he should be remembered as the father of a great poet, and that he should be remembered as the father of a great painter.

The next day was the painter's afternoon At Home, and so Oliver opened the door to us there and introduced us. Jack Yeats, a tall old man with a great bald dome fringed with white, with strong brows, sunken cheeks below the high bones, and a firm mouth, greeted us cordially. If he had ever heard of my obduracy he gave no sign. Then he began to talk, picking up canvas after canvas and telling us a great deal about each in turn. One painting I remember vividly, by style of the twenties I should guess, a low curved sandy beach and a tall peasant girl wading on the foam's edge, with a creel of kelp balanced on her head, a caryatid sort of figure. The summer that he saw her so, John Synge was with him, and John Masefield arrived and stayed, and Synge said and Masefield said and he said and then they did so and so and he did so and so, and as the story billowed, airborne, away from the painted girl, I saw the painting become more and more interesting before my eyes; and I kept saying to myself 'Nevertheless, it is still a bad picture'. Years after, I saw it again, in the lounge of a fashionable Dublin hotel. It was still a bad picture. Well, at any rate, not very good.

His talk was lovely, full of life and colour, bred of years of affectionate observation of his fellows, embellished with excellent mime, lit with vivid vignettes, as of how a man in a teashop, if he has bony wrists, will twist and turn his ankles so, as he raises his cup; this to demonstrate some theory Yeats had about the unity and coherence of personality, physique and gesture. But captivating as his words and movements were, I was able, over our teacups, to take a good look round the studio, and to notice the paper rose twined to the easel which was part of the legend of the man, like the pipe-cleaner looped round the door handle to signify that he was working and not to be disturbed. On the evidence of that afternoon I should place him among the good talkers; yet a conversation between him and his friend Tom MacGreevy on the Third Programme once, fell flat, and ever after he refused the microphone.

Zoltan Frankl took to Yeats early in his Irish collecting career, and acquired a number of fine paintings, from the early *Jockey* to *A Race in Hy Brazil* with a brown horse in it as good as any Gericault, and *The Whistle of a Jacket* to name only those that in time became my favourites. It was in the small upstairs sitting room in his house that I began gradually to accept the old man's quality and applaud his skill, for there must have been at least seven Yeats paintings and no others on those jewelled walls. But though Frankl loved Yeats and his pictures, visited him often and framed with delight the pen sketches the artist used for Christmas cards, he always harboured some doubt of his ultimate standing. Often he would enquire 'Tell me, Hewitt, is Yeats a great artist or a great Irish artist?'

Certainly, although Yeats could not have enjoyed a higher reputation in his own country, there has always been some difficulty in exporting his fame, as if his were a wine that does not travel. In spite of exhibitions in Paris and New York under impressive auspices, and in the Tate, his name has never found its way into the reference books. Of course, these have, for a long while been selective, loaded, tendentious, Paris-centred, though, in recent years, the absolute domination of the School of Paris wears thin, as the importance of Munch, Ensor and the Germans penetrates and now the tides of American paint soak through. Even so, Yeats is not named in the widely accessible and handy Penguin *Dictionary of Art and Artists* (1959), while Frank Brangwyn, Muirhead Bone and Augustus John, to name only his contemporaries, are.

When Yeats had his show at the Tate in 1948, Eric Newton would venture to assert no more than that he was a painter of importance, and used up the rest of his column proving that he was not 'slap-dash'. Only John Berger, that young man of courage, declared his belief that Yeats was a great painter suggesting, to my mind not very perspicaciously, that his 'kind of romantic but outward facing expressionism is the natural style of art for previously exploited nations fighting for their independence'. Whereas, in myself applying something approaching a Marxist analysis, I suggest that Yeats' style suited a phase when some sort of stability has been reached in such a development. Berger also declares 'Further, it is Yeats' Irish background which explains why his direct influence on younger European painters would be a dangerous one, leading to theatrical mannerism'. This would be difficult to substantiate, for the younger painters anywhere seem never to have even heard of him, and anyhow to hold his 'Irish background' against Yeats is either to condemn all Irish artists out of hand or to cling to a very limited xenophobia.

When the Conference of the International Association of Art Critics was held in Dublin in July 1953, soundings were anxiously taken by those deeply committed, from the assembled experts. Special buses were booked to take them to see the generously strip-lit Yeats collection of a wealthy race-horse owner out of town. In courtesy to their hosts, the foreign critics made friendly noises, and, when pressed, seemed generally to set Yeats somewhere after or between Kokoschka and Ensor, as some unspecified sort of an expressionist, not a very penetrating or precise assessment; although when I first saw the former's *Vienna from the Wilhelminenberg* (1931) in the Vienna municipal gallery it struck me, at first glance, as not unlike the Yeats of Frankl's *Hy Brazil*, particularly in the lightness of its calligraphic figures. But, on a second seeing, when it was included in the Kokoschka Arts Council Exhibition at the Tate in the summer of 1962, I realized that the similarity was not very deep and that the composition, based, as the painter asserts, on an analysis of Brueghel's *Children's Games*, was much more complex than Yeats could ever have achieved.

When I went to Dublin in February 1955 for the latest Yeats Exhibition at Waddington's, it was in a more receptive mood. None of the paintings I had seen before, so that I could come towards them without the spangled curtain of words, associations and memories between us. I was able at last to feel that they were speaking to me without reserve; and that I could, in some measure, understand what they said. I was still cautious enough to note and criticize one or two which I thought bad pictures, muddled, unresolved; but, making my report in the *Belfast Telegraph*, I set out my recantation with some relief:

> The overwhelming effect is of richness of imagination, of human heartedness, of marvellous colour, and the masterly manipulation of a highly personal style.
>
> With my sceptical northern nature, it has taken me a long time to come to terms with the Yeats enchantment: now I have to admit that the man is a magician.

The next year, in February 1956, we had the first Yeats Exhibition in Belfast. He had shown his work in London, at the Tate and the National Gallery and at Wildenstein's, in Leeds, in Washington,

Boston, San Francisco. Now when he was eighty-four, the Wee North gave its tardy salute.

I might have been inclined to hold myself to some degree responsible for the delay; but circumstances proved that the Belfast City Council was scarcely ready for him yet. The display of forty-five paintings was drawn largely from his last ten or twelve years. This was Victor Waddington's choice. I should have preferred, remembering my own struggle, a retrospective anthology, so that an unfamiliarized public could move from the early, more easily acceptable works to 'the last quartettes', or as near them as possible.

Since the rejection of *Morning in the City* nineteen years before, no painting of Yeats, early, middle or late, had been considered for inclusion in the Gallery's permanent collection; and in that period his prices had increased steeply – I think myself, far too steeply: but, then, price has never been a significant factor in my estimate of the value of a work of art. So, with a little misgiving, I put forward a small canvas for the committee's approval, its price £300. The Art Sub Committee could not agree, and the matter was passed to the full body. When I had made the remarks I thought relevant in that place, to that company, I mentioned the price and sat down. An alderman, an old enemy of mine, asked in his flat voice 'Will the Keeper of Art tell us what this works out, per square inch?' When I replied that 'I was not a quantity surveyor', he demanded the protection of the chair from my insults. The painting was not bought. But I was a little consoled when the artist, in his own fist, thanked me for what he called my 'handsome foreword' to the catalogue, and for the hanging of the exhibition, which he had heard was very good.

We arrived in Sligo in August 1961 for the W.B. Yeats International School at which I was to lecture, just in time to catch the opening of the Jack B. Yeats Loan Exhibition in the Town Hall. The last time I had set foot in it had been at the poet's funeral.

The Mayor introduced Dr Thomas MacGreevy, Director of the National Gallery of Ireland, well recovered from his recent illness and looking more than ever like a distinguished diplomat of Boston antecedents. Tom presented a ripe and characteristic estimate of the painter's personality; and I remembered, the Dublin story that, when

Jack Yeats in his last years wintered in a nursing home, every evening Victor came in to light his cigar, Tom called later to put it out.

Tom's graceful and well phrased essay was followed by James White, who stepped round the rim of the packed room and stopped beside four or five well differentiated paintings, the texts for his talk. And as I stood close to the wall, too late for a chair, listening, my gaze coasted round the sixty pictures, hung too close, uncomfortably low, recognizing, among them, many old friends, Frankl's prominent, and with a jolt of surprise that old acquaintance of 1940, *Man in a Train Thinking*. And I thought that, perhaps this was, after all, the proper way to see Jack Yeats' work, at the core and centre of the kingdom of his boyhood's imagination; and my memories turned back over the long road that I too had travelled from *A Morning in the City* to *A Room in Sligo*; and I felt the stirring of a lonely hope that I should see not this time through Yeats' eyes, but for myself, *A Blackbird Bathing in Tir-na-nOg*. But from their quick glances I was made aware that both Tom MacGreevy and James White had me under surveillance, and were, doubtless, wondering how I took it all. We Irish, as I have remarked, possess long memories and not a surfeit of charity.

28

Welsh Rarebit

Our first opportunity to step outside Ireland since the war came in 1946, when Roberta and I crossed over to London to wonder at the bombed sites and the rash of loosestrife, and to see our first prefabs. We stayed with Marie and Bertie Rodgers in their Hampstead flat, at the top of a house owned by Mrs Ullmann, the wife of the painter, the first work of his we were able to see through an open door on our way out.

The prime target for our seeing was the Exhibition *Britain Can Make It* in the Victoria and Albert Museum. In this, it was amusing to note that the display gimmick seemed to be a kind of applied surrealism, the exhibit stands being of the nature of 'found objects', and, in several cases, rubber gloves inflating or collapsing regularly gave a sinister hint of mindless being to the presentation.

A friend of Bertie's and a fellow Ulsterman, Bill McAlpine for no reason other than his abundant goodwill, gathered us into his charge and found entertainment for us in a most interesting way. First he took us to a party held in Leslie Daiken's flat. Daiken I had met when he was a teacher at Portora in County Fermanagh during the war; and I was to have dealings with him when he was getting hold of material for the Devin-Adair anthology *New Irish Poets*: and, such are the vagaries of undertakings like that, when the book came out in New York in 1948, I was included and he was not. At his party we found Austin Clarke on one of his rare visitations to London, and, for the first time, Ewart Milne, most prolific of Irish poets, whose verse I wish that I could like better, a man who, as we say, will never let his bone go with dog, an indefatigable writer of letters to editors, who will attack you if he thinks that he has cause, and just as vehemently defend you, if he thinks that you have been done an injury.

Later one memorable evening Bill took us to Soho to rendezvous with Dylan Thomas. When we had worked our way to the right pub we were very surprised to see a very rubicund Constant Lambert stride briskly in, order a drink, knock it back, and as briskly stride out again. The only other time we saw him was at Covent Garden conducting *Coppelia* with Fonteyn and Helpmann in it.

Not long after Dylan arrived accompanied by Roy Campbell and a young Scots supporter whose name I never picked up. Nevertheless I remember him as the purest type of the devotee. Throughout the evening he kept coming over to me and insisting that Dylan was his man, and once he produced his Post Office Savings Book to show us how methodically he had been withdrawing the statutory three pounds a day, and reckoning optimistically how long his sojourn in the bardic shadow would last.

Dylan rather surprised me by his appearance. He was a little fellow. The springing curls of the famous John portrait were flat and damp. He seemed a little grubby and sweaty. And straight off he took a dislike to me, remarking to Roberta that I was a bloody intellectual. Thereafter I talked with and listened to Roy Campbell, again in appearance somewhat disappointing, tall, thin, toothless, very bald, in a not very well fitting double-breasted navy blue suit. I was at that time an enthusiast for his resounding rhetoric, and had not long before read his autobiography *Broken Record*. So I was very properly amazed when he declared this to be largely fictitious, and where not fictitious in fact the life of another South African poet. He took my honest appreciation in a surprisingly gentle manner seeming genuinely grateful and pleased. I certainly could detect no hint of irony in his attitude, nor could I observe any hint or sign of the violent, brawling, opinionated reactionary gossip had made him out to be.

Save for the half dozen of us the bar was empty most of the evening, and while Roy Campbell and I talked in a corner and the young Scot wove towards us with his Savings Book and retreated to fill Dylan's glass, the bard, with Roberta and Bill, were engaged in an impromptu parody of a Louis MacNeice radio feature, Dylan providing the sonorous voices, Bill and Roberta the drums and trumpets and a rich variety of background noises, marching and counter-marching as the pattern of the allegory demanded. Dylan, apparently, had not tasted solid food for the last two or was it three days; but, so involved and caught up in this gallimaufry was he, that he drank very little. Then, very quietly and with no fuss at all, Roy Campbell took a little bottle from his pocket and gave Dylan a couple of aspirin-like pills, watched till they were swallowed, went outside and called a taxi, and when it came, packed-off the unresisting poet to Broadcasting House where he was shortly due to deliver one of his ripe recitals. All this achieved with the utmost kindness and unobtrusive efficiency.

Dylan's name I had first seen in the Poetry column of *The Sunday Referee*, that amazing journal run by the Ostrer brothers, where Victor Neuburg set and judged verse competitions. I entered for a couple of these, and for one when I was awarded a notecase for a lyric, Dylan, I think, received a fountain pen.

And in another Soho pub crammed to the walls, a seething cauldron of voices and tobacco smoke, we saw Tambimuttu, black as night, his teeth, someone said, as bright as the badge on a busby, famous then as editor of *Poetry London*; and like Box and Cox, MacBryde and Colquhoun the Scottish painters. I was introduced to both, but cannot remember which was which, for my attention was diverted by the apparition, passing holding a glass chest high, of Paul Potts on his way to or from somewhere, the creature had a purpose and his face was sweaty with it.

It is interesting that MacBryde and Colquhoun should flicker into the picture just at that time, the typical, the representative painters. For, with Minton, Craxton and Sutherland, they belonged to the Neo-Romantic movement which seemed for the moment to point the way that British painting must surely travel.

Years after, when I saw the Arts Council memorial exhibition of John Minton's work, the painted surfaces seemed arid, dry, crumbling, so much had our experience of pigment textures been modified by the Action Painters of the fifties. It has always been a shock and a satisfaction suddenly to discover some phase in or phenomenon of activity in art which had been seen to be happening, current, contemporary, abruptly stiffened into the recognizable posture of style-dated, remote, ticketted for history, yet still valid for what it was, but if imitated only as pastiche.

29

Van Gogh at Glasgow

By lucky coincidence, I was asked to give a talk in Glasgow to the members of Scottish PEN, a few days after the Van Gogh Exhibition was due to open there, in February 1948. So, to use my father's restatement of the proverbial phrase, I was able to feed two birds with the open hand. We crossed over with some eagerness to take in the opening, for Glasgow was the nearest point to Northern Ireland that this amazingly popular display was to come. Many of the paintings had become so widely known in reproduction that my attention was more deeply engaged in the sombre, clumsy *Potato Eaters* and the late, premonitory *Crows over Cornfield*, and in the less familiar drawings. We had an odd experience in this. Both my wife and I liked the painting *Almond Blossom in a Glass*, and, unbeknownst to each other, bought coloured postcards of it. The first jolt, which only deepened my mistrust of reproductions in colour, was that in both instances, the narrow red strip across the background was of a markedly different tone, and neither accurately recorded the colour of the original.

As I shall relate, we went on to Edinburgh for a few days. On our return to Glasgow on our way home, we paid another visit to the Exhibition, and when we got round to the *Almond Blossoms* again, we were both shocked to find it in actuality so small. Between our first seeing it and our second, the picture had, in retrospect, become inflated in size, far beyond its mere 9³/8" x 7½", a warning against the tricks of visual memory, or a demonstration of the vitality of the creative image.

Van Gogh is a prime example of the serious risks that wide public approbation of an artist's work can involve. For some as yet unanalysed psychological or sociological reason, his work in reproduction came to meet a deep social need. The popularity of

Sunflowers became notorious. The romantic legend of the man him-self became generally accepted, the slicing of that ear, the asylum periods, the Gauguin association, the saint of the long letters. So much so, that for a generation or longer, he became the archetype of the Artist/Genius; a satisfactory image to Admass which exists to baffle, confuse and make profit out of the bemused and apathetic general public. So long as the artist can be shown to be an outsider, our materialist economy is safe. His urgent values have no apparent daily relevance. He is our lonely lightening conductor. Keep him outside, up there, and we shall not catch fire; and Gully Guinness may shuffle away to sympathetic applause.

And with this alienation of the creative artist comes the tragic corollary, that the very evidence of his creativeness must be diluted, rendered down in the commercially successful but essentially lying and socially destructive vulgarizations of the colour reproduction, in which scale, texture and colour integral with the nature of the work of art are distorted and falsified. And, perhaps, most tragic of all, because of the acceptance of the false, the original itself becomes debased, and losing its unique impact, is rendered meaningless by repetition, and humanity is impoverished by the loss. Jack Yeats who would never allow his later works to be reproduced, once said of colour reproductions: 'The better they are the worse they are'.

So the Exhibition which I had looked forward to, with such anticipation, left me with a sense of deprivation, of something filched from me that I had counted on for nourishment.

Dr Tom Honeyman was then Director of the Glasgow Art Gallery, one of the great directors of my time. Criticise, if you like his showmanship, spotlighting Rembrandt's *Knight in Armour* buying Dali's stagey *Crucifixion* for £8,000 which, anyway, the Gallery got back in admission fees, and postcards. But set against all this, his vig-orous propaganda on behalf of those good painters, his fellow coun-trymen, the Scottish Colourists, Peploe, Hunter, Fergusson, Cadell, and his passionate desire that folk should and must be drawn in, by hook or by crook, to confront and respond to actual works of art.

Sitting over a cup of tea, my wife said 'Dr. Honeyman, what have you done to your lovely Botticelli?' 'Tell me', asked he, 'what you think I have done?' 'You've cleaned it, and it has lost its quality. It's chalky looking'. Pointing his finger at her, he replied 'There you are, just one of those who don't like cleaning. We've simply taken the glass out – it hadn't been touched for years – and cleaned that. You're seeing the picture clearly for the first time – So much for your chalkiness'.

Douglas Young had come over to Glasgow for my talk, and when it was over he swept us with him across to Edinburgh where he then lived, and for a thronged weekend he set us in the midst of the Scottish literary movement. Bards and artists of all shapes and sizes were bidden to his hospitable stove in the evening: Sorley MacLean the best living Gaelic poet, Norman MacCaig quiet and impenetrable, Alexander Gray makar and translator, Robert Kemp the playwright, Wilfred Taylor the witty columnist; and when they could not come in the evening, George Bain the gentle revitaliser of Pictish (so he calls it) design – I'll always call it Celtic – and Wendy Wood the Scottish Nationalist, fresh from some flag hoisting adventure.

Then so that my afternoon should not be wasted, I was carried off to visit old Professor Charles Sarolea with his house full of books, where we crouched in the small clearing round the stove in a labyrinth of bookstacks, tall folios in ribbed leather, *Penguins*, the famous Napoleonic collection in another room where even the table top was piled with volumes.

In Glasgow on our way back, William MacLellan, that adventurous publisher, arranged for us to meet Hugh MacDiarmid, the Muckle Makar, as Douglas Young called him, the unchallenged leader of the Scottish Renaissance. I had been a close and continuing reader of his work since I first found *Sangschaw* and *Pennywheep*, his two earliest volumes of verse, and, with *The Drunk Man Looks at the Thistle*, the peak of his achievement, about 1930.

So much of a devotee had I been that I even subscribed to the limited edition of *First Hymn to Lenin*. This cost a guinea, a large price for a book of verse in these days, and came in a cardboard case, with a portrait of the poet reproduced as a frontispiece and a foreword, both from the hand of A.E.

My grandfather in his Glasgow days had become fond of Robert Burns, and I can remember with what energy he used to recite *Tam O'Shanter*, banging his fist on his thigh and bellowing the climacteric couplet:

'Well done, Cutty Sark!
And in an instant all was dark.'

My father, born in that city, although he was brought to Belfast as a
small boy, kept in memory a wide canon of Scots, and was a handy
glossary for me as I grew up and my reading proposed questions of
translation. Of course, in the North East of Ireland, the area planted
by Scottish colonists, we have a tradition now unfortunately waning,
and this, and my researches into the vernacular bards of the coun-
tryside developed this side of my otherwise not very subtle linguis-
tic curiosity. Anyhow, MacDiarmid I took easily, and because of the
contemporary quality of his ideas and responses, in spite of conven-
tional opinion, I held him to be of the front rank among the poets of
my time; and although my Scots pronunciation is far from satisfac-
tory, I can still for my own amusement and interest repeat maybe
half a dozen of his lyrics without the book. But I have failed to find
that memorable resonance in his later pseudo-philosophical works.
But unquestionably MacDiarmid is a remarkable phenomenon; per-
haps most of all resembling a Colin Wilson with lyrical genius, a
provincial polymath whose tongue, for a brief spell, the gods
anointed with song.

We met in a pub and settled in one of these compartments which
in Ireland we call snugs. MacDiarmid, or Christopher Murray
Grieve, to give him his baptismal name, was, at first, something of a
disappointment. His features good enough in themselves seemed too
small for his face, and his excessively high mop of fair hair increased
the discrepancy. His manner of speaking, a bit truculent and queru-
lous, lacked distinction. But his humour, quick wit and vivid thought
very soon took us captive. For, for all the fixed points of his attitude,
his mind had a quicksilver speed and run. I accused him of inconsis-
tency in being both a Communist and a supporter of Social Credit,
and when Roberta suggested that he might fare badly if he lived in
Stalin's Russia, his reply was that he had been able to survive in
Capitalist Britain alright, so that the Soviets offered no more serious
problem.

30

'The Funeral of Mr W.B. Yeates'

At the September meeting of PEN I found that Nelson Browne was the only other person there who had thought of going to Sligo to be at the funeral of W.B. Yeats. We knew that the people of the south would be taking it seriously and sending official representatives, but we did not expect that the Six Counties Government would stir a toe; and the University, although the poet had received an honorary degree from it, largely run by English and Scots, to whom a poet's return to his native earth meant nothing, had probably never heard of the coming event. So, in order that the whole of his country should be represented, we agreed to make the journey together. That it was to be on Saturday the seventeenth, was highly convenient, for Nelson, as a schoolmaster, could be free from Friday evening, and I could take time off. We had both grown up in the long shadow that Yeats had cast over the writers of Ireland. Nelson, some years later to publish the only recent study of Sheridan Le Fanu, the macabre novelist, had been a contemporary of mine at Queen's, had devoted a good deal of time to Irish literature, and what was rare among us, was a sensitive and judicious critic. Deeply interested in music too, he had a concern for the arts and was an early collector of Colin Middleton's paintings. Appearing to many as a quiet, courteous, serious man, with his great friend Rowel Friers the cartoonist, he had a less public aspect of high spirits and lively humour.

Travelling on the rocking little train from Enniskillen to Sligo, past the deep lochs famous to anglers, with the dark mountains behind, at one of the wayside halts, three or four railwaymen off duty came into our carriage. As this was not long after the Costello Coalition had taken over the control of the Free State from de Valera and his party, I asked them what they thought of the new

Government – one gave a characteristic reply, 'Well, we haven't riz up agin them, yit'.

We got into Sligo at a quarter to eleven so that we saw little of the town in our urgency to find a hotel. The only evidence we had that we were in a strange place was the pervasive smell of burning turf blown across the streets. Next morning at breakfast a woman at a table next to ours annoyed us rather unreasonably. She was approaching middle age yet wore slacks and sandals, a garb at that date, unusual in an Irish country town. She talked in a Southern English accent so loudly that we could not but overhear. She wondered why Irish towns were so drab and dirty. They are; but we do not like English people to tell us. She had been over here for three weeks on a cycling holiday, and had only prolonged her stay so that she might attend the funeral. We wondered edgily what right an English tourist had to do that. It was our affair. He was our man, not theirs. Looking for local colour likely, to add to the wake, the cattle fair, the tinkers' cavalcade. Surely she would have a camera. She knew W.B. Yeats. We thought of possible circumstances, the literary lunch, the evening lecture. All this urgent gabble produced no response in her table companions, a silent Indian lady in a sari, and a middle aged middle-class couple from the North on a motoring vacation, more interested in the cheaper petrol this side of the border. So we ate quickly and slipped out, determined to give the lady in slacks a wide berth. Sligo is a decent town, more like a northern town of the same size, with prosperous shops and not much secular building prior to 1820. The winding river with its broad bridges added interest, for at first we were perpetually crossing it, seeing the backs of tall warehouses and hotels from different angles. There were back streets with grass sprouting out of the low thatches, and many bells that clanged the quarters, not always synchronizing. Dutifully, we found St John's Parish Church and gaped at the Pollexfen headstone, noting, inside, the alabaster ruin of a sixteenth century relief and the shabby British military standards hanging limply from the poles.

The funeral procession was not due to arrive until noon, so we still had time to see the interior of the Roman Catholic Cathedral, a dull and massive pastiche, cold and unevocative, with surprisingly pleasant roundels set in the high windows.

When we found our way back to the centre of the town already there were signs of activity. An officious garda, in front of the Post Office, a low red brick building, was hurtling lorry men and carters and diverting motorcars. It was here that we encountered Barbara and Oliver Edwards who had come over from Bundoran by bus. I should have guessed that they would be here. Oliver knows more about Yeats and his work than any man alive, and so generous has he been with his scholarship that his name inevitably appears in every list of acknowledgements in the volumes that the American professors, associate professors, assistant professors extrude in such an unyielding flow.

While we stood at the corner discussing our intentions we watched a Dublin spiv, with an open cardboard box, touting mourning cards for the occasion, little oblongs with a cross and RIP in black. One or two passers bought from him. One sturdy young woman near us just answered 'No' to the drawled solicitation. Then the fussy garda spotted him, strode over, took out his notebook, wrote name and address and admonished him sternly, while the boyo himself adopted the offended but voluble attitude of one well used to police interrogation.

It was wearing up to noon, so we edged to the kerb outside the Post Office from whence we should be able to see, past the tall pillar with the white marble alderman on top, the procession coming down the long street opposite, and turning to the right in front of us on its way round the corner to the Town Hall where the first halt was to be made. Shutters began to go up on the shop windows, for the mayor had asked that business places should be closed from twelve till four. The bank manager's family and friends gathered at the upstairs windows across the street. People began to muster along the kerbs. The Post Office doors behind us were closed, and a handwritten notice appeared, as if by magic, on one panel, announcing that business would be suspended until four o'clock, under the surprising heading of 'Funeral of Mr W.B. Yeates'. This the ready pen of Oliver corrected forthwith. Donkey carts with loads of brown turf or sacks of potatoes were urgently thumbed along by the garda. Droves of schoolchildren with the rush of the newly released, curved past us round the corner. I wondered if they knew what the stir was about, noticed two or three barefoot, and tried to remember the poet's couplet on the old roadmender, but I could only recollect the second line:

> Ireland will be free and you'll still break
> Stone.

A party of soldiers in their dusty green khaki, with steel helmets, marched smartly past, 'all of a height', as the man beside me remarked. The shops, by now, were all shut. The sidewalks were full of folk. Family groups dribbled along the narrow path behind the kerbside belt of spectators. Time limped by, for although the busy-body garda was, as my neighbour phrased it, 'lookin' for a stripe', and although a turf cart piled high with its load jolted precariously past that worst statue in the world, there were none of the loud happy calls and comments which usually fly out of a waiting crowd.

Then, almost an hour late, we caught signs far up the long street that the procession was coming. A hush came over the town, and the flap of an occasional pigeon's wings was obtrusive as a handclap. Newspapers were folded away, like two waves of breaking foam, as the feeling of the approach ran down the street. Children were hoisted on shoulders. In the stillness, for the first time I could hear far away the cry of pipes, wild and sad, and the slow distant thump of drums. Soon they rounded the corner and came down the hill towards us.

The pipe-band of local lads in their blue serge Sunday suits, tense and tall with dignity, came forward slowly step by step, the drums crêpe-wrapped and anonymous. First it was a quavering lament that I know well but cannot name; then Moore's *Oft in the Stilly Night*. I recalled what Yeats had written of Tom Moore; and yet, in spite of that, it seemed decorous and just, a tune we could all share. And somehow, I was glad that it was the local civilian band and not the brass and braided uniforms of the state. It was enough that the old poet's body had been brought back from the Mediterranean sunshine in an Irish gunboat called *Macha*, for he had been, maybe, chief among them who had made that gesture possible:

Did that play of mine send out
Certain men the English shot?

But now he was returning to the town and the countryside, once more among the named places stitched so brightly into the fabric of his verse.

The hearse with a very large bright coffin, the largest I have ever seen, half-covered by the Irish flag, was next, followed, on foot, by the Mayor of Sligo, public representatives, cabinet ministers, men from Galway University capped and gowned in their degrees, for it had been in Galway that the gunboat had berthed. Then a long file of creeping cars, with, here and there, a profile behind glass and its passing reflections, that I could recognize.

By now the procession, slower and slower, had run to a halt. Round the corner where we too moved into the square before the Town Hall, the crowd swarmed and elbowed, beating about the black cars like waves. The hearse was drawn up before the steps and was already ringed by riflemen with bowed heads and arms reversed in a guard of honour.

In the jostle, losing Nelson and the Edwardses, I ran against the dark figure of Austin Clarke, that scrupulous poet, and as we were talking, Lennox Robinson, hatless, with glinting glasses, like an elderly undergraduate, coasted past us and was hidden in the close crowd. In less than five minutes, Austin drew my attention to where the eminent dramatist had got, high on the steps, facing the firing squad of cameras. And to the right, not centred, I recognized the long dark head of Louis MacNeice, in his black oilskin coat, and beside him the pale face and large spectacles of Maurice James Craig.

By two o'clock the cars were in position; a bugle sounded advance and they rolled off again; this time without the band, the mayor and the public representatives marching in front of the hearse. The streets were rimmed with spectators, but not so thickly now. As we crossed the bridges, along the quays, they stood in little clusters. Then the rain started to fall lightly. At the town's end waiting cars gathered up the marchers, and the whole cortege moved slowly to Drumcliffe. The cloud lifted a little from Ben Bulben's flank and then closed down. At gates, at lane ends, in front of houses, knots of people stood, here a dozen, there two or three, sometimes a woman with a hooded pram. And as we drove along, beside us there was a continuous surge of young cyclists, mostly young girls with head-scarves.

The driver of our car, a local taxi-man, remarked 'There's a loch up there, Loch Gill, and he went up there and stayed a week and wrote a poem about it. O he was a grand poet.' I found it more comfortable for him to talk of weather and crops. At last we caught a glimpse of the churchtower among the trees and knew that it was Drumcliffe.

The cars pulled in to the *sheugh*. The hearse drove on down the short lane, past the broken cross, into the graveyard. We waited on the roadside until the poet's widow and son and daughter and his brother the painter, in a long dark overcoat, had walked slowly but steadfastly forward. Then the crowd closed in. Young people perched on the walls along the lane, and, at the gates, cocked their cameras as de Valera, head and shoulders above the rest, approached. In the graveyard the hearse stopped to the left of the church door; and the grave was enclosed in a hedge of crowding backs. Sightseers hung one-handed from tomb railings or stood straining and peering from convenient monuments.

All I could see under the foliage of umbrellas was the curl of a bishop's crosier. Of the service according to the rites of the Church of Ireland I heard nothing above a faint drone. Austin Clarke at my side inquired if one might smoke at a Protestant funeral. With no inclination to thrust forward into the graveside huddle, I could only look around me, peer up at the tower which seemed too high for the church, and watch men with a movie-camera recording the scene, look at the rain slanting through the trees, and find names celebrated in twentieth century Ireland for the backs – and the backs of heads, the actor, the poet, the man of letters, the politician. The crowd along the walls was noisy, ill-at-ease, waiting for the oration which never came. Behind me, two men were talking loud enough to be heard, one urging his fellow to 'come in on a good thing', for 'I can get the stuff direct from Holland'.

I could hear the sound of spaded earth. The mourners round the grave dispersed and others pushed forward to look. There was a general loosening of tension, an easy standing around. Small boys and girls threaded through the groups, autograph books open and pens tilted forward butt foremost. Austin introduced me to Dr McCartan, a smallish square man whose part in Irish affairs I could not quite recollect, but knew to have been significant. Then Valentin Iremonger, poet and civil servant, came over and said that Sean MacBride would like to meet me. I was introduced to the Minister, a pale intense man with light hair. Son of Maud Gonne, he had a right to be there. But while I was explaining that the only hope for a united country was in federation with firm guarantees for the north in regard to censorship, divorce, birth control and the place of organized religion in the constitution, I could see, a few feet away, Micheál MacLiammóir the actor, walking past. Dressed, as few of us were, in dark formal clothes and looking very solemn, he caught my eye in passing. Some years after at a party in the MacCanns', when, at Micheál's insistence we were playing the Truth Game, he asked me abruptly 'John, when you saw me at Sligo, did you think I was a bit of a cod?' And I could only answer 'Yes'. They were gathering or making small circles round us, other folk who wished obviously to shake the Minister's hand, so we drifted to the waiting cars.

> Under bare Ben Bulben's head
> In Drumcliffe churchyard Yeats is laid.

That evening Nelson and I called at Dr Tom Murphy's; his wife, Nora, also a doctor, was sister of my friend Patrick Maybin. They were hospitable people.

We found our way back to the hotel close on midnight. After some delay, the street door, with some drawing of bolts, was opened, not by the expected porter, but by the English woman we had seen at breakfast. She explained that there seemed to be none of the staff about. We thanked her, and as she turned to the stairs, I said 'I suppose you were at Drumcliffe this afternoon'. She stepped down the last treads to the hall. We found the switches and the three of us sat at a table neatly laid for breakfast, with inverted cups. We talked of the funeral, of Yeats' poetry, and then she spoke of the man. She knew that he was a considerable, even a great poet; but what mattered to her was that when she had needed help he had helped her. Years ago when, emotionally, she had been in a bad way, a friend had said 'Go and see Yeats'. She was a person of no consequence, no importance, just someone who desperately needed friendship and understanding. 'He was the kindest person I have ever known. I shall always be proud, and rather amazed that he had time for me and my trouble'. So, she, in spite of the loud voice and the slacks and the sandals, had a right to be there; more right than I who merely loved his verses and his way with words.

> Under bare Ben Bulben's head,
> In Drumcliffe churchyard, Yeats is laid.

After breakfast, Tom Murphy called for us, and drove us round Loch Gill, showing us Dromahaire, The Fiddler's Rock and Innisfree, a mophead of foliage floating on its reflection. In the afternoon we took the train home, failed to change when we should have, and sailed into Derry in the dark, the last train for Belfast gone an hour before. It was lucky that the next day was Sunday.

31

Annus Mirabilis

For my adventures among pictures 1949 proved a year of marvels indeed. After a starved decade, largely concerned with the problems of art in my own province and country, a period in which, because of the flaring-up of activity in a war-isolated community, we were probably disposed to exaggerate its value without the constant check of European standards, suddenly circumstance gave me the opportunity to move outside and beyond our island problems, and not merely reassess former standards but reach out to new levels of experience and judgement. The Arts Council organized the great exhibition, *Art Treasures from Vienna* at the Tate, and the only slightly less important *Masterpieces from the Alte Pinokothek at Munich* in the National Gallery, and it became my responsibility and delight to take the good fortune with wide eyes.

With the Vermeer *Artist in His Studio*, the Cranach *Crucifixion*, the Van Eyck *Albergati* portrait, and Velazquez' royal imps, it was hard to keep one's head. But Titian's *Nymph and Shepherd* with its quiet incandescence, his strenuous *Jacopo de Strada*, Giorgione's curiously nineteenth century *Laura* with the leaf blade background, and, a name unmarked before, Coëllo, with the still, tense faces and the fantastically intricate embroideries, gave me new points of reference.

By contrast, the Munich paintings, at first glance, looked a little uncared for, and in need of cleaning. But here too, Grunewald's *Christ Mocked* with its Nazi-like overtones, the half dozen round-topped Rembrandt Passion pieces, great in scale though no more than three feet by two, the heart chilling leer of Rubens' *Susanna and the Elders*, and the Blakeian avalanche of bodies in his *Small Last Judgement* one figure in it with the mask of Le Bête in the Cocteau film, the glitter and vibrant sparkle of Guardi's Gala *Concert*, the fat sprawl of Brueghel's *Land of Cockayne*, entered my imagination for-ever.

Then, in September, I got myself made delegate from our Centre to the PEN Conference in Venice. Passing through London we took a quick turn among the Venetian paintings in Trafalgar Square to set the tuning fork astir. At Victoria there was a carriage reserved for PEN travellers and we were hauled aboard as the train moved off. In the Gare du Lyons late that night I saw Cyril Connolly with his walking stick amid an archipelago of luggage with Cecil Day Lewis metaphorically holding his hat. When they marched down the train we were not to see Connolly again, for unluckily, he developed food-poisoning or caught the measles or sprained his ankle, and stayed indoors at Danielli's ever after.

We could not afford a sleeper but were fortunate in having a car-riage to ourselves; and after a jolting gritty night when the water in the lavatories gave out, we woke to a brilliant Swiss morning with time for coffee and rolls and the best jam in the world, and time for Roberta to meet, botanizing along the railway siding, the spare, sen-sitive Lady Vyvian, in her WVS uniform with the badges removed. Later in the day, stopping at a small station at the foot of a terraced mountain whose top we could not see, we were swarmed over by a babble of Americans, one of Brownells Tours, forty women and one man. They had already done England, France, Holland, Germany, and very affably asked us where we were bound for. We said 'Venice', and they enquired 'And where else?'

From the railway station to the Lido by *vaporetto* in the dark, we goggled at the lights in the high black houses and the passing steam-boats splattering the swirling black waters with snakes and ladders of gold. When we woke in our large room in the morning I got up and jerked back the tall shutters. The city with its domes and towers across the lagoon was a silent explosion of pink and rose, an enor-mous fragile bouquet of misty pearl blossoms, nature outclassing Turner's 'golden vision'.

The inaugural session was held in the Palazzo Ducale, and through the delays, the ministerial welcomes, the obituary tributes to Maeterlinck, the eulogy of the absent Croce, the translations, the Belgian delegates' embarrassing salute to the abashed Silone, we sat and gazed at the vast Tintoretto *Paradiso* behind and above the minute platform party in Sala del Maggio Consiglio, and it seemed to me that it would have been more fitting for us to keep silence and let that great multitude sing out from the wide wall before us.

Edging out at a convenient interval, we cricked our necks at the Veronese ceilings and stepped round a man flat on his back taking a proper look. We discovered a door ajar, whispered round it and inside, above we saw the Titian fresco *St Christopher*, a painting which came back very oddly in a long poem I made seven years later.

The Lido, with its to-ing and fro-ing, was inconvenient; our hotel, somehow, too impressive with its chandeliers and furlongs of red carpet, so, although my expenses were being paid, we transferred to a *pensione* in the heart of things, over a little bridge from the Piazza San Marco and past the baroque San Moisè with the squirming figures in the niches of its facade. That first morning apparition of Venice was not to be repeated; to demand it more than once in a lifetime would be avarice.

We walked around, to get the feel of the place; the quick-cornered alleys, the bulging buildings, the dark church interiors, the sudden release of the unexpected sunlight in the squares, the great drum well-heads, dry and carved, the stale warm smell of the scummed water everywhere, the switchback bridges, the dusty gondolas cargoed with straw and yellow bricks, and, before St Mark's, the blizzard of pigeons, and, high up, the iron men beating their bell. Our Congress, for some of its days, synchronized with an International Folkdance Festival. There was a raised platform in the Piazza, and, for a couple of evenings, passing or sitting at tables, we saw and heard the floodlit performers; and from early morning little teams in national costume, perhaps like ourselves, fugitives from the Lido with its combed sand by day and its Coca Cola neon by night, wandered among the streaming tourists and gaping natives, often, by request or out of sheer good spirits, stopping to clear the floor and give an impromptu performance to the fiddle or the pipes. Flemish, Balkan, Scandinavian, the flutter of scarves, the flicker of skirt and blouse, the signalling of sleeves, the flash of long white stockings, offered a new innocence of carnival, a new meaning of theatre in the round, to that old remembering town.

But, by contrast, past our *pensione*, one bright morning, a little procession of shabby men, with posters tacked on sticks, marched their protest of the unemployed.

Sean O'Faolain, in his book on Italy, describes the facade of St Mark's as being like the entrance to an enormous fun-fair; and when, one Sunday, we stood for the High Mass, led by the Patriarch of Venice, against the golden blaze of the altar, with small nimble boys vesting him in green and gold, as noisy trickles of country people in Sunday black, herded by their parish priests, eddied round the kneeling worshippers, gaping at the mosaics and the roof, the Irish' playwright with us exploded, 'We wouldn't stand for this in Dublin'. I felt that his comment was not directed simply at the trippers' seeming irreverence, but at the whole medley of ebullient splendour and casual unconcern. In Ireland we are all tarred with the same brush: our Protestantism is Calvinist, our Catholicism Jansenist, our Judaism Orthodox; we have never learned to take serious matters naturally.

The phrase that labelled the total visual sensationalism of Venice came from Norman Ewer, the *Daily Herald* correspondent, when he turned to me one night at our table outside Florian's, and asked 'John, what do you do, in real life?'

Counter-pointed against the talking sessions of the Congress and the sparkling evening junketing, we followed an independent campaign of picture-hunting, beginning with the Bellini Exhibition in the Palace, convenient for truants, learning to judge and love the calm normality of his vision and the masterly variations he played upon his major theme. In the Correr Museum we saw the famous Carpaccio *Courtesans* and a special display of small Sardinian prehistoric figurines, like manikins by Leon Underwood. We inquired our way from kindly but inexpert people across the Rialto to the Accademia, to the magnificent Giorgione *Tempest*, marvelling at its smallness, the Gentile Bellini Processions and Carpaccio's *Miracle of the Cross* and his *St Ursula* sequence, and Titian's *Presentation of the Virgin* with the lonely child on the long staircase, and his *Deposition*, and the several little Longhis, strangely domestic after so much of the rhetoric of great public art, so that I felt like Lemuel Gulliver back home after Brobdingnag. Most forceful of all, the impression that so much Venetian painting was about Venice, the sacred subjects given the only setting worthy of their holiness; that pictures were still in the ambiance for which they were first intended. Titian's *Presentation* had been painted for that very wall.

We had thought that it would be a pleasant gesture to light and set up candles in a church for the sake of our Catholic friends in the far-away Glens; but no church that we looked into seemed equipped to receive them. Mario Praz, that friendly man, volunteered to find out for us, and next day told us that the Frari was our place, but that we should have to buy the candles in a grocer's shop nearby. The afternoon that we set out was dark and cold, and by the time that we found the grocer's, a ponderous thunderstorm blackened and rocked the wet and threatened city. The Frari offered comfort and we did what we had come to do with satisfaction. Titian's *Assumption of the Virgin*, that soaring anthem, was a happy bonus. Then we paddled through the curtained rain to San Rocco. The mounting wonder of all these Tintorettos in their places seemed as much as we dare ask, until, unprepared, we came upon *The Crucifixion*; and from that day Tintoretto took his place as the greatest master I had yet experienced; not so Shakespearian as Titian, not so opulent in textures as Veronese; but in sheer invention, and in the subjection of his passion to painterly terms, and without any of the hysteria of his disciple El Greco.

The only other experience at all comparable to this was not in Venice, where Tintoretto stood supreme, but in Padua, in the Arena Chapel when we moved among Giottos with the toy landscapes, with the sheep-like whippets and the smiling camel, where every human gesture had been grasped and made sculptural and hieratic forever; and in that place I realized why Giotto must always be counted among the first. The appreciation of Tintoretto was, in a way, our own discovery, for fashion had not then veered towards him so strongly as a decade later; but our confrontation with Giotto had all the sublimity of a Chestertonian commonplace, that grass is green, a greatness which received no increment from our experiences in Florence and Assisi thirteen years later.

The Salute was opposite the Congress rooms in Ca'Giustinian, so we therefore knew it well, massive yet afloat, so much better looking than the Belfast City Hall, before we crossed over to visit it. When we arrived a small wedding was in progress, the bridal couple, the priest, two altar boys, and maybe eight or nine family guests, islanded in the vast interior, and without music. We sat awhile, not liking to intrude, a little sorry to have been caught spying on the small private event, yet longing to see them all go off in the two gondolas tied up at the landing stage before the steps. We had already seen a coffin and mourners on the water, and were eager to relate the great occasions of life to that elemental stream of the city's being. But the service droned on, as if the priest, resenting the intrusion of the vast, still tomb, was determined that the law must be fulfilled every dreary tittle, every tedious jot. So we tiptoed off in a wide evasive arc, about our own affairs. At first the bold baroque had affronted me, with my protestant asceticism and sense of economy, and with my visual awareness so conditioned by the strict and dry standards which my reading and thinking had led me to. But the three Titians on the ceiling, *Cain and Abel*, *Abraham and Isaac*, *David and Goliath*, when we discovered them, somewhere behind the altar, each with the diagonal of its violence, and the *Marriage of Cana* by Tintoretto, with its defiant asymmetry, made me think more kindly of the place.

A Congress excursion took us to Vicenza where I was introduced to Palladio for the first time, knowing him before at a great remove in the projects of the Ascendancy aristocrats in eighteenth century Ireland. Most spectacular of all, an opera at the *Teatro Olimpico* had been arranged for us: *The Coronation of Puppea* by Monteverdi. We sat in the tiers of backless stone seats, on paper cushions, gazed in marvel at the fixed stage, the two-storeyed backwall with niches and pilasters, with the triumphal arch and the two side arches ramping abruptly with illusory perspective, and heard Boris Christoff, firmly set in his high blocked white boots, and delighted when a cat strayed across the stage and a hand rose blindly out of a trap door to waggle it away. In the intermission, the audience rose, descended, and climbing on to the stage, wandered in and out of the arch and up the sloping boards between the low doorways distanced by the scale of carpentry.

That evening we supped well, thanks to the Municipality of Vicenza, sharing a table with Kate O'Brien, close friend of Silone's Irish wife.

We returned to Venice so late that few delegates were able to attend the first morning session. The programme being thus dislocated by absentees, I found myself summoned early, and gave my talk on the Congress theme, criticism, to a meagre company. Pamela Hansford Johnson in her report to *Tribune* afterwards, called it 'excellent, lucid and blessedly concrete', a comforting estimate. Herself the only other United Kingdom delegate to speak during the Congress, she, normally a pretty woman, had unfortunately to carry a savage mosquito bite on one of her eyes. This mishap, like the good novelist that she is, she made use of in *Catherine Carter* (1952), her novel on the Victorian theatre, when the heroine, waiting in Venice for the hero to come for her, suffers the same misadventure – 'She looked like an Asian who had been in a prize fight'.

The final excursion was to Torcello. We set out under a dull grey sky with a cold wind; and when Douglas Young, his collar up, his hat plucked down, stood beside Roberta with her head scarf tied under her chin, watching, from the stern rail, Venice recede, someone remarked that they looked like Maddox Brown's *The Last of England*. I sat beside a stout and cheerful Jew who pulled a beret out of his pocket when he was fumbling for toffees; a Graham Greene character, I thought. He disclosed himself as Louis Golding. Luckily I had read and remembered something of his early verse, even if I had never frequented *Magnolia Street*: and once again remarked how many middleaged or elderly prose writers like their verse to be recalled, the poet still enjoying a vestigial supremacy.

The first to stride along the landing stage, Douglas with his long shanks, set off like a steady breeze, for it looked as if the light was going from the sky. Derek Patmore, great grandson of the poet, himself a biographer or an autobiographer, another tall fellow, stepped out too, and with Lady Vyvian Roberta and I trotted in the rear. The island is flat, as if with an effort it had raised its sods out of the sea, bearing no more than bushes, tamarisks, along the little canals of the weary and waterlogged place. The campanile and the church beside it, seemed the sole reason for the island being there at all.

The interior of the church was gloomy, but the high tiered stone seats were impressive, and the great mosaic of the Madonna silencing in its solemnity. The awe and bare splendour, the pervasive sense of antiquity, of a rather frightening endurance in worship – it was one of the few churches that I have been in, where I felt that I ought to pray – descended upon us, but our meditation was shortly broken by an uproar outside. The cohorts of the Congress had just arrived, having had no long-legged Douglas urgent in the van. The peasant custodian refused to admit them, as official closing time had passed. So not to allow the baying rabble – there is no roar so menacing as that of a thwarted mob of multilingual congressionists – to disperse our peace, we quietly pushed through and out into the now still and golden evening, noticing that it was Carlo Levi, the painter, author of *Christ Stopped at Eboli*, who was gesticulating with the most furious abandon. We found an inn across a small canal, and taking a welcome glass of wine, watched a tremendous sunset first of greens and golds, and then of flaming gold. Men in gondolas had shot out of ditches and bushy creeks, with cargoes of grapes, crying their wares. We signalled one with a free vessel and allowed ourselves to be floated briskly back to the landing stage. A more leisurely voyage would have been more appropriate, but our boatman had an ear for the sullen mob back at the church with fares in their pockets too.

It was not till we were home in Ireland that I read the famous second chapter in the second volume of *The Stones of Venice*, and found that John Ruskin had said it all, clenched it in his image of the basilica as an ark in the midst of the waters. Seven years later Geoffrey Taylor, then poetry editor of *Time and Tide* printed my Torcello sonnet, a poem for which I have found very few to express any liking; although I still am fond of

> ... the tarnished gold
> of an unreal Adriatic day

and the closing lines of the sestet:

> the symbol of an old drowned continent
> where, on the last rood of remaining land,
> faith still outfaced the mutinies of men.

In retrospect, little remains of the many speeches, the often angry disputations which the name of Croce shuttled through like a ritual chant. Still, it was a new experience to find that literary discussion could be as emotional and bitter as a political affray. After the places and the paintings, it is the people who remain vivid: Dos Passos, a tall stout bald American, accused by the Italian journalists of treating the Congress as a honeymoon and not singing for his supper as a guest of honour should; the straw-haired Auden modest when accosted; the sad faced friendly Silone, glad to remember the package of coffee Paul Potts sent him when the war stopped; Julian Benda of the *Trahison de Clercs*, losing his way to the Conference room, and refusing to pay the attendant at the turnstile of the Bellini Exhibition, rattling his heavy stick indignantly – he had, it was rumoured, been waiting at his hotel for the taxi which never came; Spender in open-necked shirt, dashing about with his brief case; Clough Williams Ellis, the architect, like some prehistoric bird, not as proud as he should have been of the grocer's shop which he designed for the MacAlister's at Cushendun, not eager to recall that time he fell off the platform in the Great Hall when lecturing at the Belfast University.

Most heartening, most nourishing of all, was our meeting with Edwin and Willa Muir. Douglas, of course, saw to this, and later had pleasant things to say about it, in the Congress chapter of his characteristically extrovert book, *Chasing an Ancient Greek*. It started with a party one evening, which included Benno Schotz, the Scottish sculptor and his wife. Benno I had known for a good while, from before the war, when he modelled that brilliant portrait of Hugh McAleavy, the Belfast bookie, in one strenuous weekend, and when the Belfast Art Gallery bought a bronze head of his wife. The Muirs' just then were based in Rome, where Edwin was in charge of the British Council.

As everyone must have, I realized straightaway the goodness of Edwin Muir. A small shy man, he listened and smiled and spoke with quiet compassionate wisdom. To me, it was as if my father had come back enriched and informed by the unimaginable disciplines of death. His charity and humility made me feel brusque and coarse-grained, even, in a way, gross, beside that gentle sensibility. I knew his poems well. I knew *The Story and the Gable*: and so I was able to find confirmation for what I had taken to be crisscrossing threads which bind the two, his verse and his autobiography, into one of the most impressive and meaningful literary and spiritual achievements of our time. It was unnecessary, but deeply gratifying, that he should have liked my long poem *Conacre*, published not long before in Grigson's anthology. Willa, on the other hand, seemed more like a companionable, clever aunt, with an edge to her tongue almost Irish in its temper. Roberta had about six months before found and enjoyed Willa's novel *Mrs Ritchie*, so that my reverential regard for Edwin was justly balanced by Roberta's eager interest in Willa. Together, the Muirs created something greater than its parts. I have met maybe three saints on earth; Edwin Muir is of that number. I have met, I should reckon, not above half a dozen great women; Willa is among them.

They were staying with Peggy Guggenheim in her palazzo on the Grand Canal. This may sound out of character; but the palazzo was actually two restored ground floor blocks tied together with a flat concrete roof. Peggy Guggenheim, celebrated of course, as an art collector, had a display of sculpture in her garden: Arp's firm bosoms, Viani's sharp pointed plaster breasts, Brancusi's tapered space birds, Pevsner's scored flanges of metal, Moore's, Lipschitz' bronze people, all comfortably scaled, on their pedestals, under the flicker of leaves and sunlight. Giacometti's little *Piazza* of trudging figures will never look better than there.

In the open patio between the houseblocks a Calder mobile swung, every fin and fan alive and vibrant in the ceaseless stream or tunnel of air to the garden from the terrace fronting the canal. Out there Willa was sitting reading. Beside her Marini's naked man on horseback, embellished with a phallic broom handle, challenged the passing water-traffic. When we were introduced to her, Peggy Guggenheim was wearing mobile ear-rings, the work of Calder, also.

Towards the end of the Congress, in a ground floor room of our headquarters at Ca'Giustinian, we came upon an exhibition being hung by Giorgio Chirico. I knew that he had reneged on his earlier loyalties, but was shocked by these recent paintings, clumsily drawn, in slimy pigment of an unpleasant surface and in drab lifeless colour, like faded linoleum; still lifes of Roman helmets and bunches of roses, small groups of pseudo-classical horsemen and warriors.

It looked to me as if he were endeavouring to produce Old Master paintings with no grasp of Old Master techniques of underpainting and glaze. I could see no connection with the canvasses of his great period, with the compelling compositions of the lolling ovoid-headed philosophers, the solid geometry of the doom-imminent empty city squares, the surrealist collisions of railway trains and cabbages. I recognized the artist from his self portrait in Reynal's book, but had not the heart to salute him.

When the Congress ended we stayed on wondering if our money would spin out as far as Florence. But the news of likely devaluation of the pound, and a strong belief that it would be wrong to rush there for no more than two or three days, kept us where we were, and we did not see Florence until 1961.

So we went back to the Accademia, grew more accustomed to the city, found, through a friendly cafe-contact, a little dealer's gallery full of Morandi's pale-ale jug and bottle arrangements, cool as cucumber, and Campigli's wasp-waisted ladies with parasols, warm as sun-baked earth. And, one evening, the same contact, a quick and intelligent Italian woman took us to the Café Columbo to see the proprietor's collection, hung round the walls and stacked in private rooms, Carra, Rosso, a couple of early Chiricos Utrillo, and a tumultuous Kokoschka roof-top view of Venice. We were very relieved to discover these, for any work in the art shops in the more frequented alleys was clearly aimed at the tourists, bad, glossy, bright, academic in style, obvious in subject; and it had seemed that art had died a long time ago.

At last we headed homewards, cashed our last traveller's cheques in Paris, where the foreign exchange departments were closed for a day till the rate was adjusted; and it was with a pleasant shock that we ran into Benno Schotz once more, and one wet evening saw the Italian film *Le Voleur de Bicyclette.*

In the Orangerie, that time, we had the delayed Centenary Exhibition of Paul Gauguin, my first opportunity to see any considerable range of the great Post Impressionist's work; so, I had little thought of the surprises before me. The first was a painting of the Seine, which looked to me like a good Sisley, but utterly outside the expected canon. *The Fight of Jacob and the Angel* I had seen in Edinburgh in the Scottish National Gallery and liked greatly. *The Yellow Christ* stood up to this in quality, but as we moved from painting to painting in his later periods, I became aware of a deep inner unrest. I was disturbed first, by how so much his method had become the commonplace of poster art, second, by the frequent unpleasantness of the colour, but, most of all, by a frightening sexuality, cynical, hard. The demonstration of an evil nature, in three or four of the paintings, gave me unavoidably a violent reaction to the not simply implied but here clearly exemplified personality of the artist. I had read his *Journals*, had taken him for the romantic rebel, the hero of Maugham's novelette, an extreme example certainly, but of a known kind. Now I knew him still to be in his works an evil spirit. My reading and thinking, I had believed, had long taken me beyond all questions of morality in art, and consequently this sudden intuition struck me with unexpected force. In spite of my non-conformist, puritan pedigree, I had learned to enjoy the fondling sensuality of Boucher, and not to be affronted by the florid carnality of Rubens. Bosch with all his compassionate obscenity, I could accept as inhabiting the deep unconscious of us all, his sharp violence somehow becoming ecstasy in the process of the dialectic of feeling. But only with Gauguin, and only with these green paintings, have I ever experienced this particular sensation of fear almost, of supreme nastiness, of evil positive.

The recent works of Matisse in the Museum of Modern Art were a serious disappointment. Blatant colour in oils, trivial paper cutouts, a carelessly showy calligraphy, they seemed the blundering gestures of an overblown but essentially flimsy decorator. I had never really accepted Matisse as of much durable significance; but in the Twenties and for a while after, it had been the convention to set Picasso and Matisse at the top of the list, the Heavenly Twins of the Modern Movement. This abrupt coupling of contemporary names had been a great fashion from Victorian times; Dickens and Thackeray, Keats and Shelley, Tennyson and Browning, Hardy and Meredith, Shaw and Wells, were the normal pairs, and I am old enough to remember with what effort we contrived to think of either alone. But the interesting way in which critical fashion has now dealt with these who were once considered equals suggests, perhaps, in addition to the altered assessments, that this momentary pattern of pairs is no longer required to meet some odd need in the aesthetic imagination of forty or more years ago.

The Picassos which we saw in the temporary UNESCO build-
ing, were also a disappointment. Starved, deprived as we had been
for a decade, I looked unthinkingly for the abundant life of that great
imagination, the rich, the comforting, the nourishing, the benevo-
lent. I had failed to realize that Picasso too, in a harsher context than
ours, had come through his own dark night, and should not have
been expected to arrive like a beaming Santa Claus at my bed foot
with a brimming sack of presents for a good boy. Consequently, I
found his paintings, spiky, angular, hard, brutal in their distortions,
of lamposts and children's tricycles and what looked like battered
bins, disturbing, not as in the Gauguins for the evil of their maker,
but for the discomfort, the pain, the agony of his comment.

Of course, it may have been that, having in a concentrated experi-
ence, risen in my heart to meet and be lifted higher by the Venetian
marvels, above all, by the Tintorettos in San Rocco and the Giottos in
the Arena Chapel, the art of our modern masters must have seemed a
retreat, a defeat, an art that in a shorter perspective might have
appeared satisfactory enough. But it was not until 1960 in the great
exhibition at the Tate Gallery that I came to my own estimate of
Picasso, setting aside as far as I could the whole force of persuasion
and propaganda which has accumulated round and behind his name.
Certainly, the originality and power of his perception, his imagina-
tion, was so evident that in those crowded rooms after a time you
came to feel not only that some of the motionless, silent, framed pres-
ences on the walls had a greater reality than the less palpable figures
moving round you, but that face after face thrusting out of the melée
of spectators had a Picasso look about it, particularly the dark women
with the large noses. Here, of course, I touch on the vast mystery of
style, a notion with me for years, but now more recently assuming the
power of a commonplace; that something, working through the cre-
ative artists of an epoch first, establishes the modes of our seeing, and
that, after, the image-making of all of us, including the scientists, slips
into the now accepted but unanalysed convention which they have
compelled us to utilize: and it is this conceptual conformity which
makes sense of a generation's identity.

The first conventional opinion on Picasso which I had to shed in
dogged defiance of the reiterated chorus, was that he has always

been the supreme virtuoso technician, the matchless master of all painterly skills. This is simply not true. His works in general are not, painting, collage, assemblage, very well made. He displays a coarseness, a heavy-handed strength, with no affection for his materials, with no caress. His pigmented surfaces are often as unpleasant as a plastic table-top. Perhaps in this he presents the archetype for our synthetic age.

But more fundamentally, the truth that I came to was that Picasso has a profound and expansive human sympathy unequalled in our time, and very likely since that other Spaniard, Goya. His gentleness, his tenderness, his pity is obvious in his early phases. But it is always pity for the lonely individual, the smallest family. It never stretches out to include society; and it is only in society that human reality exists. Picasso's sad little acrobat or solitary drinker have something in common with Wordsworth's monolithic Leechgatherer. But having at some time faced utter disillusion and despair, being no longer able to expose the tendrils of his sensitivity to the winds of his world, he retracted them, shut up like a hedgehog, and tried to satisfy his straining awareness with the discipline of formal problems, smashing the world of his terror into a thousand fragments, continually mocking his own pity, by violating his true nature with violent distortions. Picasso's is the art of the bitten lip, of the fist clenched upon the lacerated palm, of the stigmata.

And because of the intensity of his despair, of his occluded pity, Picasso's is also a great comic art, for, in truth, the opposites must hold their equilibrium.

I remember when, before the war, an Ulster born painter had his first One Man Exhibition on his return from the centres of influence, I asked him how he would describe himself, and he replied 'as a disciple of Picasso'. I could scarcely conceal my amusement at his pretention, and retailed his remark for my friends' delight. Nowadays, although Picasso is still alive and has produced the greatest body of visual invention that any artist in history can lay claim to, his example no longer would be admitted by any young practitioner. Already the style-images of this epoch predicate another set of creative forces. Yet, of all the paintings seen that year, it was one which I should hesitate to put among the supreme masterpieces that had, ultimately the deepest effect upon my feeling for art history; Titian's twenty-five feet wide *Presentation of the Virgin*. This large work spanning two doors and still on its intended wall in the Accademia, states its point so dramatically by the contrast between the crowd at street level on the left and the almost empty mounting steps; by the placing of the little girl against the pillar, by the emphatic broadening of the step which she is about to leave, by the strange blunt diagonal running counter to that of the steps, made by the old woman with the basket of eggs and the great craggy landscape. Seeing it, I could not but feel its mastery, its immediacy, its authority of realization.

Then, when in February 1959, when I was in Dresden going round the Gemalde Galerie, myself not sure of what to expect beyond the big Raphael and the Giorgione, I suddenly found myself in front of that other *Presentation* by Cima da Conegliano. This was certainly the biggest shock that a picture has ever given me. Instantly I remembered the Titian, and bit by bit I noted the similarities, the high priest at the temple entrance, the infant on the steps, the crowd at the bottom, the old egg-woman, the distant landscape.

The plagiarism was blatant, overbearing, as if Titian had brushed Cima aside with the back of his hand, and said: 'This is the way it ought to go'. I was, in the formulation of my ideas, fronted and faced with this problem of honesty. Titian was the thief, sweeping all his predecessor's properties into his own satchel. But he had made of his theft something greater than all that he had stolen, broadening that step, organizing his architecture, getting rid of the turbans and the fancy dress, introducing a loved and known landscape rather than a stage prop, but keeping the egg woman. Compare, for example, the resolutely marching little woman of Cima with the breathless hesitant little girl of Titian. The ideas jostled in my mind; has art its own or has it no morality? Is not this what Shakespeare did too? Is not the only point which matters, whether a work of art is good or bad? And what does one mean by good or bad? And mingled with these shoving and shouldering questions I had a distinct sense in myself of having reached an important foothold or ledge in the development of my aesthetic and pictorial experience, when I could instantaneously bring together two clear and true experiences separated in time and space, and measure one against the other with confidence.

I had noted similarities in works, recognized borrowings, influences, stylistic affinities, but this was far more moving, more significant, an almost mystical realization, as if, in the Marxist jargon, quantity had become transformed into quality. I felt in an innocent humble way as if I were beginning after so long to know something about pictures, touching the ripple's edge with my toe of that vast ocean wherein the great scholar disports himself like behemoth.

32

From Chairmen and Committee Men, Good Lord Deliver Us

As the time for the Director's retirement approached, although he gave no hint that my hopes of the succession were not well-founded, I realized instinctively that something peculiar was in the air. Roberta had always warned me that I was not invariably a reliable judge of character. A great politician in the museum profession's affairs, he had of late found himself elected or co-opted to ancillary bodies and became closely tangled with others like himself who had interests in the British Association. The B.A. was due to meet in Belfast in the autumn of 1952, some months after his retirement was statutorily due; but he secured an extension designedly to allow him to fulfil his onerous commitments with and responsibilities for the conference. And for this, he conscribed me to serve as secretary for his section, a medley of voluntary societies, and individuals interested in antiquities, botany, bird watching: it was, in fact, an enclave for the less strenuous camp followers who had not the equipment to keep up with the expert papers and demonstrations. My other colleagues, George Thompson and Douglas Deane, were more properly involved in the deliberations of more academic sections; and so the museum and the gallery were crammed with projectors, folding chairs and trestle tables. For myself apart from shepherding stout ladies in tweeds and frail old gentlemen with white moustaches, I found opportunity to slip out to the university for an hour to listen to and partially comprehend that alarmingly clever man Dr Bronowski on The Theory of Experiment, who, with a blackboard and nimble chalk, played havoc with his 'micro-hoyles'.

During the week, the Director's silver haired, naked-faced cronies were much in evidence as his office became a sort of headquarters for their convivial consultations. But as the days passed I became aware that not one of them, although I had been acquainted with them for years, ever suggested to me that as the Director was about to depart, I might be wished well as his successor.

The Chairman of the Libraries, Museum and Art Gallery Committee, Percy Tougher, golfer, shirt manufacturer, son of a once well-known pawnbroker in the city, had the misfortune to be unwell at the time, and viewed with evident dislike the Vice Chairman's lavishly provided hospitality. It was with some curiosity I learned that the most silver-haired and naked faced of the museum professionals went out to spend an evening with Tougher, for it seemed hardly likely that their conversation should not, at some point, touch upon the Belfast succession; but of this I heard nothing.

When the coming vacancy was advertised and the candidates mustered, some good men of my generation of known skill and distinction whom I had thought possible contestants did not apply. This, I have some reason to believe, because they considered that my claims were not contemptible. Eventually out of an odd bundle of disengaged clergymen and others scarcely any better qualified, only one name emerged as a possible rival, W.A. Seaby, F.S.A., Curator of Taunton Castle, a local society's museum. With Alfred George and myself he had been one of the very first batch to be awarded the diploma of the Museum's Association, by examination a year or two before the war. After service at Reading, he had gone to Birmingham Museum, but had, I believe, spent some time with his brother's firm, the well known numismatists, for numismatics was his speciality.

It seemed odd therefore that, in the prolonged interval between the closing day for applications and that fixed for the deciding interviews, partly or entirely due to the Chairman's insistence that the appointment should not be made in his absence, the Director, as one of the Carnegie Trust advisors, should make a special journey to Taunton to inspect the castle museum's eligibility for a development grant. At this stage the Director and I ceased to communicate with each other on anything other than strictly day to day business. It was not from him that I learned of his Taunton trip.

About a week, or maybe a day less, before the interviews were to take place, while I was at home for lunch, the telephone sounded. A very guarded voice enquired if I were I, if I could guess who was speaking. I was. I could. Something greatly to my disadvantage had blown up. Could I possibly leave the Gallery for a short time this afternoon? About three? It would be better for us not to be seen together. Could I be on the Lagan Embankment at the end of King's Bridge, at three, then? The car would pass and stop a little way along the road, out of town and wait for me. This air of conspiracy, this schoolboy plan, puzzled and shocked me. I have never believed in secret societies, for, as Jamie Hope said, 'Oaths will never bind knaves'. On the other hand, I had been schooled by living in Ireland for so long, to keep a discreet tongue in my head, never speaking to anyone of any confidential matter, unless the other man mentioned it first, or unless I felt sure that he needed to hear it; so, although the situation seemed hard to believe, and difficult to speak about afterwards, it remains a clear memory, not requiring the storyteller's shaping.

I took up my position at the time appointed. The car passed and pulled up fifty yards on. I followed and got in, and my fellow conspirator murmuring 'We can't talk here. Let's go somewhere safe', we drove off. When the driver came to a cul-de-sac of newly built as yet unfinished, unoccupied houses, we stopped.

Then he unwound his story. The Chairman, inevitably a Unionist, was going round the City Hall, showing Council members a letter he had received from Mrs O'Malley (a member of the Irish Labour Party which provided about half a dozen councillors representing wards with strongly Catholic populations), and in this letter she stated that, as she could not be present at the next meeting of the committee, she wished, if it were in order, to be recorded as supporting me. This was a personal letter to the Chairman but he was making more than private use of it. Further, my informant declared, Tougher was asserting that I was a Communist, and, in addition, that I 'was one of the Tomelty clique'. Joseph Tomelty, just then starring in an American play *The Trouble Makers*, in the West End, had been one of the Group Theatre company, and a contributor to *Lagan*. As one of those most vitally concerned with the arts I could not help knowing him, even if he were a Catholic; and that, of course, was my offence. On the other hand I knew of but had not then met Mary

O'Malley or visited her company, *The Lyric Players*, who performed in the tiny theatre at the back of her house.

This was the situation. I had admittedly Catholic support; I had Catholic friends, and actor-authors at that; I was a Communist; and these allegations were being widely canvassed among the people in whose hands the appointment lay. My informant could do no more. It was for me to deal with the matter as best I could. My mind, flickered through with shots and snippets of Westerns and Tammany ward heelers, was still clear enough for me to thank him heartily for his kindness and for the trouble he had taken. So he drove back, and near but not at our first rendezvous, I got out.

This was the epoch when McCarthyism was in the news: guilt by association; the smear; the lie. I could not help feeling a sort of identification with its victims. In any society with standards of public decency, this sort of thing could not happen. I was being branded both as Communist and pro Catholic. My years of gallery experience, my education, my long practice as lecturer on art, my reputation, such as it was, as broadcaster, my service on cultural committees, these lay outside the reckoning. Then, as I walked slowly back to the Gallery through the Botanic Gardens, I considered my informant and his motives. He had his career and livelihood to think of. Perhaps he felt that he owed me some gratitude for a small service my wife and I had done him years before. Perhaps his sense of fair play had been disturbed. He had done the best he could. He was by his own standards being amazingly brave, even foolhardy. While he would not run, he had at least whispered in the hare's lug and given it a yard or two start.

Although I was in a turmoil of rage, consternation self-pity, incredulity, and bitter amusement, all in kaleidoscopic patterns, that evening my wife and I set about trying to stem the attack. I went out to call on W.R. Gordon, my only personal friend on the Committee, house-bound with flu. An old man of no political influence, suspect maybe himself for having been a play-actor in the past, a singer of folk ballads and an artist into the bargain, he could only sympathize and promise that he would be at the meeting, come hell or high water. My wife communicated with her sister's husband who could talk frankly to a non-council member of the Committee. The next morning, hating her errand and the necessity for it, she visited an elderly councillor, widely respected as an honest man, under whose chairmanship she had served for some years on a hospital management committee. He admitted that Tougher had been displaying the letter to all possibly interested parties, accepted her word that I was a socialist, not a communist, and promised his support.

I disclosed the whole dirty story to my friend Zoltan Frankl who had been looking forward to the day when I should be Director with a more absolute confidence than myself. Infuriated, he enlisted another man who knew me, a relative of a council-member who set out bravely on a counter canvass. Frankl, giving up his business completely, for a couple of days, drove furiously round the city, catching the more prosperous aldermen, councillors and others known to belong to groups of some influence in Unionist affairs, at their offices, at their clubs, at lunch time, or at their homes in the evening; all this with a troublesome heart, returning to pant up the long stairs to the flat, grey-faced, to report the day's calendar of evasions, prevarications, rebuffs. By the afternoon of the second day the other man gave up. It had obviously become not a matter of decency or fairplay, but of the Chairman's standing. The Unionist caucus in the council had met and decided to back him and order all dissidents to heel, all, that is, except that elderly councillor who had given his promise and would not be budged. Still, Frankl drove doggedly on with sinking confidence in his powers of persuasion. We told him that he had done more than enough; his heart would stand no more. Then he found that the charge against me was shifting. Decent folk outside hearing rumours of the affair were telephoning members of the council, protesting that I was no emissary of the Vatican or the Kremlin, that surely in this age sectarian aspersions were no longer an acceptable procedure, that to accuse a man for having Catholic friends would look like bigotry in the opinion of sensible people. So to meet these objections another card had to be played. When Frankl asked for evidence that I was Communist or pro-Catholic, the answer was 'Whoever suggested that he was? In point of fact, Hewitt is no good at administration. The Director says so.'

The day for the interviews arrived. The committee was to meet in the forenoon. My brother-in-law's contact had been at pains to switch an important business engagement to the afternoon. By chance I found myself travelling to the City Hall in the same bus as the Director. I sat down beside him and we talked of the weather. When I arrived at the Committee Room, I learned that as the cross-channel steamer had not yet berthed because of fog, the interviews had been postponed until the afternoon. The Director had been telephoned and told of this just before he left the office, and the committee clerk who informed me expressed some surprise that I had not been warned.

I met Bill Seaby in the members' reading room. We recalled meeting each other somewhere. A tall fair pleasant looking fellow, clean shaven, with wavy hair. With not much between us to sustain a conversation for very long, we listlessly lifted and flicked through the illustrated magazines from the leather-topped table. I was called first. The Chairman asked the questions. There were several supplementaries from here or there. The room seemed very gloomy and I had no opportunity to fix and name each face round the wide table. I answered with, I thought, competence. Then it was Seaby's turn. Alone in the reading room, I examined the shelf of new library books placed there for the members' convenience, and thought that they fairly represented the taste of the City Fathers. Then Bill returned. After a time, I shall never know of what duration, he was called in again by the committee clerk. This is the normal routine. I had lost, unless by some remote chance the other candidate made conditions for acceptance which the committee could not accept. I remained alone. That notion, for it was not even a hope, vanished. Should I slip away? Or wait till I was formally told? I would wait, for I have a stubborn streak which makes my retreats few. Then, at the far end of eternity the committee clerk put his head round the door and said 'O you're still here! I suppose you know that Mr. Seaby's been appointed?' I gathered my coat and going out of the building through the swing door, encountered W.R. Gordon and Morris Harding the old sculptor. They stopped with funeral faces, and Gordon blurted out 'It's a bloody scandal. You were beaten by the Chairman's casting vote'. Just then another non-council member, Dr MacDonald, no friend of mine, thrust past us without word or glance, and Gordon said loudly 'That bla'guard should be ashamed of himself'.

With the bitter angry words of sympathy from the two old artists, I went out to catch a bus home, and tell Roberta that what we feared had happened, and that once again the Belfast Museum and Art Gallery had an English director, once again without a university degree.

Afterwards I pieced it together. The committee was divided seven to seven, evenly and neither side would budge, so the Chairman 'exercised his prerogative'. Had the meeting been held in the morning I should have got by by one vote, and what would the Chairman have had to do then? One nice point: the man who had met me, that crazy day, on the embankment, at the end of the meeting, rose and thanked the Chairman for his efficient conduct of the proceedings. The voting had been by ballot, not by show of hands.

The Council's confirmation was completely a party routine. Mary O'Malley raised the matter; the Chairman replied briefly, and that was that.

An interesting piece of Irish silver was coming up at a London sale, the day after the Council meeting, so the Director suggested that I should go over, inspect the item, and bid, if I thought proper. He must have considered this a small consolation prize, for neither he nor his predecessor had ever before proposed a London business trip for me; all my journeyings to London and to the Continent had been at my own expense and in my own time. Perhaps, the Director only wanted me out of his sight for a spell. So a few hours after the Council meeting I boarded ship for Liverpool. When the steamer had edged past the lights of Carrickfergus and Bangor and the flashing beam from the Copelands, and was pulsing away into the blackness, I could not go below to my berth. Round and round the deck, I marched fighting over every known thread of the intrigue. And when the last clumping sailor had pointedly called Goodnight and gone below, I still marched on, round and round the deck mechanically.

Once I stopped at the rail and looked down at the troubled waters sliding, folding over, and turning past, and, for a minute or more, I was nearer suicide than I hope I shall ever be again.

I did not like the piece of silver so made no bid; and in the evening after the play I went backstage to Joe Tomelty's dressing room at the Strand Theatre. The next day I had lunch with Howard

Sergeant who had made generous reference to my verse in his *Cumberland Wordsworth* not long before. He heard my story with kindly patience; and then, in his pleasant North Country accent, remarked 'John, if I were you, I'd get out of that God forsaken hole'. But I knew that when I went it would be in my own good time.

In the weeks which followed my return my wife and I felt utterly alone. Of course there was family indignation, rage of colleagues. Of course, a few of the people met by chance in the street, murmured their sympathy. Our friends, the Rosenfield sisters, journalists, attempted to make something of a fuss in their newspaper. But, generally, there was a feeling of remoteness and isolation. The subject was dead. And, perhaps, most cutting of all, when business took me into the City Hall, men in the public service whom I had known for years, dodged down corridors or dived round corners to avoid me, to avoid being seen near me by any of their employers. One fellow of supposedly progressive views, stumbled and nearly broke his neck on the marble staircase in his flushed stampede.

Some time after, the committee had its annual visit of inspection of the museum and art gallery, and I took a wicked pleasure in compelling the Chairman to introduce me to Mary O'Malley. We became good friends thereafter. Later she told me that when in Dublin a short time before the business she mentioned my name to her friend Valentin Iremonger, the poet, and he had told her to support my candidature as I was a decent chap and the right man for the job. Hence that unfortunate letter.

33

Stanley Spencer

Of the Lloyd Patterson Collection for a long time hung together in a small room, it was Stanley Spencer's *The Betrayal* which best survived the erosions of familiarity. Even the fact that this was the painting most queried by visitors and so having to be explained and justified a thousand times, or that it was in demand for borrowing by exhibition organizers elsewhere never diminished its interest for me. Painted in 1922, it belongs to the artist's best period, expressing his originality with none of the suggestion of crankiness which sometimes interfered with the impact of later works.

Later, we were given, through the Friends of the National Collections of Ireland, as being, very likely, the only gallery in the country not too hidebound to accept it, a long canvas *The Bridesmaids* which had been commissioned by the present Lord Moyne from one of Spencer's sketches for his *Marriage of Cana* sequence. A parlour choked with heavy Victorian furniture, swarming with young girls and children, and, under the table, a fat infant crawling over the open pages of a wallpaper compendium, it became known to our attendants as *Arses and Legs*.

Stanley had a brother, Harold, who lived in Belfast, in whom the family likeness was strong. He was a musician; I recall him first playing the violin in the tiny orchestra at the Little Theatre before the war. His daughter Daphne, a small slender pale blonde girl, was a secretary in the local region of the B.B.C., and a great favourite with her uncle. After the war, Stanley went over to stay with Harold and his family, and after Harold's death he continued his annual visits.

I had no trouble in getting to know him, for *The Betrayal* proved a firm bond; and, in addition, he came a firm friend of Zoltan Frankl who acquired three of his paintings, *The Adoration of the Old Men*,

Christ before Pilate and *Caulkers*, one of the Clyde shipbuilding series. Consequently my memoires of this powerful artist merge into one experience, the strands not to be disentangled or dated with any precision. A very small man with a red shiny nose and cheeks below the wide sparkle of his glasses and the long grey fringe of hair, there was something boyish or urchin-like about him. I never thought of him as elderly or even middle aged, and while gloriously solipsist, he retained a childlike innocence and cunning, never adopting the rhetoric or pomposity of the Great Man.

He was sufficiently interested in the work of other artists to look and comment, demonstrating, to me, for instance, just how well composed Lavery's *Twelfth of July* really was; and once having been taken to an amateur painter's exhibition, he declared 'I like these. I only hope he doesn't get any better'.

My first broadcast interview with him took place, for acoustic reasons, in the large goods lift at the Gallery, a matter of only a few minutes. But when John Boyd wanted a full scale job, we met in a B.B.C. studio, where Stanley talked for about two hours, my questions being rather supererogatory. However, in preparing my brief, prompted by the hint of Stanley's early *John Donne Enters Heaven*, I recalled Henry Vaughan's *The Retreat* and looked it up, and then found that he accepted my application of the lines, that he was indeed one who

> had not walk'd above
> A mile or two from (his) first love

The recording had, of course, to be trimmed to a fifteen minutes' span, and I still, probably in vain, hope that the full tape is preserved in the vaults; for when later he broadcast on the Third Programme, his talk lacked the direction that my questions had supplied before. He certainly was, as a released prisoner I once met on the Heysham boat said of himself, 'addicted to the talk', but always of an autobiographical kind.

There would be little point in my attempting to retell the stories he told me, for hundreds must have heard them too, and as they say, biographers must eat. I shall risk mentioning a couple of anecdotes, as perhaps more typical than others: Roy de Maistre recalling a great Garter service in Windsor Castle, and when the notabilities were waiting for their cars at the end of it, the whole flow of traffic was dammed for Stanley pushing his famous perambulator with his painting kit piled in it; and Stanley's own note on a Royal encounter, when in 1950 he was bidden to the Palace for his C.B.E., and took a picture for the Queen in a paper bag, disconcerting the flunkies and upsetting protocol. And in Belfast where we know the ways of shipyard folk, we enjoyed his remembering being in Port Glasgow as a war artist, and liking the working people that he lodged with, and when he drew a number of their portraits and presented them, these became by far the best framed works of his he ever saw; the best of craftsmanship and the best of material going into their making. One story, however, of an Irish provenance, deserves to be set down for fear it should be lost. Staying at Annalong with the painter-poet Patric Stevenson one day the two artists were out sketching in the wooded fringes of a large estate, when the lady of the manor, tweedy and brogued, tramped in upon them. Patric introduced Stanley as the Royal Academician, knowing his lady. After expressing her interest in art and her love for all things beautiful, she invited Stanley to call on her at the big house, sometime, adding 'And remember, Mr Spencer, the front door'. Which, for me, fixes forever that urchin appearance with the too long, unbrushed overcoat, the uncombed fringe and the umbrella.

Once when we had tea at Harold's widow's flat, Stanley took me into his bedroom to show me what he was working at. A canvas was pinned to the wall, low down, and he explained that he sat on the floor to paint. It was one of the Cookham Regatta series. The drawing was finished, and he was applying the pigment carefully so that a definite section of the painting was complete while the rest remained bare canvas. He was, as he called it, 'doing his knitting'. Although more detailed in Spencer, the dry deliberation of the surface marked a whole generation of English painters. It was only when, years later, I saw a retrospective exhibition of John Minton's work at a time when *tachisme* was all the rage, that I realized just how dry his finish was, for even by then my eye had come to expect some variation and vigour in the paint surface.

I always admired his landscapes and enlarged flower or plant paintings and portraits; but these he dismissed as pot boilers, moving on to speak of his real work, the work which he never could afford to do. But I was glad that no difficulty arose when I had a half-length portrait of Daphne which I had seen at Tooths, sent over for the Art Sub Committee's approval. So with three of his paintings in the gallery's collections, with Frankl's by now four – a fine *Self Portrait* of 1951, painted in Belfast having been snapped up, and with several other locally owned canvasses and drawings, I arranged a small Spencer Exhibition in June 1954. One scarcely known piece, a *Crucifixion* belonging to Everard Spence, proved an exciting demonstration of his idiosyncratic Bible-Cookham merger, the cross constructed of an iron crowbar and a wooden slat, the crown of blossoming wild roses, set in a meadow outside his native village.

I have always felt the essential Englishness of Spencer's work, the Pre-Raphaelite particularity of his vision of nature, the Dickensian tendency to caricature in his people, a Rowlandson coarseness, one aspect of which still persists in seaside comic postcards, the heavy Crabbe-like concern with tombstones and small plants. But it was not until I had lived in England for a while that I realized the full richness of the national quality in him. For in the lovely carved undersides of the best misericords in many an old parish church – we do not have the like in Ireland – I saw the English tradition to which he so inalienably belonged.

And not only in his art but in his personality was he English of the English, not least in his addiction to talk, for it is one of the most erroneous of beliefs that the English are a silent, reserved people; in fact, their most characteristic expression is the monologue. Expression, I say, not art form, for in spite of some magnificent but infrequent triumphs in the mode, such as Wordsworth's *Prelude*, their talk lacks rhythm, colour and invention.

I have sometimes thought of planning an exhibition of four painters to epitomize the national qualities of the main groups in these islands. Stanley Spencer beyond all question for his folk, and Jack B. Yeats for ours; but which of the Scots is so indigenous yet so emblematic, Peploe, Fergusson, Anne Redpath? And what Welshman dare sing out in that company, Ceri Richards, David Jones, Kyffen Williams?

Then in June 1958 the Spencer Exhibition in Cookham was announced. We set off down the map along the roads with hawthorn blossom beginning to tarnish on the hedges, and the young corn *brairding* in the fields. When we pulled in for petrol, a cheerful mechanic, a rooted man in spite of his calling, made sure we saw the limestone spread of the White Leaf Cross and instructed us to turn left up the hill towards Lacey Green, if we wanted a 'priddy' view of the Chiltern Hundreds. Much sooner than we had anticipated, we observed the yellow arrows of the Automobile Association, and following their points we parked in a sandy lane in a drift of cars, and walked to the church grounds.

Paying our halfcrowns at a wooden hut, we equipped ourselves with catalogues, leaflets, a good little history of the church, and the current issue of the parish magazine, on its cover a photograph of Stanley looking up to the Vicar. Towards the back of the magazine there was a paragraph which hit the right note: 'During the exhibition of Mr. Spencer's pictures we want to keep the flowers in church specially attractive and fresh. If anyone during this period has flowers they can spare, will they please contact Mrs. Vanderfleet (Bourn End 505)'.

In the vicarage, three rooms had been cleared of all movable furniture and hung with about forty paintings. There were some old friends among these,

Swan Upping and *Kings, Cookham Rise* with its thicket hedges and the labelled standard roses, and that magnificently vulgar portrait of a Mayoress; and, at the foot of the stairs, a small landscape of the tide's edge, a stony beach, and white walls. We recognized the place; the title was *The Foreshore at Whitehouse, N. Ireland 1952* and a note read 'painted while staying in Northern Ireland with my brother, Harold'.

The catalogue had a sketch plan of the village, with every name carefully placed, with arrows marking the artist's stance and the view he saw therefrom; a unique document no parallel to which could easily be compiled for any other British painter, for who else 'has not walk'd above a mile or two from his first love'.

All the while Stanley had been working at an easel in the church yard. The painting when finished was to be auctioned for church funds. When he took a break, the picture on its easel was carried into the vicarage hall, and a note attached to it giving the highest offer to date. When we were there it was £375, and an embarrassing incident occurred, when a tall stout lady in a felt hat misreading the figure as £3. 7. 6., marched round loudly looking for Stanley to offer him £3. 10. 0.

He was clearly pleased to meet us again and crowed and chuckled, introducing me to everyone in sight as 'This is my friend John Hewitt. He and his wife have come all the way from Coventry to see my exhibition'. While I was talking to the art collector Sir Beddington-Behrens, to whom I had just been introduced, Stanley drew Roberta aside to complain in a low voice, pointing his thumb over his shoulder, 'He left me for Kokoschka'.

As we walked from the vicarage to the church, I noticed how many of the tombstones in the freshly mown grass had scrolls and winged cherub's heads, and how one in particular, with a flying angel blowing a trumpet, looked as if it had jumped, straight out of the artist's most characteristic imagining.

There were groups of young people sprawling among the slabs eating a picnic lunch, and when I drew Stanley's attention to them away from his endless flow of talk, he said 'Yes. They do look like a buckshee Resurrection'.

In the church, a good type of the English Parish Church, with its merry jumble of architectural and decorative styles, Tudor reliefs, Regency marbles, Victorian glass, were hung the religious paintings and they looked at home as never before. Threading round the pillars and pew ends, along the aisles, Stanley kept up his expository monologue, pausing now and then to greet an old friend, introduce us as from Coventry, and say, when we had left them, something like 'That's Dot Wooster, from *The Visitation*'.

I did not like the new *Crucifixion*, painted for the Aldenham School Chapel. It seemed to me too brutal and eccentric, with the ugly nails sprouting improbably from the hammer-men's mouths; but the eight small paintings of *Christ in the Wilderness* intended to be followed by thirty-two others to make out the forty days and fill the lattens in the chancel roof, which had seemed so odd before and unrelated to Spencer's *oeuvre*, now became relevant and right; when we came upon them propped round the chancel walls and, with a flick of the eye could lift and set them where they should ultimately belong.

And when we left the church to see the village itself – Roberta also wanted to visit the Nursery School, a very special example of its kind and celebrated throughout the movement – it seemed hard to tell reality in this context. You may know the Constable country from the gallery wall or from over the Suffolk/Essex hedges, but the artist, as a person, glances only briefly from the memoirs and the anecdotes. Paradoxically, although John Constable could say and write highly individual things, in his painting he appears a force of nature like a strong slow flowing stream, or a rushing cloud, anonymous, inevitable. Here at Cookham for a brief June afternoon, place, man and work were held in a unity of being and feeling, an experience never likely to be repeated, but to be remembered as long as life.

After that I only saw Stanley once. He was commissioned by the staff and former pupils of the Teachers' Training College in Coventry to make a portrait drawing of Jane Brown the Principal. One afternoon Stuart Robinson, head of the College Art Department, and, I suspect, instigator of the commission, called at the Gallery to tell me that Stanley was outside in the car and would like to say hello.

Just at that moment the presentation ceremony was taking place in the entrance hall, of a very handsome Standard Car of 1907. So I urged Stuart to drag Stanley in, if only for five minutes. When he came in, he looked tired and old, for he had had a serious illness not long before. The car was being handed over to the Museum by Alick Dick, at that time, the boy-wonder of the Motor Industry. So when I brought Stanley over to see the great yellow vehicle, I suddenly thought that it would be amusing to introduce the artist to the tycoon. I did. And it was evident that neither had ever heard of the other. However, Stanley, unabashed, plunged back to the always springing fountain of his early memories, and said that he remembered how the doors of the old well-made motorcars always made the same sound as a horse carriage door on shutting, and asked permission to open and bang the high car door. That is my last memory of him, individual and in character.

Always an irritant or troublesome problem to the fashionable art critics of his time who had no pigeon hole the right shape for that dove of the spirit, but who nevertheless could not easily ignore his power and originality, Stanley received his knighthood, and died not many months after the door-banging. And the sting of death was as so often in the official biography which only intermittently and for brief passages revealed the likeness of the man I knew.

34

Silver Jubilee

July 1954 signalized the twenty-fifth anniversary of the opening of the Museum and Art Gallery building, and so we had to celebrate the Silver Jubilee. A special exhibition of our principal possessions was organized, and the opening of this by the Governor of Northern Ireland, the head of our little state, was to provide the appropriate occasion for the speechifying.

As Bill Seaby, the Director, was so far as Belfast was concerned, not yet even a two year old, and as Alfred, senior of us all in service, had not been in good health, the responsibility of providing the factual commemorative summary devolved upon me who had seen twenty-three and a bit of the twenty-five years worked out in practice. So I said nothing to anybody and went ahead preparing my oration. I did not fear any competition from the public representatives, for, in my day, the level of municipal oratory was miserably low.

Now, the Governor, Lord Wakehurst, a big, handsome, florid man, was also a cultivated person, by far the best of the three Governors Northern Ireland had had since its inception. The first of these, the Duke of Abercorn, had been one of the large landowners associated with the Unionist Party in its struggle against Irish Home Rule. As a member of the insurgent Provisional Government which had threatened a take-over of authority if the Asquith Cabinet persisted in its legislation, when the country was partitioned and the Six Counties cut off from the rest of Ulster and Ireland, he was awarded a job, this job. It was when studying an old photograph of the rebellious team, for they had had a postcard made of it, that I learned from my father that invaluable adage:

> Treason never prospers. What's the reason?
> When it prospers none dare call it treason.

The Duke whose family had been known in local history as the Hungry Hamiltons, occupied his high office with no noticeable distinction for many years. His successor, the Earl of Granville, who graduated from the Governorship of the Isle of Man, came to us with the strong recommendation of being a brother-in-law of King George the Sixth, their wives being sisters. One cynical leftwing agitator referred to this appointment as being a splendid example of Outdoor Relief. He was an elderly and sick man, and could do little more than perform the motions required by the constitution.

With Lord Wakehurst, it was very different, a healthy and intelligent man in the prime of life, he had already established himself as a first rate professional, having been Governor General of New South Wales with marked success. While over there, he had disturbed the official clique by commissioning William Dobell the Wild Man of Australian Art, and no pictorial flatterer, to paint his portrait for the historical record. Indeed, he approved the rather uncompromising result so heartily that Dobell was asked to paint Lady Wakehurst. He was also a very good amateur film maker.

I knew therefore that no reasonable departure from convention on my part would take a feather out of his cocked hat; and so on that Saturday forenoon, 10th July, when it came to my turn I stood up and read a long poem in blank verse, the whole 200 lines of it.

Going back over the history of the museum idea among us, I celebrated the contributions to it of William Thompson, pioneer naturalist, Emerson Tennent, Dickens' friend and historian topographer of Ceylon, Crozier, associate of Sir John Franklin and collector of penguin skins, and Robert Patterson, ironmonger and Fellow of the Royal Society.

> The common names of these uncommon men
> should ring and sing like lilt of balladry:
> Thompson, Tennent, Crozier, Patterson;
> And yet there is no ballad of their names,
> for we have lost the ear for public song.

I spoke, something of a King Charles' head with me, of the long struggle of William Gray to force the Municipality to adopt the existing legislation.

And in a paragraph I reminded my hearers that after twenty-five years the building was still far from complete, that it had been started as relief work in the Depression, and left when that Depression persisted. I also made a little allusion to the Irish origins of the very name Stranmillis.

> The tardy hour we now commemorate
> fell in the twilight of an ebbing day,
> when the wheels, turning slowly, paused and stopped,
> and men with empty pockets stood at corners;
> then the full project, trimmed to meet the moment,
> was carried forward to a half completion,
> set the high columns fronting to the trees,
> and left the bare bricks toothed along the flank.
> And so it stands, Stranmillis, the sweet stream
> of knowledge trickling where a flow should be,
> so closely walled the spring is overbrimmed.

The ticklish part came when I had to deal with living persons. I could not in honesty avoid referring to the Curator and his successor; so I ran them off with the remark that the council had

> … summoned men whose craft it was to tend
> the crowded objects fifty years had flung
> into the dusty corners …

The rest of us I rounded up, with Alfred first;

> those summoned to the service serving long
> and others beckoned later, serving still
> in their known several ways, this heritage,
> have by the nature of the causes served
> made life the richer for this hill-rimmed city.

And so in what might have been an awkward situation, enjoyed myself by asserting the bardic privilege.

35

Amsterdam, 1954

We flew into Schipol, the airport for Amsterdam, a pleasant estab-
lishment not too oppressive in the suggested, scale of its operations,
below us, since we crossed the foam-rim of the low coast, the recti-
linear fields and the tidy farms margined and gridded with the glint-
ing strips of water and the straight roads, Mondrian's country.
Amsterdam struck us, wandering around, immediately as a friendly
acceptable and accepting city; trim and ordered; the canals parallel,
even the whores sitting framed in the lit windows of the port quar-
ter. It seemed a Protestant place, the churches infrequently evident
in the general architectural consistency. The Oude Kerke, amus-
ingly, entered through the caretaker's front door and then, back
door, one in the low thick wall of houses which hug and huddle
round the large old shell. Inside, for us, the principal interest and
surprise, the set of strongly cut and coarsely imagined misericords,
more vigorous than any I had seen before – I never go into a church
of any antiquity without tipping or trying to tip up the choir seats.

The tall tower of the dark Westerkerke across the canal, with men
at a canvas-canopied stall eating herring, in the foreground, and a
flowery barge slowly floating past in the middle distance, lodged itself
in my imagination until, two months later, I made the first draft of a
poem 'The Spectacle of Truth', to find its final shape in *New Poems
1960*, one of the very few poems of mine sparked off by experiences
or images out of my foreign travels. Otherwise, the curiosity of the
Portuguese Synagogue with the great curved brackets of its brass
chandeliers, and its, to me, novelly organized interior, made it the
most memorable building I saw there; but no poem came out of it.
Rembrandt's House, next stop on the tourist's itinerary, had, for me,
no sensation of having been lived in: that troubled spirit left no aura

there. Its sole value was in the fine sets of the famous etchings on the panelled walls. It was outside Amsterdam, in Peter's Church, Leyden, the Mauritshuis, and in Hoorn that I felt the quiddity of the Dutch thing in a more concentrated, masterly shape.

An evening reception by the Minister of Education at the Rijksmuseum gave us a leisurely and unimpeded chance to tour the galleries, for, as ever, the French never strayed at all from the buffet (froid); and here the easily taken impressions, reinforced by repeated visits, for our hotel was close at hand, were of the strength and limits of Dutch Painting. They were all present, the greater and the lesser names, the long familiar *genres*; Rembrandt with *The Night Watch*, spot lit as in a chapel; *The Syndics* forever inspecting the candidate; the tender *Jewish Bride* pulsating to the gentle pressure of hand on breast and hand on hand; the infinitely pathetic *Self-portrait as the Apostle Paul*; and the Vermeers, the sharply focussed *Little Street*; the wholesome, permanent *Cook*, the pitcher pouring eternally, the pot never brimmed; the *Young Woman Reading a Letter* as hushed as an annunciation. Of the others, Hals' relaxed *Married Couple* the textures proudly carried; Jacob Van Ruisdael's *Mill near Wijk*, archetype and ancestor of so many landscapes yet still unblemished by its degenerate progeny; Paul Potter's *Horses in a Field*, for once in the work of this genial unambitious man, as intense as George Stubbs; and Pieter Saenredam's *Interior of a Church*, as chastely and scrupulously designed as any cubist could conceive, still firmly rooted in visual experience and somehow timeless in its placidity. These for me were the revelations and extensions of my awareness; the Ostades, the Jan Steens, I accept for their evocations of grumbling squalling existence; the de Hoochs, the Terborchs with their great sophistication I approach less closely, held, at arm's length, by the obtrusive expertise. The bloom on peach, on grapes, the lemon rind, the polished surfaces of metal, the fly, the raindrop, leave me utterly indifferent. Winter scenes, even Avercamps, I can never look at without hunting for the figure at one side or in the distance making water against a wall, or a tree.

It was an abrupt contrast to visit the Stedelijk, where first the Chagalls took my attention, armed now with Atzik Manger's clue about Yiddish folklore. Then among the native painters, after the sombre Breitners, *The Potato Eaters* period of Van Gogh, the transition was easy. Then the brightening canvasses and the singing colour, the clouds and blossoms, on to the last little self portraits, each distorted in its own sad way, pinched, lopsided, grown perceptibly madder and madder, until, wrung with pity, your mind painshot, you move into the next room and greet as a welcome friend, the intelligent and supremely clearheaded Toulouse Lautrec, and take your bearings once more, comparatively sane.

My chief response was, what was the point of this? To demonstrate the headlong collapse of a fine human mind? An appeal to the morbid part of us that lives on case-histories, Krafft Ebing or *News of the World?* Or is it neurosis speaking to neurosis across the wasteland of modern society – the spectator finding in art what he brings to it? Can these then be considered works of art? They must be, by some of authority, taken so, exhibited in an Art Gallery, given the warranty of their *milieu*. And to children and willing-to-learn-but-uneducated adults, what will these signify? An insistence on the abnormal, the eccentric, as the normal, the balanced? I find it difficult enough to keep standards in mind in those areas where standards can be applied, and quality can be claimed, I, stubborn-minded, who have looked at thousands of paintings and read hundreds of books. So, in fairness to those whose minds are in the making, these paintings should not be shown on the walls of a public gallery with other paintings by other men, with the better paintings of their own maker; they should be kept in a cabinet for students and scholars of the arts and the sciences of the mind to inspect or consult. Every poet has written bad poems sometime, every painter has produced bad paintings, failures of his intention. There is so much worthwhile that we have only time for the best, who have other things to do besides look at paintings.

Yet what is that best? We are brought against a large problem of Art now: the romantic image of the mad, or, at the very least, eccentric artist, the wild one, the outsider, the outcast, a hangover from the Bohemian of last century. And now the madness has passed into the work – no longer the squalid man producing the lily of perfection seeping and spitting out in formlessness; the panels or canvasses showing violence to have been done to them, scorched, blistered, sawn, nailed, perforated, gashed, slashed, the smooth surface violated. Were Vincent's mad eyes staring in this direction? Surely not, for although however mad his work it always made an objective reference; a mad *face*, a mad *flower*, a mad *field*: and that objectivity left a foothold for sense to steady itself on, for the climb either way.

I have sometimes been challenged on this matter of standards; though not as often as I expected or should have liked. It began with Cubism, Abstraction, Collage, Surrealism, Dada, Negro sculpture, then Child Art, Art as therapy; now, Tachisme, Action painting, Assemblage, Pop Art, must be added to the list. Is it then possible to isolate and define any qualities or characteristics common to Mondrian painting, a Jackson Pollock, a Schwitter's box of oddments, an Annigoni portrait, a child's representation of himself with a balloon, a Ben Nicholson panel, a schizophrenic's drawing from a mental hospital? Yet each of these has its admirers and advocates, honest, serious-minded folk who care passionately. I attended an auction in Sotheby's some time ago, and out of perhaps a hundred or a hundred and fifty man-made objects, a Moore bronze, a Ben Nicholson still life, a Munnings' painting of a horse made the highest prices of the day. So these had certainly one quality or element in common: high desirability.

The Mauritshius at the Hague, a comely early seventeenth century mansion in the Renaissance style, is certainly one of the smaller but more pleasing of the famous galleries. From the outside, the Rijksmuseum gives no hint of its contents. Here, you expect and find lovely things, a fine Memling portrait, a characteristic deposition by Rogier van de Weyden, a strong Holbein of a man with a falcon; but it is the Terborch *Lady Writing a Letter*, the Metsu *Company Making Music* which seem most inevitably at home. Carel Fabritius' *Goldfinch* chained to his perch, the Vermeer *Head of a Young Girl* already belong to the literate world, their colour prints adorning ten thousand walls. Yet here, too, is Rembrandt's uncomfortable *Anatomy Lesson*, the bearded students looking three ways simultaneously, at the cadaver, at Dr Tulp's left hand, at you looking at the picture; his self portraits that span nearly forty years, the last, the soft, old womanly, sad one; and the free sketch of the two negroes which makes all paintings of negroes since, sentimental, vulgar, or merely superficial paint, like John's.

We were fortunate enough when the Congress was over, to find ourselves in Haarlem, marvelling at the wide canvasses of the clubbable Companies of Archers, the ruffs, the faces, the hands, the hats, the halberds, the banners, superbly organized. To know Franz Hals of the brisk, confident portraits is to know less than half of his greatness. Think of what Sargent did with the Allied Leaders of the First World War, in the National Portrait Gallery and look again at these celebrations. Yet it is, of course, that other pair of groups which establish his quality forever: *The Governors and the Ladies' Committee of the Old Man's Alms House*, the first, with the assured, the calculating, the kindly, the sodden and the sad faces, each in himself a person, and in the second, the stupid, the dull, the malicious, the hard, as tough a gang as ever whisked away the second blanket by the calendar or stopped an old man's tobacco money. When we add up the account of man's honesty, make an item of these, for you will find little to set near them in the audit, except, maybe, Goya's assault on his Royal family.

One Congress excursion took us through the sandy, scrubby National Park to Otterlo, to the Kroller-Muller Museum, a crouching building improbably sited there; in my experience, the most aptly designed for its function, its small rooms and comprehensible scope making impossible the museum fatigue of the long walls and the parquet floors. Yet it was Henri Van de Velde, who began as a contriver of curly chairarms and twiddley bindings in the days of Art Nouveau, who conceived this setting for pleasure. The collection is, what they show of it, consistently good; perhaps too many Van Goghs, but Seurat's high kicking *Le Chahut*, Renoir's fiddler *Clown*, Léger's *Soldiers Playing Cards*. Gleizes, Gris, Picasso, Braque, present the School of Paris at its essential best. It is only when you think back over it, that you realize the implied aversion from expressionism which makes it a loaded, limited judgement on the epoch of its concern; the culture is perhaps too pure to be fully effective.

Another Congress excursion of an unusual kind was the visit to Leyden where, in the afternoon, anchored within the sturdy Gothic of St Peter's Church where the ship models hang becalmed in air, as guests at the Solemn Meeting of the Senate of the State University, we were present when honorary doctorates of literature were conferred on E.M. Forster, Jean Schlumberger, and Victor E. Van Vriesland. The last, a Dutch poet, had been at both the Venice and the Edinburgh Conferences, a lean man, delicate-looking, with rimless glasses and always carrying a thick walking stick.

The Professor of English presenting E.M. Forster, read a sound essay on his achievement and importance, another experience which further confirmed my high regard of the linguistic resource of the Dutch, where, in every shop, a bright girl will respond in excellent English, and, if you stop in the street to consult your map, a lad on a bicycle will jump off and hurry over to offer his help. It was gratifying to be there when Forster was saluted, for there can be no better representative of the best of English culture than this quiet deep unobtrusive man. We had not seen him since his Belfast visit, but he remembered us with the same unaffected friendliness which he had then evidenced; and later, at the big celebration dinner sponsored by the Dutch Press, as he was passing behind my chair on his way to the top table he patted my shoulder as if giving a sign that among all these foreigners and faces we were on the same side.

Silone another of the same quality was not at this Congress, Italy being represented by the cordial, limping Count Umberto Morra. Once again there were the old regular *conferenciers;* the little Catalan professor with his manifestoes and leaflets, the Belgian professor and his English wife welcomed by and welcoming everybody whose face looked even vaguely familiar, the stout pasty faced, trundling Dane, the scrawny Indian wearing the white cap of another Congress, Czokor, with his cape and leonine head, like a music hall representation of a Middle European man of letters of the pre-1914 vintage. A newcomer was James T. Farrell whose *Studs Lonigan* had been one of our books when we moved on from Upton Sinclair and Theodore Dreiser, small, square, solid, dark, he seemed every ounce an Irish Catholic in appearance.

Charles Morgan, now filling the role of International President, was much in evidence in public and private sessions. To him I took an instant dislike. Like an aged matinee idol reduced to provincial repertory, he was altogether too smooth and bland, with, behind his diplomatic gait, an obvious conceit of himself, brass, a little tarnished, against the fine gold of Forster. Among the other English delegates, it was with lively curiosity that we encountered William Cooper at the London airport, incredibly trim, in an open neck shirt and with bathing trunks, an orange and a Penguin paperback in his string bag. And with Daniel George, that superb anthologist, again many congressional longueurs were lit and enlivened by his idiosyncratic wisecracks and anecdotes.

But looking back now with the benefit of hindsight, incomparably the most important foreigner there was Bertolt Brecht. Among the English-speaking delegates his presence caused little comment, for I presume that like myself they were ignorant of his stature. Our insularity in this was no less than shocking. But mere literary folk might be forgiven when British theatre people who should have known better were in no better case. Not so long ago John Gielgud had written, 'I did not at all care for Mr Brecht's article. It seems to be obscure, pointless and humourless. Mr Brecht presumably writes his own scripts, and it might be interesting to see a performance of one of them'. Among the continentals it was obvious that he was an authoritative figure, not that he was surrounded by disciples or admirers. Indeed, apart from Johannes Tralow his yoke-fellow, only Jan Parandowski the Polish prosewriter, seemed on terms of much cordiality with him. Parandowski is himself a remarkable person, a tall, spare, stooped man, for thirty years leader of PEN in his country, he has survived wars and revolutions with no loss of dignity or humanity. In Warsaw in 1962 I heard him not unkindly referred to as a salamander, for he has faced and outfaced dangers beyond the imagining of writers on these offshore islands whose greatest grouse is income tax or political indifference to the importance of the creative artist in society.

Brecht was below medium height, clean shaven, with a small round head, his short cropped hair dog's toothed against his brow, a cigar always in his mouth. He wore a kind of coarse grey tunic buttoned at the throat, without a tie – a military sort of attire from which it seemed all badges of rank or distinction had been removed. A friendly smiling little man, he reminded me instantly of my uncle Dick, padding purposefully round the corridors, not in any sense playing the great genius.

The international executive committee at each Congress is formed by the official delegates nominated from each centre meeting with the international secretariat, to consider the resolutions submitted for the public deliberations. It meets in private, and it was here that Brecht made his impact. Partnered by Tralow, a heavy, big, pale-faced sagging man, he kept up a steady fight to have certain resolutions adopted and others amended. The phrasing of these betrayed their political intention. Without fluster or temper, Brecht and Tralow, now one proposing, now the other, turned and swerved, line by line and sentence by sentence, as either was headed off. I saw them at times indomitable as a fox terrier and a bloodhound, heroic as a pocket-size Don Quixote and a large sad Sancho Panza. Most of the afternoon it took, but in the long and complicated run the sure discretion of the secretary steered the committee along its constitutional course. Marvelling at Brecht's ingenuity, I voted against his proposals with the majority. When, afterwards, I spoke to him of my admiration for his nimble tactics, he took my words like a shy friendly girl.

Brecht's presence at the Amsterdam Congress was due to the circumstance that he held an Austrian passport and had a Swiss bank account. Although a year or two later I saw *Mother Courage* at the Unity Theatre, it was not until February 1959, when I attended a performance of *Der Kaukasische Kreidekreis* in Dresden, that I became fuller possessed of Brecht's significance and joined the growing company of his admirers, counting myself fortunate that even for a brief spell I had seen Shelley plain.

His value for us is not only in his dramatic work, his verse or his fiction, important though these are, but lies, above all, in his resourceful attitude to life, his exercise of the Christian skills of dove and serpent. For Joyce the lifelines were silence, exile, cunning. Brecht improved on this by returning from exile when possible and necessary, to persist in his cunning, surviving the ambiguities of the Ulbricht regime and Soviet disapproval of his formalism to show theatre the way to extend its scope in a manner appropriate to the tasks and problems of the century, and to demonstrate that new circumstances require new kinds of heroism. We have moved into an epoch when romantic gestures have become irrelevant; we must be craftier than our adversaries.

Between sessions one day, I was approached by Adriaan Morriën, short-story writer and poet, tallish, dark, younger looking than his forty years. He had discovered that I was Irish, and told me of a friend of his who was contemplating a holiday in Ireland and would like some practical advice.

So it was that the next evening we met Jan Hanlo at Morrien's apartment. Jan, a very little taller than I, lean, with a red fringe of beard rimming his lower jaw, looked very like some portraits of Van Gogh, but with a much better head of hair. He was a poet, an experimental poet. That seemed to be the distinctive quality; you were or were not experimental; and so far as I could judge the experiments remained about the Dada level. Jan's most popular poem, published in a finely printed bulletin, was called *The Sparrow* and consisted of the Netherlandish equivalent of 'chirp' repeated eighteen times. But he had, of course, written more serious verses than these.

I asked about the standing of poets from the English-speaking countries. Yes, they liked Dylan Thomas and George Barker. Of the Americans, Robert Lowell, due, in a measure, to his having lectured in Holland fairly recently. I inquired about Yeats. Yes, Yeats too, but Raymond Holst, an elderly poet was most influenced by Yeats and the Irish writers. He had reconstituted some of the Irish legends in his verse. Of the experimentalists Lucebert was the acknowledged leader. And like Jan, he too was not attending the PEN Congress, which was not for real writers.

Then at the celebration dinner in Leyden, when we were all seated, a tall dark young fellow in a long coat or cloak, marched in and strutted silently round the horse-shoe of tables like a threatening demon, or somebody playing at being one, and strode out again. That was Lucebert in characteristic pose. And, quite properly, no one seemed much impressed. Since those days he has taken to picture-making, rather in a manner akin to that of Dubuffet, a kind of grimy Child Art, being included in an exhibition of Dutch painting which I handled in Coventry.

Jan, we saw more of, for he took us on several drinking excursions which lasted a long time, as, in Holland, closing times are properly late and not, apparently, standardized. As bar after bar closed, we edged to another still open. In one artist-frequented cafe, the boys and girls looked exactly like their British contemporaries, and I remember thinking it odd that young rebels should conform with such astonishing accord in garb, hairstyles and behaviour. Later I found this to be true even behind the Iron Curtain, for, in 1962, the members of the Krakow group looked very like their fellows in England and were doing the same sort of thing to canvas and hardboard, while the young girls in the coffee bar in the basement of the International Press Club, sat long-haired, tragic-eyed and blackstockinged, exactly as their counterparts in any British town with an art school were sitting at the same hour.

The upshot of our meeting Jan was that, later in the summer, he arranged to visit Ireland, beginning with the North.

He came off the overnight boat and called at my office, and as I was clearing things up before taking him to the Glens where Roberta had gone a couple of days before, he asked me very hesitatingly 'Would we see a mountain like this – and a white horse before it?', showing me a well worn section of a tourist brochure which he had found some years before and had hoarded. It was a coincidence, for 'the mountain' was our Tievebulliagh, a hill of 1,300 feet, above Cushendall, with a very characteristic profile not unlike that of a sharply nippled breast, about four miles as the crow, or, in this instance, as the raven flies to the west of the cottage. So, within the next twenty-four hours, Jan saw his mountain and the white horse. Our wild fuchsia hedges delighted him, and he took photograph after photograph of the flowers which he had only known in gardens at home.

His English was very good – teaching it was his business, although this was his first footing among speakers of our tongue. From him I learned something of the problems of a writer in a minority language, the pull of French and English with their immeasurably vaster audiences, the sense of loyalty to one's own vernacular in a shrinking company. I had, in Amsterdam, bought a small booklet of verse from a poet with sideburns called Steen, in which the poems appeared in French and English translations as well as the original Dutch, but in neither of the translations did any of them seem worth the labour of carrying over. The principle Jan accepted as one way out of the dilemma.

Besides the mountain he wanted to see a bog: the first rather obviously because the Low Lands are, in fact, low; indeed, a longing for high hills is something which we ourselves have come to experience in our sojourn in the English Midlands: the second, because he had spent his childhood in Limburg, a boggy country now drained and tidied, and he wanted to recapture the sensations and emotions of that time. We showed him what bog we could, then we directed him to other mountains more impressive than Tievebulliagh, to the Mournes in County Down, and to the wide bogs of the middle of Ireland.

Although a Catholic and a man who gave hints of fierce, disturbing religious experience, I felt close to him: he seemed a bridge to Europe; his communication guaranteed that I belonged to this age and this world. Something of a recluse, he changed his lodgings frequently, using a Post Box number as accommodation address. It was sad but not surprising that my last letters remained unanswered.

We stayed on some days after the Congress, for the Rijksmuseum is a big place, and, in addition, Roberta wanted to see how they ran their nursery schools. Then, with only twenty-four hours to go and our currency run down, I took the risky and unsophisticated step of spending most of what we had left on an American Express bus tour. Determined patiently to endure our fellow trippers who, by their unchastened accents were clearly American, we found to our surprise and delight there, one man, an oil technician returning from the Middle East to the States with his wife and young family, prove a wise and agreeable companion. He had lived open-eyed and open-minded, and was going back a true member of humanity, convinced of the inescapable part his people and nation must play in a world where the perils of war and starvation challenge the possibility of survival. And because of that just, serious man we felt more kindly towards the great republic.

So we travelled through the obvious tourist programme. At Alkmaar we watched the flat-hatted porters swing and lift the round cheeses on the sledge-shaped cradles; we attended a flower auction where the buyers sit in the tiered desks ready to press the buttons as the great hand of the clock face drops nearer the price they are prepared to bid; we climbed up inside a windmill (they are all kept simply as local colour now); we stopped beside the statue of the fabulous boy who stuffed his fist into the leaking dyke; at a workshop where a man shaped *klompen* out of the white wood; I bought a pair my size which proved useful in the muddy fields of the Glens for years after; we inspected the great model of the canals and polders of the country where an attendant demonstrated with a switch how the land had been flooded as the Nazis advanced; at Haarlem the long lunch time we spent mostly with Franz Hals; we admired the sleek mobs of black and white cattle in the rectangular fields, and pointed out to each other the trestles on which the cut hay was piled, interesting to us who are familiar with other ways men have learned to save the hay in a wet country.

36

Brendan Boy

I was undressing for bed, my braces off my shoulders, when the telephone rang downstairs. I was asked in a thick Dublin accent 'Is dat John Hewitt? Ye won't know me but I'm a friend of Ben Kiely's. Me name is Behan, Brendan Behan. I'm ringin' ye to find out if ye could let me have a bed ...' I asked him where he was telephoning from: 'The top o' the Falls', that is, the Catholic side of the city.

In about half an hour the doorbell rang. When I opened it, a burly fellow lurched in, and, in the dim light of the hall, drew out of his pocket and showed me a letter from Radio Eireann to himself, as his visiting card. When we went upstairs to the flat, Roberta was up and had revived the ashes. She asked him if he would like a cup of tea, but as by an odd circumstance we had a single bottle of stout in the cupboard, he took that for preference.

His shoes were splattered with whitewash; his blue suit was crumpled; his open necked shirt not fresh that morning; from his upper lip a piece of sticking plaster hung by a single corner. I inquired about this. 'Och, John. I ran inta a bit o'bother', and that was all I ever learned about it. Regarding his shoes, he explained that he was a housepainter by trade, and was in the North, whitewashing lighthouses. This seemed to me so improbable an assertion that I felt instinctively that it could not be other than true: although there are, in fact, no lighthouses 'up the Falls'.

Once we had established each others' *bona fides* by way of cross reference, we settled down, we to listen, and he to talk. And it was soon clear that we were in the company of a master. Many of his stories that evening have since appeared in his published work, and although they may communicate to the reader, I feel, remembering that night and the stout fellow with the fat noble face and the

black curls, talking and singing melodiously, effortlessly, as the old
mother of James Hogg the Ettrick Shepherd, who said of her own
stories and songs that 'they were made for singing and no' for read-
ing … An' the worst thing o' a', they're nouther right spell'd nor
right setten down'. But one sustained exercise has not so far to my
knowledge been recorded. This was the description of the career
of an imaginary young Irish Republican politician in the wee
North; the sedition, the speech from the dock refusing to recog-
nize the court; the prison months; the martyr's home coming; the
election, and the refusal to take his seat in Parliament; the taking
of his seat and the seizing of the Mace in protest; the suspension;
the re-election; and finally the seconding of the Speech to the
Throne: each of these stages fully documented with news flashes,
speeches, appropriate songs. And the whole performance, rich in
its comedy, had also the cynical edge of one who knows how the
bright ideals tarnish in the common air of day. We went back to
bed about three o'clock.

In the morning by common agreement we let Brendan stay in
bed; but talking over breakfast, we both thought that, although he
had said nothing, he would very likely be hard up. So I left a ten
shilling note with Roberta to give him if it seemed appropriate.
When I returned at lunch time our guest had gone. He had had his
breakfast, and when Roberta was ironing he had sat and chatted for
awhile; then, suddenly, without warning, he leaped to his feet,
grabbed her hand and shook it, said 'T'anks a million' and fled
downstairs. Roberta was very put out that she had not had a chance
to give him the note, and kept on reproaching herself for not asking
bluntly if he stood in need of it.

Then a couple of days later, Brendan telephoned us from Dublin
to thank us for our hospitality. This pleased us greatly, for nowadays
the old custom of the bread and butter letter is dying out, and to
have this courtesy from the great talker was more than we had
expected. That overnight stay in its way became a little legend,
which came back to us enhanced by its journey: one version ran that
when Brendan rang me first, I asked where he was, and *sent* my car
for him. At that time we had no car. The second version was that we
not only sent the car for him, but pressed a five pound note in his

hand when he departed. It is strangely flattering and embarrassing to have been given out as more generous than in fact you are.

Maybe six months later I was telephoned at home, one lunchtime. It was Brendan. 'Where are ye ringing from?' 'Portstewart' (a town on the north Antrim coast about eighty miles distant). 'What in the name of God are ye doing there? 'I'm on a greyhound farm'. Greyhound farm or whitewashing lighthouses, an uncommon man must follow uncommon employment. It was for a bed that night, that he was ringing. He arrived very appropriately at tea time. The greyhound farm he made no effort to explain; but his presence in the North, over the border, was easily explained. He had had some difference of opinion with a *garda* in Dublin, so that his absence was necessary from that place for that time. After tea, as we had no stout in the house, I suggested that we adjourn round the corner to the Club Bar, where Mick the barman, who always called me doctor, was an affable man. On our way, Brendan stopped and said very quietly 'Before we enter this adjacent hostelry, John, I'd have ye know that I'm flat.' This was fair enough. I had invited him. And so handling no more than a single pint of porter, Brendan kept Mick and me, for it was a quiet, scarce night, with very little custom, in a continual tide of merriment. These incidents I report, partly to establish that when we knew him Brendan was the most temperate of men, and that his talk did not suffer any loss thereby.

So far it was only as a poet in Irish that Brendan had any standing as a writer. I was told by those qualified to give an opinion that his Irish verse is of high quality, and certainly the poem on Oscar Wilde, translated by Donagh MacDonagh has the right ring about it. But the first direct writing in English that I saw of his was when he became a columnist for *The Irish Press*. One article, in particular, was memorable, when, after the flooding of the Tolka, Brendan was going over the consequences and paid a kindly tribute to the *gardai* for their speedy and generous help to the stranded or unhoused inhabitants. The cordiality with which he congratulated them had all the more warmth coming from where it did.

We met him again in Grafton Street, Dublin. I asked him what he was engaged in just then. He explained that an organization, the name of which I have forgotten, but which existed to further the

Irish language, was sending him to the Aran Islands to gather the material for a book. 'For', said he, they're tryin' to wean me from me native tongue'. For all the bravura of his imagination and talk, with Brendan there is always a strong core of relentless honesty, as in that remark he insists that English is the spoken language of the nation. Similarly, he was, forever, declaring that pastoral Ireland was a legend, that the countryside was decaying, that the only life in the land was in its large towns and cities, that the future of Irish literature was as an urban art, that the great representative Irish writer of our time was Sean O'Casey, who found the creative springs of his drama in that very urban context.

The next time that we saw Brendan again, *The Quare Fellow* had established his name. For the first night of its production at the Group Theatre, Brendan was there, but we passed him unrecognized; and after the final curtain, when he made a tearful little speech, he fell off the stage. Often, I have thought of the fine talk that night by our hearth from the stranger who knew Ben Kiely and had rung our number with confidence 'after his bit o'bother'; and I am gratified that my wife and I are known to be hospitable folk.

As an addendum to this: some years after Brendan's visits, it was near Christmas time, Hamish Henderson, by now field collector of folksong for the School of Scottish Studies at Edinburgh University, called in unexpectedly. We asked what fortune brought him again to our fireside. He was, he said, on his way to Dublin to call with the Behans. Brendan, we supposed; but no; he had just heard of him. It was the old father and mother whom he sought, fountains of balladry, and the most important of the clan.

37

Vienna, 1955

Schwechat the airport for Vienna seemed a primitive sort of place after the slick functionalism of Zurich. The runways appeared all grass with small but, to my excitable imagination, hazardous haycocks littered about. The airport buildings were large wooden huts; and when we were inside the place swarmed with Russian soldiers, solid chunky little men, their uniforms familiar from press photographs. But in customs and passport control they were brisk without being officious, so that we found our bus without delay. Here, however, the fact that Vienna was still under the Four Power Control was made evident, for when the bus filled up, a British Army redcap with a gun slung over his shoulder, climbed in, shut the door and sat down beside the driver, for we were within the Russian Zone of occupation.

Amused a little by this hint of *The Third Man*, I wondered vaguely what use that single gun would be in an incident. Was the redcap there to repel a Soviet attack on us, or to make sure that no one jumped off our bus and escaped behind the Iron Curtain? But then the whole occupation had its comic side too; a great deal of the comedy arising from Russian insensitivity to the absurd or at least, the inappropriate.

The wellknown square, the Schwartzenberger Platz, had a tall pillar dedicated to the Unknown Red Army man in it, and at the base of this the first soviet tank to enter the city; and the square was now called The Stalinplatz, a piece of ostentatious provocation that, with the greatest sympathy, one could not overlook. Then beside the Danube, at the end of a bridge, was a brick coloured obelisk, memorial to the Red Navy, a shocking piece of nonsense.

The Hofburg was the centre of Allied Control; each of the four powers occupied a portion of the great block, and when each in turn was in control, the appropriate national standard was hoisted over the central flagstaff. Otherwise, the broad building was without token or sign of its temporary tenants, save on the extreme left, where over the Russian part were displayed two enormous photographs of Marx and Lenin. Here and there too in the Russian sector of the city were little showcases or stands with propaganda photographs and slogans exhibited in them. One which irked me in particular, had to do with workers' housing in some city in the U.S.S.R., photographs of buildings, tables of statistics, explanatory captions. To one who could remember reading of them, it seemed impertinent and without sensitivity to cry up Soviet achievements in the very place which had seen workers' housing pioneered in the great flats of the Karl Marxhof, the Lassallehof, the very flats which had been besieged and battered by Dollfus and his reactionaries, which had been, for a generation, a powerful symbol of the spirit and the strength of Social Democracy between the wars.

All in all, the Russians seemed to have been tactless, heavy-handed, without a saving sense of humour. And as this was my first direct experience of them, I was deeply disappointed. The Soviets had been savagely criticized so long as I could remember, since Dr Edward Coyle, my grandfather's physician, wrote a pamphlet declaring that Trotsky and Lenin were alcoholics and that the October Revolution had let loose an orgy of drunkeness on mankind. But with my innate scepticism I had offset this endless flood of malice as capitalist chagrin. I had not even wavered during the Russo–Finnish War. But now these little evidences of dullness, of insensitive authority, shot through with pompous megalomania, provided a startling lesson on how not to win friends and influence people. Yet I still ask myself if it would be possible for a government or a state to possess a sense of humour. And, if it were possible, would it be wise?

The famous Opera House was being rebuilt, but the company was performing elsewhere, and so we had the luck to hear Eric Fuchs in *The Magic Flute*.

Along the north of the city by the Danube there was still a good deal of war damage to be repaired, and the Prater with its great Orson Welles wheel, when we visited it, was sparsely attended and very dull.

Now, we had found that the bus tour in Holland on our last day had proved a venture well worth wearing the label of tripper for. So it seemed sensible to repeat it in Vienna. One evening a busload of us was bundled out to Grinsing, where, on our earlier passing that way we had seen the green wreaths hung over the tavern doors – good wine needs no bush – signifying the *heuriger* or the new vintage: and at Grinsing we were set down at a long table, given a small glass of bitter stuff, played at by a fiddler with a feather in his hat and bare knees, and then whisked off. At a Hungarian restaurant, we had a bowl of goulash, while a trio, again with feathers in their hats, but this time in red waistcoats, tore through a short repertory of familiar gipsy tunes. By now we realized that ours was only the first of four busloads of tourists, and that we were all tethered to the same round. So, after several other calls when we waited for the benches to fill up with our followers in the slower coaches, before the new wine was forthcoming and the fiddles began, we were brought to the peak of our tour of the Night Life of Vienna, a cabaret in a garish club with mirrored walls and ceilings, an enlarged version of a Parisian bordello I once visited. Here once again the public for the cabaret came almost entirely from our four buses. Bus parties can, in some circumstances, be the occasions for frolics or fun, if they are street excursions crammed with neighbours, or club excursions bulging with bottled journeymen of the same craft or interest; but from busloads of miscellaneous tourists with no common talking or singing point, no spontaneous sense of solidarity or companionship can emerge; so we hurtled and were herded through the night, growing colder, wearier, more isolated. The cabaret was, in fact, not at all bad. The principal dancers, clad only in jewels, a glittering diamond in each navel, were shapely and lithe. A woman performer got across the language barrier as an Austrian Gracie Fields, raucous, natural, good humoured, sentimental. The other singers, the jugglers were adequate. But the whole thing, except for those navel diamonds winking and sparking in infinite regression around and above us, was a flat end to a dreary evening.

Vienna with its imperial Baroque, the Hofburg; the Ringstrasse, the churches and the arcaded streets in the heart of it, was the first true capital I had seen. Paris, London, Amsterdam, Brussels, each has its character; but Paris has something of anonymous bureaucracy about it; London is a mess becoming a menace; Amsterdam, a well devised bourgeois republican town in spite of its monarchy, is a place in which I believe I could live with comfort and satisfaction, but its visual effect is not imperial, the heavy palace at the Dam has no lease in history. Until we saw Rome, Vienna had no rival in my mind.

Stephansdom seemed less of a man-made building than a cavern with lit altars, memorable chiefly for the harshly carved saints round the pulpit; the skinny Hieronymus with the flat hat, the kinder Ambrose with mitre and the wrinkled gloves, Augustine chin in hand, the fingers prodding his cheeks, and the scowling Gregory fingering a medal. These and the high half length of the sculptor himself, Anton Pilgram, peering out of the wall above our heads, remain for me the essence and quality of that great church. But with Karlskirche I can recollect hardly anything of its bleak interior; it is the outside, the portico flanked by the unattached Roman columns, their secular strength adding the authority of the state to the witness of the dome, which places the architect Fischer Von Erlach for me among the better inventors of the Baroque.

The little Schotterikirche in the huddled heart of the old town had a fantastic case of flesh pink wax figures writhing in Purgatory as its chief item of interest. We had gone in remembering that Ireland once was called Scotia, and that the medieval Scots among the wandering scholars were indeed Irishmen, the greatest among them, Johannes Scottus Eriugena the last of the Platonists. We were hoping that something, some hint of light or tilt of symbol might reach over the centuries and touch with a friendly finger. But there was none. Only the name was not alien. Mario Praz remarked that not even in Sicily, in the deep Italian South, would you find any display of religious figures of equal barbarity or naïveté. And by degrees I began to realize that Vienna was the strange focus of the Italian element, the German element, and what, because it was new to me, I supposed to be the Slav. It was precisely this assertion of barbarity as in the Purgatory tableau, so also in the splendid crown jewels in the Schatzkammer, the tenth century crown, Rudolf's crown, Stephen's crown, sceptre, monstrance, chalice, which carried overtones of the galloping hordes from the steppes, stemmed, stopped and absorbed just here.

The Schonbrunn, for all its scale, has nothing of this barbarity or brutality; its proportions are controlled, so that in spite of its size it is a friendly looking building. And inside also, for all its 1,400 rooms the lovely rococo is friendly too. The Congress had a big reception there, delegates, at the top of the stairs, shaking the hand of the Federal Chancellor Raab. Here too at the buffet the French were true to form, almost smashing doors down, elbowing tight along the tables, shouldering back all other races, first to snatch at the plates, last to shuffle away replete, for publicly the French are the worst mannered and greediest of people. In Congress sessions it is easy to tell even at a distance if the speaker is French or using that language, otherwise the French delegates chatter and gabble regardless of the comfort of others.

The Schonbrunn has many little rooms, or large alcoves, leading one off the other, each decorated superbly in period. While sitting with Patricia Lynch and R.M. Fox in one of these rich with Chinese objects, porcelain figures or jars on lacquer shelves adorning the walls (the figures securely fixed. I tried them) an American woman drifted in and gaping round with open mouthed awe, drawled 'Wonderful'. 'There can't be another room in the whole world just like this'. Roberta got up and taking the American by the arm, said brusquely 'Come with me', and firmly marched her across the intervening long gallery to the identical twin apartment on the other side, which she had discovered for herself in her curious peregrinations. At Schonbrunn too we had the elegant pleasure of attending a concert in the little Schlosstheater of the music of Scarlatti, Mozart, Schubert, with an additional note of historical appropriateness in an aria by the Emperor Leopold the First.

But no building in Vienna had the surprise and wonder of the Abbey at Melk. A mountain of masonry on a mountain of rock hung above the Danube, as impregnable as the ports of Heaven, as picturesque as an Alp, inside it the air was chill as ice, visitors' breaths clouding and thinning out against the complex and tremendous glories of altar, pillars, ceiling. Here out on the platform of a lower storey cliffed over the water, as we ate our hot sausages, I had the pleasure of introducing W.N. Ewer, the famous foreign correspondent, author of the memorable quatrain. 'How odd of God to choose

'The Jews' to Mario Praz, for they had unaccountably missed meeting in Venice six years before.

But though we found the city hammering at our senses and sensibilities at all levels, from the expensive but excellent chocolate cakes in the fragrant coffee-houses, and the wandering minstrels busking in the beer cellars, and the polite children in the street cars, one dainty infant shaking hands all round before her father could entice her off at her destination, the art galleries demanded full attention. Visiting the Kunsthistorisches Museum, I was able to greet a good many old friends from the London Exhibition of 1949. But here the most abiding satisfaction was in seeing the great roomful of Breughels, for the bulk and best of these had been deemed too fragile to travel to the Tate. And we spent a long time reading them like print: *The Massacre of the Innocents, Children's Games, The Combat of Carnival and Lent, The Carrying of the Cross*, and the others, and thought how generous the artist was in cramming and crowding his panels with such a teem of life, and yet how skilfully organized the apparent tumble and tide of his moving figures; fun, pity, satire, love, protest, every emotion not spilt or splashed, but loading and charging the complicated plotting of his forms with meaning beyond the fundamental appeal of the intricate geometry, and all laid down, stated and described with a sign-painter's steady hand. And all this accomplished on manageable panels; events, not monuments. In any single one of these a thrifty figurative artist of today could find material enough to set him up for a long and careful career. Brueghel, for me, among the great masters, is, in retrospect, my escape from, and challenge to the parsimony of the abstract; how often I look and long for the appearance of a twentieth century genius equally abundant in his giving, equally interested in and committed to his world as in his time, but then, to span from Chaucer to Edgar Lee Masters, 'It takes life to love life'.

The Brueghels were an experience apart. One or two oddities, such as Archimboldo's faces composed of fruits and vegetables, known from illustrations to books on Surrealism, although not well hung, caught my attention. But walking in the galleries of the three dimensional objects, the Italian bronzes, the rock crystal vessels, the amazingly worked half length bronze busts, Cellini's *Salt Cellar* more relevant and impressive here than in London, gave one an awed sense of tremendous opulence, of art for emperors, consistent with the emphatic feeling we had received of the great city. I had always been predisposed to estimate works of art singly, in themselves or either in relation to a religious function or a national need, even if expressed in terms of social class preserving the national accent; from folk to court through every level or degree; but here it was the ample treasure of the Holy Roman Empire with, which one was confronted, supranational, imperial, Catholic.

In the Academy, within its smaller compass, we found the magnificent Bosch triptych, the unusually violent drama of Titian's *Tarquin and Lucrece*, remembered from the Tate, the low angled poise of Barent Fabritius' *Self Portrait with a Halberd* – at least, that is what I should call it – and Guardi's *Piazza of San Marco* with the tall flag poles asserting their verticality against the horizontal courses of the wide buildings with as much precision and a deal more life than any Mondrian; and, in the absurdly short time that we could eke, we dare look, in the Albertina, at no more than Dürer's famous watercolours, probably the most demanded drawings there, wondering at the freshness of the washes.

But for the national quality it was the Barockmuseum in the Lower Belvedere which introduced me to paintings of Rottmayr, Maulbertsch and Kremser Schmidt, another version of whose *Holy Family* I saw four years later in that ice-cold gallery in Graz, and borrowed for the Old Masters Exhibition when the Herbert Art Gallery opened in Coventry. In the Orangerie the Museum of Austrian Medieval Art contained a wealth of paintings and, in particular, wood sculptures which took me beyond the few fine things remembered from the Victoria and Albert Museum, in variety and quality remaining unchallenged until 1962, when I visited the collections in Warsaw and in Krakow.

For the moderns, in the Secession Gallery a big show of Klee, the largest I had so far seen, disappointing in the oil paintings, exciting in the few early elaborate mythical drawings, still left me my opinion of him as an interesting mind but a minor artist, over-praised, perhaps, because he was so articulate. Kokoschka's portrait of the Chancellor asserted once more his supremacy in that sadly depleted field; this, all that I can recall from a current contemporary Austrian display. An exhibition, *European Art Yesterday and Today* presented the main lines and tendencies of the last century in a boldly expository fashion. From Daumier to the Impressionists, this was largely through the media of prints and drawings. What to me was most valuable was that while the School of Paris was fairly represented, the expressionists, Ensor and the Germans, Marc, Nolde, Kirchner, Hofer, were given due attention. Indeed the half dozen or so items of Edvard Munch were actually the first originals of his that I had seen, for, in my earlier years the modish fixation on Paris kept him off stage while many lesser talents were paraded and exposed. It was here that we saw the Kokoschka which reminded us of Jack Yeats, just as a Nolde recalled Colin Middleton. The sculpture included several names which I had only seen in print; Archipenko, Barlach, Lipschitz, Lehmbruck: Zadkine I had first encountered in Dudley Wallis' collection in Manchester over twenty years before.

In the Congress, the theme of which I have completely forgotten, there were the by now very familiar faces: Czokor, his fine mane no less magnificent, very much on his home ground and enjoying it; the De Backers essential congressists, universally affable, without attitudes; Parandowski; Neumann; Kastner; Hans Redeker, Dutch Christian existentialist, with Englishman's moustache and incongruous meerschaum; Andre Chamson, doing whatever he had to do, even if it were only entering a room, with intensity.

Charles Morgan, International President, was still as smooth as ever, moving around as if, my old mother would have said, he were giving the town a treat, showing temper only when the photographers swarmed up and got mixed with the platform party at the inaugural session in the Josefstadt Theater.

In the deliberation of the executive I thought him too obviously being seen to manage and manoeuver the discussion and the resolutions when they were about to become pertinent to the vital problems of writers in the world of 1955; and when Silone, that reliable man, made his plea for tolerance and humanity above and beyond the letter of the constitution, I was angered that his honest, heartfelt speech should evoke no more than sneering whispers about his Rotarian's French, from the hollow, flannel-suited men.

38

Exeat

In the summer of 1956 I saw the advertisement that Coventry required an Art Director for the gallery in process of being built. All I knew of Coventry was that it had been Godiva's burg, that Tennyson had got off the train there on his way to Stratford, that it had been hammered by the Luftwaffe, that it had a Labour Council which had made a bold attempt to rebuild the blitzed city centre in a modern idiom, and that, not long before, the same council had struck against spending useful money in a fallacious scheme for civil defence. So it seemed to offer an interesting prospect, a place where, at any rate, my political ideas would no longer be a social and economic handicap.

I had not wanted to run away from Belfast after the debacle. I had felt that I should stand my ground, and be, as it were, a walking reproach to, a thorn in the consciences of my enemies. Bill Seaby was a pleasant fellow to work with, and did all that he could to make my subordinate position tolerable, leaving me master in my own field. But, one by one, the committee rascals died off. The Chairman, in fact, did not last very long, and part of me, uncharitably, could not help feeling that the troubles of the affair had had something to do with shortening his days. I know that this was a malicious thought; but I should have been a hypocrite not to have admitted it to myself.

But by 1956 I had demonstrated that I could stand up unabashed, and, further, I had enough worldly ambition not to remain professionally a subordinate throughout my career. Yet if I went off I wanted it to be somewhere out of the ordinary run of gallery jobs, and the idea of an absolutely new building with the exciting problems of devising a new and appropriate policy for its use offered a challenge which attracted me. It would, if I were successful, mean uprooting us from a context in which Roberta and I had our own places and interests; but she had frequently in our early days urged me to break away from Belfast, for she never had had the strong self-identification with its past and its future, which had provided so much of my deep concern and my intense effort at comprehending. So I sent in my application, as a gesture of my feeling of independence from the restrictive climate, nominating Tom MacGreevy, Director of the National Gallery of Ireland as one of my referees.

Some time after, I learnt from the secretary to the University that the cautious Coventry folk had been checking that I was indeed a *bona fide* graduate. In the early autumn I was called for interview. The train journey which took me through Crewe and Stafford to Birmingham proved rather disheartening, for it was not a part of England that I had seen before. The raw backs of old factories, the dirty canals, the grime-blighted railway sidings, the end-on mean streets, chilled my spirits, and I could not help thinking that if Coventry were to be like this too, part of the mess and detritus of the industrial revolution, I could not fairly ask Roberta to leave our hills and green fields for such a future. Someway out of Birmingham, the landscape improved, and pleasant, if flat country supervened, and when Coventry hove up before me with the tall blocks of the Tile Hill housing estate on the skyline, I felt less disconsolate.

In the couple of hours before my Council House interview, I wandered round the new city centre, struck a little by the smallness in scale of the new buildings, but impressed by the open pedestrian precinct, and, supreme novelty to a Belfast man, clear evidence of a civic plan. Then down a side street I came upon an eating house called *The Farmer Giles* and imagining that nothing could be more English than that, went in and sat down, to discover that the tables round me rang with Irish voices and that the menu was handed to me by a man who looked and spoke like an Italian.

On a slight rise of the ground beyond the new buildings I observed an old church with a spire. The notice board named it as Holy Trinity, so I climbed the worn steps and went in. I could see at once that it was of some antiquity, though much restored and with Victorian pews, older far than almost any church in Ireland which is not a ruin. I remarked the fine stone pulpit, the handsome brass lectern; and then on the wall beside the West Door my searching eye took notice, first of one, then of three tablets. The middle tablet, the largest, with classical pilasters, was to the memory of the Honourable Ambrosia George and Elizabeth Hewitt, dated 1796. The right hand tablet, a Victorian Gothic shape, was for James Third Viscount Lifford, died 1855. The left hand tablet, a plain rectangular slab bore the name of Juliana, wife of Rev. John P. Hewitt, died 1827. I had known of the Lifford Hewitts and that they had not come to Ireland until the eighteenth century, so being there a younger stock than mine; but I had not known that they haled originally from Coventry. Yet, seeing the surname cut in stone and dated, I had an odd friendly feeling, as if, in some way, part of me had come home, that I stood in that place with some sort of right, and, from that moment, I knew, in my heart, that I should, later that afternoon, be appointed the Art Director of the Herbert Art Gallery and Museum, Coventry, in the county of Warwickshire, England.

Index

Dates given are those birth and death, where known.